C. E. Singletary

Communication and Social Behavior: A Symbolic Interaction Perspective

Communication and Social Behavior: A Symbolic Interaction Perspective

DON F. FAULES
DENNIS C. ALEXANDER
University of Utah

ADDISON-WESLEY PUBLISHING COMPANY
READING, MASSACHUSETTS • MENLO PARK, CALIFORNIA
LONDON • AMSTERDAM • DON MILLS, ONTARIO • SYDNEY

This book is in the
Addison-Wesley Series in Speech Communication

Frederick W. Haberman
Consulting Editor

Music score shown on p. 89 from "For the Unfor-
tunate" by H. Owen Reed, copyright 1975, Neil A.
Kjos Music Company, Park Ridge, Illinois, Edition
No. B394. Used by permission.

ISBN 0-201-01982-5
ABCDEFGHIJ-HC-7987

Preface

The major purpose of this text is to increase your understanding of the role of communication in human interaction to enable you to improve exchanges with others. This requires that the study of communication be grounded in a useful theoretical and philosophical perspective.

We selected the theory of symbolic interaction because it is a communication theory of human behavior. This perspective has the capability of integrating traditional, behavioral, and humanistic approaches to the study of communication. It is our feeling that symbolic interaction not only integrates, but also highlights the significance of communication in determining human behavior. Our intent is not to claim that all human behavior is accounted for by communication, but rather to assert that when one focuses on social behavior, a priority must be given to the symbolic forces that are operative. People learn by associating stimulus and response and by the reinforcement processes in the environment. They may also possess "insight" that leads to learning without the aid of symbols. However, social behavior is complex verbal behavior and cannot be adequately accounted for by associationist theories. We focus on the process that underlies human exchanges and what affects that process.

The text includes broad social situations, but a major emphasis is placed on the interpersonal setting. Although various forms of communication are discussed, the person-to-person oral exchange is dominant. In keeping with the symbolic interactionist position, we believe that organizations and societies are made up of the interactions of their respective members. The study of person-to-person exchange allows one to see the formative process of communication and the impact on participants.

The traditional symbolic interaction approach has been descriptive in nature and has been used to provide insight into human social development. We take the liberty of suggesting possible applications to communication behavior. In addition, we suggest a philosophical position for the practice of communication. Practical applications are integrated with theoretical discussions. We have attempted to provide suggestions that enhance interpersonal communication skills for students in their present setting and, in addition, to show how such skills are used in professional and societal settings. Examples are chosen from a variety of communication contexts. The text engages a number of issues that are inherent in the study and application of communication. We discuss not only how communication works, but also how it should work, and consideration of human values is very much a part of this text. Because communication can be looked on as a tool of exploitation, we felt it important to suggest ethical guidelines.

The plan of the text is to move from a foundation of theory and philosophy to an application of that basis to the everyday and professional setting. Part I introduces principles of symbolic interaction and key ideas of communication. Three fundamental propositions are derived for use in the text. Part II examines the interdependence of communication and social behavior. Concepts that are central to both symbolic interaction and communication are explored. Part III explores some primary purposes of communication. Both the "relational" and "content" purposes of communication are discussed. Part IV moves into applications of the text material to larger contexts. Both the external and internal uses of communication by organizations are considered.

It is our conviction that a textbook should operate as a springboard and not be regarded as covering all aspects of a subject. Our footnotes not only indicate the sources used, but also some of the sources examined. The sources are cited for the student who wishes to explore further or who wishes to look at another point of view. In addition, we have included "problems and issues" at the conclusion of the chapters. Some of these problems and issues are appropriate for immediate discussion; others could form the basis for a term project or group discussion. We are relying on the instructor to provide the necessary assistance for such projects and discussions.

Writers who attempt a theoretical, philosophical, and pragmatic approach in one text need much criticism and advice. We are indebted to Fred Haberman for his suggestions and initial reading of the manuscript. Leonard Hawes gave thorough and tough-minded criticism which made us focus on central issues. Several individuals read all or part of the text and provided additional material and insights. Our thanks to Jerome Gamache and Charles Waugh. We also thank our wives, Dee and Edwina, who typed manuscript, gave support, and listened to endless hours of discussion about this text.

Salt Lake City   D.F.F.
July 1977   D.C.A.

Contents

Part III
Communication Purposes

Part I

Introduction

This text is organized around a symbolic interaction perspective. We selected this approach for two reasons. First, symbolic interaction is a broad, theoretical framework that deals directly with the concerns of communication and human behavior. Second, we are committed to discussing communication from a coherent perspective rather than merely presenting communication concepts from disjointed points of view or "minitheories" of human behavior.

In Part I (Chapter 1), we will start with our most basic assumption (the underlying premises)—the theory of symbolic interaction. We will then discuss our view of communication. Finally, we will offer some propositions that tie together symbolic interaction and communication.

Chapter 1

Communication and Symbolic Interaction

This chapter introduces our views on communication and the larger theoretical perspective of symbolic interaction. In addition to examining the key ideas in symbolic interaction and communication, we advance several derivative propositions that combine communication and symbolic interaction. Before turning to these key ideas and propositions, however, two questions must be answered: (1) Why and how are we using symbolic interaction? and (2) What is symbolic interaction?

SYMBOLIC INTERACTION APPLIED

We have chosen the theoretical perspective of symbolic interaction because it is compatible with our view of communication. Symbolic interaction concepts, such as process, negotiation, interaction, symbolic behavior, emergence, and a holistic view of human behavior, offer a framework for discussing communication. This framework allows and encourages a deep investigation into human communication behavior. But since we are not writing a textbook on symbolic interaction, we shall not deal with all of the issues of symbolic interaction. Instead, we shall apply symbolic interaction as a broad format for discussing human communication behaviors.

An underlying premise of this text is that the more one understands the process of communication, the more one understands both self and others. This in turn increases one's capacity to see alternative ways of interacting with others and the means by which to enhance the quality of interaction between people. Although symbolic interaction is a descriptive method of viewing human behavior, it can be combined with communication concepts to offer guides for enhancing the behavior between people. Although ours is not a "how to do communication" text, we will point out throughout the text the implications certain concepts may have on your behavior.

A SYMBOLIC INTERACTION PERSPECTIVE

Symbolic interaction is essentially a sociological-psychological perspective of the entire spectrum of human behavior. This perspective seeks to explain the "activities of interacting individuals. . . . Even when the individual is the focus of attention, his [her] behavior is conceived as a consequence of past interactional episodes."[1] Such a statement focuses on four concepts inherent in the symbolic interactionist's view: negotiation, process, emergence, and holism. Each of these concepts will be discussed briefly to provide you with a basic understanding of the symbolic interaction perspective.

Negotiation

Negotiation is an attempt to reach some degree of agreement about the meaning of an object. People negotiate by interacting with others by means of symbols (usually words, but other types of symbols, such as mathematics and music, may also be used). The symbols help people define their meaning or the reality of an object in a particular social setting. For example, a wife and husband are discussing whether or not their 11-year-old daughter should be allowed to read *Playgirl*. The father does not want to grant permission; the mother holds the opposite view. In part, at least, their discussion is an attempt to negotiate agreement about what the magazine means to an adolescent.

Process

By its very nature, interaction implies process and sequences of symbolic acts. The analysis of communicative behavior cannot be static, but must deal with a dynamic episode. In the example just cited, we should not focus only on the outcome. The decision the parents reach is best analyzed in terms of everything each had to say to the other; in other words, we should look at each statement in sequence. If we look only at their decision to let their daughter read the magazine, we miss seeing the concerns the parents have about what the neighbors will say or the effects on their daughter of seeing photographs of nude men.

Emergence

In the symbolic interaction perspective, emergence is defined as the continually growing or changing meanings a person assigns to objects. If we assume that communication is a process, it follows that a string of symbolic acts will always lead somewhere. In the parents' discussion about *Playgirl,* the husband, who finally comes to agree with his wife, must change and grow. He must change the meanings he holds for such things as the double sex standard, his "little girl," and male models. The wife too changes and grows. She changes the meanings she has had for her husband and her ideas about sexual freedom. Although not every communication event will produce such dramatic change and growth, of course, people do nonetheless grow with every interaction.

Holism

Many theories about human behavior locate the reasons for activity either externally or internally to the individual. External theories of human behavior argue that people are guided by variables and forces outside themselves, e.g., role, status, social groupings, and cultural norms. On the other hand, behavior may be explained in terms of a group of internal variables, e.g., needs, drives, and psychological demands. By contrast, symbolic interaction "stresses neither the interior nor the exterior influences to the exclusion of the other but considers both as parts of a single dynamic process."[2]

Because the symbolic interaction perspective stresses both interior and exterior influences, concepts such as meaning, symbols, self, role, interaction, group activities, and behavior in larger social settings need to be exposed. We now turn to a discussion of how such concepts develop a particular view of communication.

KEY IDEAS OF COMMUNICATION

Communication Defined

Communication can be defined as *symbolic behavior which results in various degrees of shared meanings and values between participants.* Because much of the content of this book revolves around this definition, we need to explain key terms.

Symbolic behavior Symbolic behavior refers to a person's capacity to respond to or use a system of significant symbols. For example, language is an organized set of significant symbols. Other organized sets of symbols are illustrated in the photographs in this text—art, math, and music. The use of significant symbols allows humans to engage in complex behaviors. The possibilities of response to a given situation are extended because one can respond in terms of not only previous experience, but also the accumulated learning experiences of others, both living and dead. When individuals use language, they elicit responses in others *and* in themselves. A symbol "stands for" something else—another stimulus, another response, some combination of stimuli and responses, or some relationship among a combination of these. The complexity of symbolic behavior becomes even more apparent when one considers that people not only elicit responses from others through symbols, but also converse with themselves and are able to present situations other than the immediate situation to themselves symbolically and to act on them.

Shared meaning Shared meaning occurs when two people perceive a symbol in the same way and attach a similar meaning to that symbol. But what is *meaning,* and why have we used the term *degrees* in our definition of communication? Shared meaning occurs to the extent that symbols elicit the same response in the sender and the receiver of the symbol. The term "degree" suggests that the sender and receiver are unlikely to make the *exact same* response to the symbol. One might even argue that because responses are different, the symbol cannot be the same. In this sense the statement "People look at the same thing and see something different" may be misleading, because the "same thing" is *not* the same to those perceiving it.

Consider the following scenario. It is a hot, humid day in a small town on the western plains. Someone rushes into a shop and yells "tornado!" Some patrons run for cover, some seek the inner walls of the building, some simply watch others run, and one person casually walks to the middle of the street and watches a roaring black funnel dump debris within arm's reach. The symbol "tornado" elicited various meanings or responses in the shoppers. They all may have shared the notion that a tornado is a phenomenon of nature, and to that degree they shared meaning. However, some may have previously witnessed the grisly destruction of a tornado, and therefore the meanings they assigned to "tornado" would have differed from those of people who had not had that experience.

How does one know what a symbol means to another person? When has shared meaning occurred? Although there is no precise measuring instrument, responses—whether action or language—can be examined in order to measure meaning. In other words, a person may predict the degree of shared meaning with another by what the other says or how he or she acts.

Values Values consist of both norms and ideals. *Norms* are expected patterns of behavior that receive assigned meanings from the participants in a social situation. *Ideals,* or standards of conduct or reasons for doing things, may not be shared or may be only partially shared because of a differing order of those standards for each participant. The meaning an individual attributes to a message is highly dependent on one's values and the priority of those values.

Between participants The communication act is interactive. That is, the degree of shared meaning is determined by what the participants bring to the exchange—their abilities, attitudes, and experiences. When two people communicate, each contributes to the content of communication and each influences the outcome. Recently one of our colleagues was fishing on a lake and was having rather consistent success with a lure called the Super Duper. A less fortunate angler on the other side of the lake called out, "What are you using?!!!" "A Super Duper!" "A super duper what!?" "Just a Super Duper!" "#*!$%, grumble, grumble." The amount of shared meaning in this exchange did not permit a fruitful outcome for both participants.

Implications of Definition

It is difficult *not* to communicate. According to our definition, certain levels (degrees of shared meaning) of communication take place whether or not they are intended. Individuals in a communication usually share a common language and adhere to norms and thereby create common meanings. These meanings may arise as a result of physical appearance, the clothing one wears (or even the fact that one is wearing clothing), and both the spatial and time aspects of a culture. A certain level of communication occurs between people all the time, because significance is attached to symbols either consciously or unconsciously, and there is a common basis for that significance. Who has not heard a speaker say, "Before I start, I would like to say . . . " In actuality, such a speaker "starts" when she or he appears in the presence of others.

Meanings are in people, and these meanings must be created and elicited. A person who is conscious of this tenet will ask how much shared meaning occurred after an exchange. One who is not sensitive to respondents will place too much faith in speaker skills and message construction. When this happens, communicators tend to believe that if the message is constructed in the proper form, the recipient will respond in an appropriate manner. If the results do not confirm these beliefs, the communicator simply assumes that the meaning is in the message and that it might be necessary to repeat the message so that everything becomes perfectly clear. One of the authors attended a faculty senate meeting during which a proposal was read with great zeal. Later a member of that senate asked what a particular statement meant. The proponent replied, "It means just what it says!" Most of us become so attached to our own messages that we can forget the function they are to perform.

The nature of communication should not be confused with its evaluation. Thus far we have emphasized the concept of shared meaning as the basis of communication. "Effective communication" could be treated as a separate concept and examined from several points of view. In addition to asking about the extent of shared meaning, one might evaluate an exchange on the basis of selection, comprehension, acceptance, recall, and use of message. Another procedure might be to question whether the communicator influenced, persuaded, or negotiated as he or she intended. All of those outcomes of an exchange are relevant to this text. In our definition, communication takes place to the extent that participants share meaning, and the focus is on understanding rather than on agreement with a particular position advocated.

"Momma," by permission of Mell Lazarus and Field Newspaper Syndicate.

For example, in the "Momma" comic strip, the basis of communication has been confused with one of its purposes—persuasion. From Momma's point of view, "effective communication," defined in terms of persuasion, has not taken place.

Participants in acts of communication are active. A communicator may influence behavior, but have more difficulty in controlling behavior, because respondents too contribute to the content of communication. For example, students are not information bins into which teachers can pour information. Teachers may believe that since they are "covering" a certain amount of material, a corresponding amount should be found in the students. But respondents to a message—in this case students—have as much to say about the amount of shared meaning as the initiators—teachers—do. It would be fruitless to ask a teacher if he or she gave a good lecture unless some criterion were used that included the student.

If meanings are in people and if the people change, then meanings change. We contended at the outset that meaning is highly dependent on the norms and values of a society. As the norms and values of a group change, the significance attached to symbols changes. When one of the authors was quite young, his grandmother talked about freedom and the right to wear what one wanted. For some time the boy thought that it was just another one of her "immigration" speeches on the values of America. Later he discovered that when her family was poor, someone had given one of her daughters a bright red dress. The daughter was thrilled, but members of the community were not. She received a visit from church members and even a minister who feared that the daughter would be misunderstood. In their eyes, a red dress was symbolic of a "loose woman." Today the grandmother would be pleased to see that red dresses are acceptable and probably quite surprised at the changing definitions of a "loose woman"! In short, it is not useful to talk about "correct" meanings. Meanings are correct only insofar as there is social agreement about what something means.

Types of Communication Settings

As communication settings differ, so too do the number and type of factors that impinge on participants. All of us find ourselves in a variety of communication settings every day. An individual has moments when she or he talks to self, talks to one other person, interacts with a group, represents one group while interacting with another, and receives communication via newspaper, radio, or television. Although certain elements of communication may be common to all of these settings, there are also differences, and theorists have focused on one setting or another to spell out the constraints of each. Our aim here is not to elaborate on the numerous pictorial models of different settings of communication, but rather to discuss briefly the major differences among the commonly recognized classes of communication settings—intrapersonal, interpersonal, group, public, mass, and collectives.

Intrapersonal Intrapersonal communication is simply holding a conversation with oneself. The individual has been referred to as a self-contained communication system, and some theorists have construed the cognitive structure as a model of the communication process. In other words, thinking, or information processing, has been made analogous to internal dialogue and labeled intrapersonal communication. Whether one can consider internal symbolizing as communication depends largely on the definition of communication employed. If one emphasizes "shared meaning," the notion of intrapersonal communication requires a special interpretation. Ruesch and Bateson[3] describe intrapersonal communication and also make a critical distinction between internal behavior and interaction:

> The consideration of intrapersonal events becomes a special case of interpersonal communication. An imaginary entity made up of condensed traces of past experiences represents within an individual the missing outside person. However, a crucial difference exists between interpersonal and intrapersonal communication with regard to the registration of mistakes. In the interpersonal situation the effects of purposive or expressive actions can be evaluated and if necessary corrected. In intrapersonal or fantasy communication, to perceive that one misinterprets one's own messages is extremely difficult, if not impossible, and correction rarely, if ever, occurs.*

Intrapersonal communication, then, does not involve interaction, correction, accommodation, or the establishment of a social situation in the same sense

---

* Reprinted from *Communication: The Social Matrix of Psychiatry,* by Jurgen Ruesch, M.D., and Gregory Bateson. By permission of W. W. Norton & Company, Inc. Copyright © 1968, 1951 by W. W. Norton & Company, Inc.

that interpersonal communication does. Therefore, the term "communication" as applied to internal cognitive processes may be misleading.

Interpersonal Interpersonal communication is characterized by feedback and accommodation between individuals. The unique aspects of interpersonal communication are summarized by Barnlund: "The study of interpersonal communication, then, is concerned with the investigation of relatively informal social situations in which persons in face-to-face encounters sustain a focused interaction through the reciprocal exchange of verbal and non-verbal cues."[4] This description emphasizes interaction between individuals on a face-to-face basis and in which all communication cues are available. In addition, the informal social situation allows for the mutual exchange of verbal and nonverbal cues. For example, a public speech contains aspects of interpersonal communication in that it is face to face and nonverbal cues, such as gestures, are available to the speaker. However, the interaction is restricted because there is usually no verbal exchange between speaker and audience.

To some, the term "interpersonal communication" means more than the setting in which communication occurs. For example, Stewart contends that:

> ... (1) interpersonal communication is communication of the special quality; (2) that quality is the noninterchangeability which characterizes genuine encounters between two or more unique persons; (3) the first step in achieving that quality is to recognize that human communication is transactional, which means that you are constructing and being constructed by each other in the communication-situation-as-it-happens; (4) it also helps if you realize that you cannot not communicate; and (5) you should work to make your communicating meaning-centered instead of message-centered.[5]

This particular description focuses more on the outcome of interpersonal communication and what should happen. In other words, the Stewart definition implies that interpersonal communication is relating to others.

Although the study of interpersonal communication is sometimes limited to the two-person exchange (dyadic communication), the characteristics of interpersonal communication can be applied to larger groupings as well. Distinctions among settings are made on the basis of complexity as well as on the different factors that may be operative in a setting. Thus the definition that we used to illustrate interpersonal communication (face-to-face, reciprocal exchange of verbal and nonverbal cues, etc.) could be applied to the group (three or more people). We choose to categorize group communication separately because of the difference in level of complexity.

Group Group communication is illustrative of the axiom that the greater the number of individuals who enter into an interaction, the more complex the relationships operating in the setting become. One might argue that one-to-one communication is still operating and that the framework of the interpersonal setting applies. However, the accommodation between individuals changes, and the interpersonal model is not adequate to describe the adjustments that are taking place. The interaction is face to face, and there is a mutual exchange of verbal and nonverbal cues—dependent, of course, on the size of the group.

The contrast with one-to-one communication can be seen in the alliances that form within a group, a change in the quantity and quality of communication, and in the norms that participants adhere to. For example, imagine that you are talking to a woman friend in the cafeteria about mutual interests and that the two of you are deciding what to do during the weekend. When another individual joins your conversation, you feel obligated to hear his interests. (Your personal talking time has been reduced.) Suppose that others join you and your friend and start to take sides about what activity should be pursued over the weekend. (Alliances have formed.) Because of the variety of people who have joined the group, you try to adapt to a variety of interests. (The values have become more complex.) Others have taken over the leadership in the group, and you are reduced to giving information. (Your role has changed.) Because time does not allow each person to develop specific, individual views, it is necessary to simply respond yes or no to a proposal. (The form of communication has changed.) Suppose that earlier, when you were interacting with your friend, she chided you about a particular proposal. Now imagine that she did the same before a group. Would your reaction be different? These are only some of the dynamics of the group setting that have an impact on communication behavior.

Public Public communication involves the sending of messages to large groups of people in a face-to-face setting. Public speaking is the primary tool for this type of participation. Public communication is characterized by a lack of verbal exchange between speaker and audience, large groups, less personal adaptation to each participant than in the interpersonal setting, a more general language, and typically a more formal approach to communication.

Mass Mass communication, also known as mediated communication, is an exchange involving the use of print or electronic media—newspapers, radio, television, and film. This setting differs from the others in that it does not involve face-to-face interaction. There is no opportunity for immediate mutual exchange of verbal and nonverbal cues between the initiator of a message and the recipients of that message.

Politicians sometimes complain that although television reaches masses of people, it also entails a handicap for the speaker, who cannot see the immediate audience response and adapt to it. The response of the recipients is delayed and can be either direct or indirect. For example, a reader of a newspaper might respond to the policy of that paper by writing a letter in response to an editorial (delayed and direct) or by cancelling a subscription (delayed and indirect).

A successful television program usually spawns a number of programs with similar formats. Advertisers are reluctant to gamble on untested formats because by the time they learn of the outcomes (delayed feedback), product sales may have declined (indirect feedback) and huge investments have been lost. Mass communication is a setting that is complicated by the fact that the recipient of a message may react either alone or on the basis of others' reactions. In addition, the intended recipient may not in fact come in contact with the message.

One of the most controversial aspects of mass communication is its "selectivity" and consequent power. The flow of information to the general public is screened by the media. In other words, when an event occurs, people in the media decide what information will be reported and how it will be reported. It is not our purpose here to elaborate on the many issues associated with the nature of the media. But it should be apparent that the issues involved in this setting are different from those inherent in other types of settings.

Collectives Collectives of communication refer to larger settings and present a broader scope of study with greater complexity. In other words, when one examines large collectives, such as an organization, it is necessary to consider all of the foregoing settings, plus the unique outcomes that are produced by the interaction of these settings.

Interaction schemes within an organization include individual to individual, individual to group, group to group, group to organization, organization to organization, and organization to public. In addition to the constraints that exist in any one of these settings, more are generated by overlap within a larger system. In other words, the parts of an organization are interdependent, and communication networks tend to overlap. Individuals within this larger setting cannot speak just for themselves without considering the impact that their words may have on the total organization. For example, a professor must consider the impact that his or her messages may have on students, immediate colleagues, other departments, college policy, university goals, and community demands. Any one individual's interaction with another goes beyond person-to-person communication because of group and organizational constraints.

Most individuals are affected by the norms and values of groups and the larger organization. In informal social situations, individuals may generate many of the rules that govern their behavior. This is true to a lesser extent in the formal organization. However, a formal organization must have given rules to restrict people's behavior in such complex environments.

Implications for Communicators

The importance of settings Although specific forms of communication do not fit neatly into one setting or another, the differences among settings should alert the communicator to the dynamics and demands that operate in a particular situation. Thus the messages for one setting may not be appropriate for another. Interpersonal communication allows for highly individualized message treatment and exchange, whereas mass communication demands a more general treatment which can be understood by all of the recipients.

Most of us are quite demanding in the interpersonal setting and want to be treated as unique persons. Much of the exchange in such settings is based on what "happens" between people and the immediate feedback that is operating. For example, what if your favorite television announcer appeared at your front door and simply stated the same words that you had heard him or her deliver so many times before? How do you feel about the salesperson who reads the company sales pitch? In the mass-communication setting, more emphasis must be placed on prediction and message construction. An individual who talks at a very general level, does not generate feedback, and does not listen in an interpersonal setting probably does not fully understand the opportunities presented by that setting.

Settings can alter both the content and the interpretation of messages. In the group setting it becomes more difficult to allow time for highly individual treatment. Therefore, those responsible for leadership must find ways of communicating that make group activity both productive and satisfying for the members. For example, a group of one hundred people could be divided into smaller units for preliminary discussion, thereby giving each person an opportunity to participate. Some of the particular content offered by each individual may have impact on the group's ultimate decisions. A message that is mildly received in the interpersonal setting may be interpreted as threatening in the group setting.

Settings that represent large systems make more demands on the communicator, who must be sensitive to both individual and system needs. For example, a manager in an organization must be sensitive to both individual needs and to system survival, growth, and continuity. It is highly unlikely that one can always make decisions or communicate in a way that is pleasing to all.

Communication as a social process A "nostalgia craze" might well be the result of the desire to freeze time and return to less hectic days. A general awareness of change and the rate of that change is reflected in such titles as *Stop the World I Want to Get Off* and *Future Shock*. Perhaps less dramatic, but no less important, are the dynamics of the communication process. The most succinct description of the term "process" as it applies to communication is advanced by Berlo:

> If we accept the concept of process, we view the events and relationships as dynamic, on-going, ever-changing, continuous. When we label something as a process we also mean that it does not have a beginning, an end, a fixed sequence of events. It is not static, at rest. It is moving. The ingredients within a process interact; each affects all of the others.[6]

A complete explanation of this description of process would go beyond what is intended here, but let's look at some examples of the key ideas.

What is meant by "events and relationships [are] dynamic"? Suppose that you have been asked to speak before a group. You may well write out a manuscript or an outline of your speech. That manuscript or outline is not the speech itself. The speech is what *happens* during your interaction with that group. Communication is a dynamic process, and you would probably find yourself reacting to that group and to the members' reactions toward you. Could you give the "same" speech to the "same" group again? According to the process point of view, you could not, because the dynamics would differ— you would not be the same, the speech would not be the same, and the group would not be the same at another time.

The complexity of a communication event seldom allows one to place behaviors in a simple cause-and-effect model. It may be done in a hypothetical way so that certain factors can be emphasized. However, as the description of process has indicated, ingredients within a process interact, and each affects all of the others. In an ongoing interaction, a person may be a sender at one moment, a receiver of the other person's responses at another moment, or a sender and receiver at the same time. For example, Miller and Hintz have studied the activity of persons moving from a condition of behavioral independence to one of interdependence. Part of the process of this activity includes reciprocally acknowledged attention, mutual responsiveness, projection of identities, and shared focus.[7]

In most cases, cause-and-effect factors influence one another, and the interaction among those factors makes it difficult to determine which is cause and which is effect. For example, do you communicate with an individual because you are attracted to that person, or has your communication created the attraction?

The complexity is increased when one realizes that communication is a social process. People do not exist in boxes in a diagram and do not respond in isolation. They respond on the basis of meaning that is screened through a social structure that is in continual flux. People's meanings and values are anchored in the groups to which they belong or aspire to belong. For example, you may read a message in the school newspaper and then test its validity by talking to friends, family, or members of your religious or political affiliation. In fact, these groups may have decided whether you read the message in the first place.

Because communication is a social process, a communicator must, first, be sensitive to what is happening in an exchange and not be tied to a pre-determined formula of what should happen. Thus the concern is with both the act of communication and the action that is occurring. Second, each communication exchange has its unique elements because of the individuals involved and should be approached with that awareness. Finally, meanings and values are social products, and as such they change. Communicators must have an awareness of such changes in self and in others. People must continually tell others who they are.

Thus far we have looked at some of the key ideas in communication. We now combine some aspects of symbolic interaction and communication to arrive at several propositions that form the symbolic interaction perspective.

PROPOSITIONS DERIVED FROM SYMBOLIC INTERACTION AND COMMUNICATION

Although a number of other propositions could be drawn from our preceding discussion, the three cited in this section are, we feel, particularly important to the study of communication.

1. One's Interpretation and Perception of the Environment Depend on Communication

During the past ten years it has become increasingly fashionable to "experience everything" and to follow the slogan "Experience is the best teacher." However, even though what one experiences "directly" is limited, people do and can learn by direct experience.

Perception of experience How one experiences something is dependent on what meaning one brings to that experience, which is mainly a product of learned symbol systems. Response to an experience is partially in terms of the learning experiences of others that have been communicated through a shared system of significant symbols. Language, one such system, allows a person to pattern what is experienced, and in that sense it organizes one's behavior. Symbolic systems help individuals to categorize experiences and to make sense of them. This suggests that one's social reality is made up of symbolic systems.

One theorist has gone so far as to contend that "the limits of my language are the limits of my world."[8]

Access to information There is much information that cannot be obtained by first-hand experience. In a complex, information-dependent society, it would be not only impossible, but also dangerous, to attempt to experience all events directly. Individuals must rely on others for a primary function of communication—the reduction of uncertainty in the environment. Individuals must rely on others to process vast amounts of information and make generalizations that can be understood. Therefore, deliberate misinformation given out by high government officials or agencies sends shock waves through a nation. When the public trust is violated by the "uncertainty absorbers," all of us recognize our vulnerability.

Impact of media on social reality The mass media constitute a dominant force in the construction of one's knowledge of the environment. Mills writes:

> Very little of what we think we know of the social realities of the world have we found out first-hand. Most of the "pictures in our heads" we have gained from these media—even to the point where we often do not really believe what we see before us until we read about it in the paper or hear about it on the radio. The media not only give us information; they guide our very experiences. Our standards of credulity, our standards of reality, tend to be set by these media rather than by our own fragmentary experience.[9]

The media have the capacity to expose certain aspects of an environment and to create strong vicarious experiences. By August 1975, for example, 50 million people had seen the movie *Jaws,* whose plot is about the life and times of a great white shark that terrorizes a beach resort. One of the more interesting aspects of this movie is the way in which it was marketed and the subsequent events that perpetuated the marketing process. This sequence of events might be summarized as follows:

1. The movie was adapted from a best-seller book.
2. The paperback's logo (a shark rising to attack a swimmer) was used in the advertising campaign.
3. Reporters were lured to the movie location every day for five months.
4. Release of the film was delayed until the summer months.
5. A television campaign coincided with the wide release of the movie and consisted of a prime-time blitz.
6. There was a marketing of "Jaws" T-shirts, shark pendants, etc.
7. A *Time* cover piece occurred during the week of the movie's release.
8. The movie immediately started making $1 million a day.

9. Because of its stunning success, the movie became news, and the media contributed to the publicity with news stories. Newspaper features were written about audience reaction. Many shark experts emerged, and their commentary was sought for both newspapers and television.

10. Shark sightings became more newsworthy, and it was not uncommon for newspapers and newscasters to mention "Jaws" in reports.[10]

This example illustrates just how much focus can be placed on a single event in the environment and how the reinforcement process can structure one's reality.

Implications Reality is a social product arising from communication. Therefore, one's view of "reality" will always be limited. Communication can be used to limit realities as well as to extend them. One's social reality is composed of symbol systems and values. In order to discover one's reality or the reality of another, it is necessary to understand the symbol system and what those symbols mean to the person using them.

2. Communication is Guided by and Guides the Concepts of Self, Role, and Situations

Self Probably everyone has, at one time or another, dealt in some self-examination after a social exchange. The internal conversation might have gone something like this: "I sure didn't represent myself very well. Why did I say those things!? That wasn't me!" It is clear that all of us have certain expectations of ourselves and believe that the "self" contains certain qualities. These qualities have been given to us via the labeling process that occurs in social interaction. Many people spend a lifetime trying to live up to a label or to live down others. How much individuals communicate to others and the nature of the communication are very much dependent on who they think they are. An individual may be either aggressive or reticent in communicating with others, as a result of a particular self-image.

Role We have devoted a chapter to the concept of "role" as well as one to "self." Without developing those concepts in detail here, we merely note that certain communication behaviors are attached to the roles, or "parts," that one "plays" in our society. In other words, roles are one aspect of behavioral patterns that make up societal expectations. Roles are socially defined and are maintained through communication. Individuals must conceive of the roles that they execute, as well as those that others play and how they define those roles. One of the principal components of human interaction is "role taking," or being able to empathize with another and know where that person is "coming from." Since roles generally demand certain qualities, individuals are placed in the position of matching "self" qualities with those demanded by the role. How well a person executes a particular role, or even if he or she holds that role, may well be determined by what is communicated.

During the early part of President Ford's administration, for example, many people were concerned that although he was trustworthy, he did not show the strength and vigor of a president. There was a feeling that although he would probably not take rash action, he would just as likely not take any action at all. After the American withdrawal from Viet Nam and during the evacuation of refugees from Cambodia, an American ship was seized, and President Ford ordered the Marines to recover the ship and crew at once. His popularity in the public polls shot up immediately. His act communicated a role expectation—the quality of strength and resolve in a president.

Situation The roles one selects and the qualities of self that are communicated are a function of the way a person defines a social situation. Individuals' behavior changes as they move from one situation to another. For example, most people behave quite differently in a religious setting and on a "company picnic." You might think carefully about what behavior you engage in to validate your role of student in the classroom setting. Perhaps this behavior varies across classes because each situation is defined differently.

The setting of an exchange can condition one's definition of the situation and guide the communication. For example, a colleague of one of the authors lived next door to a lawyer. One day when he was trimming his hedge, he held what he thought was an "off the record" conversation with the lawyer. Much to his dismay, he found himself in court repeating that conversation. He had defined the situation as an exchange between neighbors; the lawyer, on the other hand, had viewed the situation as a professional interview.

The communication that occurs in a situation can also help define that situation. For example, some job interviews may seem more like interrogations than a mutual search for compatibility. Later we will develop the notion that certain communication behaviors do indeed lend themselves to posing a threatening situation.

Implications Communication is affected by the expectations that individuals hold of themselves and of others. These expectations are conditioned by definitions of self, role, and situations. In order to achieve shared meaning, it is necessary to understand the defining process of the participants.

Self, role, and situation are identified by the symbols attributed to them. The symbols become associated with self, role, and situation by means of social interaction. The perception of self, role, or situation can be altered only if the individual undergoes a redefining process. This process is aided by changing symbols or the significance attached to former symbols. For example, the song "I Am Woman" has almost become the national anthem for the "women's movement." It stresses the capability of women and represents a communication attempt to redefine the term "woman."

3. Communication Involves Complex Interaction

As we pointed out earlier, the simplest level of interaction occurs when one person acts and is responded to by another person. If one were to consider this description as representative of the communication process, it could be depicted as

Stimulus → Response or Sender → Receiver.

However, our concept of communication as a process has stressed that it is difficult, if not impossible, to identify cause and effect, actor and person acted on, beginning and end; in an ongoing interaction a person may be a sender at one moment and a receiver at another or both simultaneously. We will develop our discussion of communication as complex interaction by explaining some basic concepts. These concepts become more clear when contrasted with the S-R perspective.

Linearality versus mutual influence The S-R scheme presents communication as a linear concept. Someone is doing something to another person, and the influence is moving in one direction. In other words, the power resides in the person who sends the message. Bauer contrasts the concepts of linearality and mutual influence as follows:

> It (first model) is a model of one-way influence. The communicator does something to the audience, while to the communicator is generally attributed considerable latitude and power to do what he pleases to the audience. This model is reflected—at its worst—in such popular phrases as "brain washing," "hidden persuasion," and "subliminal advertising." The second stereotype— the model which *ought* to be inferred from the data of research—is of communication as a transactional (*complex interaction*) process in which two parties each expect to give and take from the deal approximately equitable values.[11]

A complex-interaction view of communication suggests that an audience is active. Messages must be altered to fit the meaning/values of the recipient. Audiences play an active role in deciding what the messages will be and in determining if they will achieve the desired response.

A certain mythology attributed to the control of others can bring about an unreasonable attribution of power to those who "send" messages. For example, in exploring the notion of symbolic leaders, Klapp delves into the question of whether "stars" can be manufactured artificially. He quotes film producer Wald as saying:

> This is absolute nonsense. There is no Geiger counter you can hold up to a girl and then say, "This one I can make into a star." Sam Goldwyn spent a million dollars trying to make a star of Anna Sten and failed. Cohn himself tried it with fifty girls and succeeded with only two—Rita Hayworth and Kim Novak. Why, there were six other girls who came to Columbia at the same time as Kim. They were all given the same opportunity, the same buildup. None of them is setting the world on fire . . . [But] the minute she [Kim] appeared on the screen, people began to put their money down to buy tickets—and nobody could manufacture that.[12]

It would appear that a public has a great deal to say about the messages it receives.

Participants in an interpersonal setting may influence each other to the extent that they create the rules for interaction. For example, husbands and wives, lovers, etc., generally know what they can talk about, at what times, and in what situations.

One may argue about how the power is distributed in a relationship and who has received the most out of an exchange, but the factor of mutual influence cannot be overlooked. A bargaining process is taking place within the dynamics of the communication process. Darnell observes:

> Because men collectively can affect the environment in ways that men individually cannot, because the resources provided by the environment are apparently limited, and because the adaptive capacity of the individual man is limited, *men are interdependent*. Men are interdependent—there is reciprocity of effect—sometimes by choice and sometimes not, in a variety of different ways, and in varying degrees.[13]

The linear concept of communication ignores such mutual influence and reciprocity.

Message- versus meaning-centered The S-R scheme implies separate units in the communication process. For example, a message or stimulus is delivered to a receiver, who responds. It is easy to infer from this scheme that there is meaning in messages and that individuals will respond to such messages in much the same way over time and in different contexts. However, a cardinal principle of human communication is that meanings are in people and that these meanings cannot be delivered. Meanings must be generated and evoked in others. The S-R model tends to underplay the level of involvement that is required for fruitful communication.

Relationship and complex interaction The S-R perspective fails to give proper emphasis to the relationships that exist in a communication situation. The importance of relationship to the complex-interaction view is indicated by Hulett:

> The relationship of any biological organism to any environmental object is a dynamic one in which the properties of the object that are involved in the relationship do not inhere solely in the object itself but emerge from the *relationship* that exists between organism and object.[14]

Now, let's simplify by example. One of the authors has had a number of discussions with a colleague about the merits of Jonathan versus Delicious apples. The discussion centers on which apple is crisper, more flavorful, etc. Such a discussion cannot be resolved, because the properties (flavor, sweetness, etc.) do not inhere solely in the apple, but rather in those who are tasting the apple. A complex interaction is taking place in which certain objective properties (level of sugar as determined by chemical analysis) may be in the apple and are reacted to (level of sweetness as attributed by tasting), after which there is a reaction to one's reaction. ("This apple always turns me on!")

When two people are communicating, they are attributing meanings to messages, reacting to each other, reacting to the other's reactions, and reacting to their own reactions. If the apple example did not "stir you up," apply the same principle to an interaction with someone whom you particularly like. You will probably discover that it is difficult to separate objective content of what is said from the relationship that exists between you and the other individual.

Any stimulus properties that an object "has" are put there by the perceiver. These stimulus properties depend on the existing relationship between object and perceiver. The same is true of the relationship between message and perceiver and that between the participants involved in the communication act.

Communication is situational The complex-interaction approach maintains that people are not the same in different communication situations, because relationships change. Meanings are bound up in these relationships; thus a message in one setting may take on an entirely different meaning in another. Communication is a formative process and even though a certain amount of repetition and predictability are present, each communicative exchange has its different aspects.

Types of messages and interaction Because of our emphasis on complex interaction, we must delineate two types of messages. (A message is the proper ordering—syntax—of symbols to convey information.) The two types of messages are *product messages* and *interactional messages*. A product message is an ordering of symbols that is permanent and less susceptible to change. Written messages such as poems, letters, reports, and novels are product messages, as are sensory messages such as art objects and musical compositions.

The reasons for the lack of change in a product message are minimal feedback and the distance between initiator and respondent; these two reasons appear concomitant. In writing a letter, for example, you may try to place yourself in the role of the respondent, but you still lack feedback as to his or her exact responses and interpretation of your message. The public speech appears to be largely a product message for these same reasons. The public speaker practices and rehearses exactly what will be said, and the bulk of the feedback received comes after the presentation of the message.

The interactional message is a symbol structure that continually changes until the participants agree that meanings have been shared to their full potential for a particular event. Participants reorder their messages to each other until both are satisfied that the outcome is as complete as can be expected. In the particular sense of interactional messages, satisfaction and full potential do not indicate a completely effective communicative event; rather, they are the points at which further interaction appears fruitless.

Because our concern is primarily with complex interaction, most of this text will focus on interactional messages.

Implications

Communication consists of complex interactions that have both "content" and "relationship" components. Reactions to messages are highly dependent on the relationships that exist between participants. Communication outcomes are affected by the interdependence of participants, mutual influence, and the situation.

SUMMARY

We have selected symbolic interaction as the broad perspective within which to discuss human communication behaviors. Our concern is with how people accommodate to one another and how they can improve that process. The key ideas of symbolic interaction—meaning, activities, interaction, self, and action—emphasize how people coordinate their behaviors in social interaction (communication).

Communication occurs when two or more people engage in the use of symbols that produce various degrees of shared meanings and values. The definition suggests that: (1) it is difficult *not* to communicate; (2) meanings are in people; (3) the nature of communication is different from its evaluation; (4) participants in acts of communication are active; and (5) meanings are subject to change.

Communication settings have considerable impact on participants and on the communication process itself. Each setting provides a different set of constraints that arise from differing levels of complexity and operative factors. Settings not only make differing demands on communicators, but also can alter both the content and interpretation of messages.

Communication is a social process characterized by action. All of the ingredients (participants, setting, situation, messages, etc.) interact, and each affects all of the other ingredients. Communication is active, and participants respond to one another and to themselves on the basis of meaning that is screened through a social structure that is continually changing. Each communication exchange has its unique elements and meanings; values are social products that change.

Three fundamental propositions can be derived from the key ideas of symbolic interaction and communication. (1) One's interpretation and perception of the environment depend on communication. To a considerable extent, individuals perceive on the basis of their prior communication experiences. Communication allows for the reduction of uncertainty without direct sensory experience. The media are a primary source of indirect experience and for that reason have impact on the construction of social reality. (2) Communication is guided by and guides the concepts of self, role, and situations, and these concepts generate expectations in the communication setting. (3) Communication is complex interaction involving action, interdependence, mutual influence, meaning, relationship, and situational factors.

One overall maxim from our initial discussion is that communication is easy—if one does not care about the results. In this text we are concerned about communicators as practitioners and decision makers. In the final analysis we all act on the basis of the best information available, because we must act. We will offer guidelines for behavior on the basis of empirical studies and also on the basis of theoretical constructs. Development of the theoretical framework of this chapter should provide you with anchor points from which you can select alternatives for action.

NOTES

1. Alfred R. Lindesmith, Anselm L. Strauss, and Norman K. Denzin, *Social Psychology*, 4th ed. (Hinsdale, Ill.: The Dryden Press, 1975), pp. 4–5.

2. *Ibid.*, p. 8.

3. Jurgen Ruesch and Gregory Bateson, *Communication: The Social Matrix of Psychiatry* (New York: Norton, 1968), pp. 15–16.

4. Dean C. Barnlund, *Interpersonal Communication: Survey and Studies* (Boston: Houghton Mifflin, 1968), p. 10.

5. John Stewart, *Bridges Not Walls: A Book About Interpersonal Communication* (Reading, Mass.: Addison-Wesley, 1973), pp. 16–17.

6. David K. Berlo, *The Process of Communication* (New York: Holt, Rinehart and Winston, 1960), p. 24.

7. Dan E. Miller and Robert H. Hintz, "The Elements and Structure of Openings," *Sociological Quarterly* **16** (Autumn 1975): 497–499.

8. Ludwig Wittgenstein, *Philosophische Untersuchungen,* trans. G. E. M. Anscombe (Oxford: Blackwell, 1953).

9. C. Wright Mills, "Some Effects of Mass Media," in *Mass Media and Mass Man,* ed. Alan Casty (New York: Holt, Rinehart and Winston, 1968), p. 32. (Selection from C. Wright Mills, *The Power Elite,* New York: Oxford University Press, 1956, p. 311.)

10. Summarized from Al Haas, "Marketing of a Movie Monster," *Salt Lake Tribune,* August 29, 1975.

11. Raymond Bauer, "The Obstinate Audience: The Influence Process from the Point of View of Social Communication," *American Psychologist* **19** (May 1964): 319.

12. Orrin E. Klapp, *Symbolic Leaders* (Chicago: Aldine, 1964), p. 28.

13. Donald K. Darnell, "Toward a Reconceptualization of Communication," *Journal of Communication* **21** (March 1971): 7.

14. J. Edward Hulett, Jr., "A Symbolic Interactionist Model of Human Communication," *AV Communication Review* **14** (Spring 1966): 11.

Part II

Interdependence of Communication and Social Behavior

$$G_n = \frac{1}{T/2} \int_{-T/4}^{T/4} f(2t) e^{-jn(2\omega_0)t} dt$$

changing variable, let $x = 2t$; $dx =$

$$G_n = \frac{1}{T} \int_{-T/2}^{T/2} f(x) e^{-jn\omega_0 x} dx = F_n \quad ;$$

coefficients are invariant with the

$$G_n = \frac{1}{T} \int_{-T/2}^{T/2} f(t-2) e^{-jn\omega_0 t} dt \quad ;$$

let $x = t - 2$; $dx = dt$;

$$G_n = \frac{1}{T} \int_{-T/2-2}^{T/2+2} f(x) e^{-jn\omega_0(x+2)} dx$$

$$= e^{-j2n\omega_0} \frac{1}{T} \int_{-T/2}^{T/2} f(x) e^{-jn\omega_0 x} dx$$

$$G_n = \frac{1}{T} \int_{-T/2}^{T/2} e^{j\omega_0 t} f(t) e^{-jn\omega_0 t} dt$$

$$= \frac{1}{T} \int_{-T/2}^{T/2} f(t) e^{-j(n-1)\omega_0 t} dt \quad =$$

In Part I we explored the key ideas of symbolic interaction and communication, and the discussion led to some derived propositions. The three chapters in Part II use the previous material to examine three ideas central to both symbolic interaction and communication.

Chapter 2 examines how people use symbols to communicate. The symbolic process may be understood by placing it in the larger scheme of sign systems. Chapter 3 explains the importance of self and communication. Communication plays a role in the development of self. A person communicates his or her "self" to others in order to accomplish relationships. Moreover, one may use a concept of self to analyze communication events.

Because people live in social contact with many people, self must be presented in accordance with some social rules. The rules of social presentation may be viewed as roles—the topic of Chapter 4. Role is explored as a means of acquiring and executing the social rules of communication.

Part II of the text explains how a symbolic interactionist views the process of communication. Part III focuses on the purposes of communication.

Chapter 2

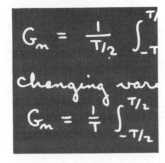

The Symbolic Process in Communication

INTRODUCTION

The concepts of symbolic process, self, and role behavior constitute the basic elements of a symbolic interactionist perspective. The symbolic process is important to this perspective because symbols are the tools people use in interaction. Self is important because the internal being gives meaning to what is communicated. The importance of role behavior lies in the idea that a relationship takes place within societal rules for behavior.

Philosophers have long argued about what makes the human animal unique. To the symbolic interactionist, the answer lies in the human being's ability to use symbols.[1] Although members of other animal species are able to communicate with one another, only humans can interact by means of symbols. Most people take for granted this uniquely human and highly complicated process of symbolizing, except for those few instances when they cannot find "just the right word."

SIGN SYSTEM

To discuss the concept of symbols, one must start with the generic concept of *signs*. A sign is any element used to represent another element. In the language of psychology, signs are at least conditioned stimuli (CS). In the familiar example of Pavlov's dog, the dog's salivating at the presentation of meat powder is a reaction to an unconditioned stimulus (UCS). No learning is necessary for the dog to emit the response; the presentation of the unconditioned stimulus always evokes the same response. However, if meat powder (UCS) is paired with a bell ringing (CS) over many trials, the dog will eventually respond to the bell as if it were the meat powder, i.e., by salivating. In simplistic language, we say that the dog has learned to treat the bell (one element) as a representation of meat powder (another element). The dog has learned a *sign* for meat powder.

Of course, not all signs elicit a singular response, but all things used as signs are different from the things represented. In other words, signs are always representational of something else. A stop sign is not a clear picture of a stopping action; the word "woman" does not look like a particular woman; and so on through the entire list of signs people use. A sign is a sensory impression that conjures up an image of an object or idea.

Signs may be classified as either natural or artificial. *Natural* signs are physical phenomena used to represent other phenomena. For example, more hair on horses, early hibernation of animals, and deep folds in the jetstream are regarded as natural signs predictive of a harsh winter. The meteorologist, more scientific, is nonetheless still observing natural signs—changes in temperature patterns, sunspot activity, etc. *Artificial* signs are phenomena that have been constructed. However, an artificial sign is valid in representing the "thing" under consideration only if the participants agree that the sign is a representation. For example, if you make up the word "ghoti," it is useless as a sign unless you tell people what your new word represents. However, if the people with whom you are communicating know that "ghoti" is George Bernard Shaw's optional spelling of "fish" (the *gh* from enou*gh*, the *o* from w*o*men, and the *ti* from na*ti*on), your "word" has become a sign.

A major distinction between natural and artificial signs is that natural signs are active, whereas artificial signs are interactive. Active signs are used for a personal interpretation; interactive ones are designated by two or more people as representing a "thing." For example, suppose that a friend is teaching you how to know when a woolly worm is extra woolly. Your friend tells you that when you see very woolly, woolly worms, there will be a hard winter with lots of snow. Sure enough, the winter is harsh, and your area is devastated by snowstorms. The following autumn you see a woolly worm that is twice as woolly as the ones you saw the year before. You know what kind of winter is on the way. To warn people, you do not hold up the worm and go racing through town, shouting, "Look, Look." Instead, you speak to them, possibly even trying to convince them of your woolly-worm theory. To you, the woolly worm was a natural sign, an active one you used to make a personal interpretation. But when you then spoke to other people about the meaning of the woolly worm, you used words (artificial signs) to communicate to others (interaction).

Signals

Artificial signs may be classified as either signals or symbols. A *signal* is an artificial sign that produces a *predictable response* in the listener. When you are driving and encounter a red traffic light, you stop automatically (or at least we will predict that you will stop). A red traffic light has become a signal for you. As such, it is a means by which you and the city traffic engineer interact. Both you and the traffic engineer agree precisely on what the red traffic light represents. Moreover, you have become so conditioned to this representation that it elicits a single response: "Stop." By extension, artificial signs that produce only one accepted response to the representation are signals.

Symbols

Symbols, the second category of artificial signs, produce a *degree of ambiguity* in the listener and therefore diminish the predictability of the response. Suppose that you encounter an amber traffic light while you're driving. The degree to which your behavior can be predicted is less than if the light were red. Immediately you begin to calculate answers to a variety of questions: How long has the light been amber? Can I get through the intersection before the light turns red? Where is the nearest policeman? Should I stop or go? Although only two responses are available to you—stop or go—we cannot be sure which action you will choose. The caution you exhibit at the amber light is an indication that your mental processes are more active and that behaving in a reflexlike manner is inappropriate.

Symbol responses are learned but are not conditioned. A learned response is always made on the basis of the organism's unique experience. A learned response may be represented as stimulus to organism to response (S-O-R). A conditioned response, by contrast, is represented as stimulus to response (S-R). The filtering of the stimulus through an organism is what differentiates symbols and signals. Signals elicit conditioned responses; symbols elicit learned responses. Such a distinction naturally leads to the conclusion that all artificial signs start as symbols and that some symbols are repeated and reinforced so many times that they become signals. Consequently, distinctions between signals and symbols must be based on their functional response rather than on any inherent properties either may contain.

It is neither appropriate nor possible to construct a list of signs that are invariably signals and those that are invariably symbols. Even a red light conveys different meanings, depending on whether it's at an intersection or over a porch alongside a Nevada highway. Thus the context in which a sign is presented is important in determining a person's interpretation of that sign. To write the word *fire* and say that you should discuss its relation to forests is quite different from shouting "fire!" in a crowded, dark movie theater. In the first instance you would probably treat the word as a symbol; 588 people were killed on December 30, 1903, in a Chicago movie theater when they treated the cry of "fire" as a signal. The distinction between and classification of signs can be summarized as in Fig. 2.1.

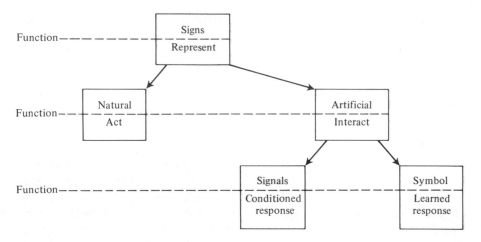

Figure 2.1

RELATIONSHIP OF SIGNS

Much of the distinction between signals and symbols is based on the concepts of linguistics. Charles W. Morris, a linguistic scholar, is interested primarily in how humans use the entire sign system.[2] He offered an idea of how people deal with signs and of the implication of the relationship of signs. These relationships are of three types: (1) *syntactic*—sign to sign; (2) *semantic*—sign to signified; and (3) *pragmatic*—sign to sign user. But Morris argues that this statement of relationship is incomplete. Specifically, he states that the relationship is such that we consider the

> syntactics studying the ways in which signs are combined, semantics studying the signification of signs, and so the interpretant behavior without which there is no signification, pragmatics studying the origins, uses, and effects of the signs within the total behavior of the interpreters of signs.[3]

The three categories above are a useful way to approach the study of signs; they offer fairly distinct categories and demand that human behavior be recognized in each category. Although the language above emphasizes the concept of sign, we are concerned primarily with symbols.

Syntactics

Syntactics includes the concepts of both performance and competence. Syntactic performance, known as linguistic analysis, focuses on how people combine symbols. If you were to do a sentence diagram of the preceding sentence, for example, you would be undertaking a linguistic analysis. The importance of syntactic performance for communication should be readily apparent; performance is the linking together of symbols to construct a message. Thus this entire book may be viewed as a syntactic performance by the writers. Because messages link initiator and respondent, communication involves syntactic performance by the participants. It should also be noted that performance pertains to the external behavior of people. Performance is concerned with how the symbols are arranged in an organized way. For example, a teacher of English composition may focus on sentence fragments, poor tense agreements, and run-on sentences in students' writing samples.

Competence is associated with psycholinguistics. Psycholinguists are not so much interested in how symbols are combined as they are in what internal states produce the combinations. Perhaps the best-known psycholinguist is Noam Chomsky.[4] "Chomsky is working 'from the inside out' rather than 'from the outside in.' "[5] Competence, in Chomsky's theory, deals with the internal syntax that we hold inside ourselves.

Competence starts with the proposition that the human being is innately endowed with the ability to handle language syntactically. The psycholinguist, interested in explaining this innate "mechanism," contends that ideas are first held in relatively simple sentences which are then transformed to single units for performance. For example, the following sentences are kernel ideas: "The car is red. The car is going fast. I love speed." These sentences may be transformed into the statement: "I love that fast red car." Competence is an internal concept because it offers a way of explaining how people operate syntactically at the mental or interpretative level. Linguistic competence offers a view of how humans organize their thoughts in order to communicate.

Both approaches to syntactics are useful in explaining how humans arrange symbols for communication. Although the approaches differ in several respects, both state that syntactics and meaning are inseparable. Chomsky's much quoted sentence, "Colourless green ideas sleep furiously," appears to be stated in good grammar, but it is meaningless. The sentence violates selection rules of words, and therefore it is both meaningless and poor syntax.

Syntactical rules constitute the organizing principles of language. Language becomes meaningful only to the extent that syntactical rules are understood and employed by all members of a language group. If you choose to put all verbs at the beginning of sentences and a close friend decides to place all adjectives there, the two of you will have problems communicating.

Syntactical rules do not apply only to word-symbols. Many nonverbal behaviors are symbolic and must therefore be considered too. Birdwhistell's study of kinesics, for example, is largely an attempt to identify how eyebrow movements combine with other facial movements to become expressive.[6] Similarly, much of the study about personal space is attempting to establish the ways in which people arrange their bodies with regard to physical space.[7]

Little attention has been given to the ways in which individuals correlate nonverbal behaviors to verbal behaviors to convey meaning. For example, spoken in a hostile tone of voice, the sentence "I want you as a friend" is said to be "ironic," because the two separate cues—the words and the tone of voice—are discrepant. However, irony is only one such correlation, and little is known about the many other methods by which verbal and nonverbal cues can be combined.

Semantics

Semanticists, who attempt to answer the question of how humans treat the relationship of the word to the thing, often use the analogy of map to territory.[8] There are several problems with this analogy, however. First, a map does not look like the territory it is supposed to represent. A road map of your state would be of little help if you used it to try and identify your state as you circled Earth in a spacecraft. Second, a map does not include everything in the territory. Your state road map does not indicate every city street and rural gravel trail. Thus, according to the analogy, a sign is not identical to or inclusive of the thing represented. The word "radio," for example, cannot tell a person what the thing looks like or name all of its parts and elements. In short, symbols are artificial creations, and they seldom, if ever, resemble the thing represented.

According to the so-called semantic-triangle theory, meanings (images) are in people. That is, a sign and a thing are related only because a person is present to create the relationship. Using a modified version of Ogden and Richards' semantic triangle, we can use a broken line to show that the link between sign and thing is weak (not identical and not inclusive), as in Fig. 2.2.[9] The strong link exists between the thing and the image an individual has of it, as well as between the image held and the sign.

A person's location in this image-sign-thing relationship has a tendency to create intensional orientation.[10] Intensional orientation is the phenomenon of believing that the sign is the thing. For example, if you were given an ordinary wafer cookie but were told that the recipe included a pinch of steer manure and 100 ground black ants for every 20 cookies, you would probably begin to feel ill. Your reaction would be based more on the sign than on the thing; consequently, we could say that you were intensionally oriented.

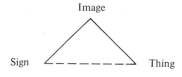

Figure 2.2

Euphemisms and dysphemisms also involve intensional orientation. A euphemism is a label that enhances a thing or makes it more pleasant; a dysphemism, by contrast, denigrates a thing or makes it unpleasant. For example, suppose that you see "Beaf steak 'tartar' " on a restaurant menu. You decide to splurge $6.50 on this item; the label sounds good, hints of French cooking, and the restaurant offers Continental cuisine. Your reaction to the *thing*—raw ground beef with a raw egg in the middle—might be much different from your reaction to the *label*. When you tell a friend about your experience, you may go to the other extreme and use a dysphemism to describe what you were served—dead ground-up cow with an oozing raw egg. In marketing products, by contrast, the sales staff and advertisers may use a euphemism as an enticement. The Lincoln automobile ads say "previously owned Continental," not "used car." Jerry Della Femina, in his delightful and insightful book on advertising agencies, mentions that many products are created because a great name was thought of for a product.[11]

Another concept within semantics is the notion that signs are self-reflexive, whereas things are not. A person has the facility to use one sign to talk about another. One can use words about words about words. However, there are no methods by which one thing can stand for another thing. It appears impossible at this time that any one thing can refer to any other thing without re-creating one as a sign for the other.

The semanticist also studies the levels of abstraction in terms of how signs are related to things. Young children learn that each thing has a label; however, their label repertoire is smaller than the number of things about them. Moreover, their category systems may differ from that of their parents. Thus parents may become embarrassed when their child says "Daddy" to the mailman who comes to the door. Each thing has several labels (signs), depending on how many like things are in the category. Daddy can also be a Mr. Smith, an American, a man, a human being, an animal, and so on.

Brown has suggested that categories can be differentiated on the basis of criterial attributes, or properties of the class of things which are important for identification.[12] Although the concept of criterial attributes seems simple enough to understand, they are so internalized that a person may have difficulty stating them. As an exercise, you might try stating the criterial attributes for the category "book." Once you have them stated, can a few friends use your statements to place newspapers, notebooks, sheafs of paper, and magazines into the category?

Pragmatics

The third area of study in the relationship of signs is the origin, uses, and effects of signs on human behavior—pragmatics. Several theories of the origin of language have been proposed, but here we will only explore some uses and effects of being symbol users.[13] Some of the effects of the relationship of sign to sign user are described in the Sapir-Whorf hypothesis, also known as the linguistic-relativity hypothesis. Whorf stated:

> The background linguistic system of each language is not merely a reproducing instrument for voicing ideas but rather is itself the shaper of ideas, the program and guide for the individual's mental activity, for his analysis of impressions, for his synthesis of his mental stock in trade.[14]

Whorf argues that language affects thought. In a broader sense, we may argue that language, thought, and environment covary to produce a world view for the language user. The only dilution of "pure" linguistic relativity is to eliminate the single linear direction of language affecting thought. Instead, we suggest that each of the three elements may affect any of the other two elements; consequently, the system is a process of mutual causality.

Complete proof of linguistic relativity has not been offered in research up to now. Much of Whorf's research has been criticized on the basis that he sought descriptive proof to already stated theorems and was possibly engaging in an academic form of self-fulfilling prophecy. However, Carroll reports studies which show that because the Zuni (Southwestern Indians) language labels a different color range than does English, children of one culture could not make the distinctions or remember the color within the range of the other culture.[15]

Carroll states that the English language requires a high amount of gender expression.[16] This may be a reason that the women's movement urges the elimination of labels of gender distinction, so as to make English less sexist. The basic idea is that by changing labels, such as "chairman" to "chairperson," and by using neuter pronouns, such as "one" instead of "he" or "she," American society will become less sexist. In other words, changes in language are being urged as a means to change a world view.

Another part of the linguistic-relativity hypothesis suggests that a person's "realities" are perceived in terms of this generated world view. One begins to see things in terms of one's needs and language. For example, one of the authors came to Utah from generally warm climates and took up skiing. Prior to this time, he had regarded snow as just snow, but his interest in skiing changed his needs, and the language of skiers began to force distinctions among packed, powder, dry snow, wet snow, corn snow, etc. Earlier, all of these designations would have been meaningless, but now his world view, language, and thought have changed because his environment changed.

Symbolic interactionism argues that every object a person perceives is filtered and interpreted through self. People see only what they have been taught to see or expect to see. Haney, in writing about perceptions, says that people never directly contact reality, that instead they are always directed by their backgrounds, experiences, biases, and so forth.[17] Selective perception simply means that people see the environment in the way that they were trained to see it. A child in an agrarian Hopi Indian culture sees time as a continuously repeating cycle. A child in a highly technological society sees time as measured into equal units that form a linear continuum of past to present to future.

Another aspect of the pragmatic relationship is that the American advanced technological society has moved from the industrial revolution to the information revolution. It is trite but true to say that all of us live in a vast sea of symbols and information. American institutions and culture are made up of, indeed supported by, symbols. People in American society were once thing-oriented; now they are symbol-oriented. General Motors exists not only because it provides transportation, but also because it markets and promotes its products to the public and uses objectives and master symbols within its own organization.

Master symbols are of extreme importance, for they express the norms and values of institutions. The American flag is a master symbol. It represents not only the United States, but also, as most American children are taught in the elementary grades, significant national traits: courage (red), virtue (blue), and purity (white). To university instructors, "academic freedom" is a master symbol. If you attack academic freedom and argue that it should be taken away, most professors will say that without academic freedom, there can be no such thing as a university. Businesspersons are committed to free enterprise. Each time the federal government attempts to control an industry or freeze prices, the business community asserts that because free enterprise is being threatened, so too is democracy. Master symbols become the representations that are held with a sacredlike grasp. To attack a master symbol is to attack the people who hold it. To invoke a master symbol is to immediately call for people to follow.

A given culture can be supported only if its members are taught the values and norms as expressed in the master symbols of that culture. This symbol-oriented human culture can function only if its members understand the symbolic process and realize its uses and effects.

Values and changes in value systems are transmitted from generation to generation by means of symbols. To speak in the pragmatic sense, the symbol user creates culture and transmits cultural values by means of a symbol system. For example, an early benchmark of educational progress is when children learn to tell time. They are taught that time can be evenly marked off into nanoseconds, milliseconds, seconds, minutes, hours, days, weeks, etc. Teachers continually reprimand students for being tardy. In English class, students are drilled for years in the difference among past, present, and future. No wonder that life seems dominated by clocks. Indeed, time is such an important concept that most people wear wristwatches in order to "know the time" as they rush from one clock to another. Time is important not because it is there, but because people teach and communicate it as a cultural value—time is money, promptness is a virtue. Time is only one value communicated by such means. The list is long and contains most of the things that shape human life.

THE FUNCTION OF SIGNS

Having explained the classification of the sign system and reviewed basic approaches to studying the sign system, we can relate these discussions to a statement of their relevance for communication. *Signals are used to regulate normative behavior in a society, and symbols are used to facilitate communicative behavior in a society.*

Because signals have the functional aspect of highly predictable responses to a particular stimulus, societies construct and teach signals as a means of eliciting typical (normative) ways of human behavior. When the traffic light turns red, drivers will stop. When a bell rings at the beginning of class, students stop their individual actions and engage in classroom activities; when a bell rings at the end of class, they stop class activities. Appropriate responses are so important to a society that it places sanctions on a person who deviates. If you run a red light, you may be given a traffic citation. If an instructor ignores class bells, the students will become disapproving; if the violations are serious, an administrative officer will deliver a reprimand to the instructor.

Normative behavior ensures the smooth operation of societies, and laws and statutes are written to govern the uses and responses to signals. Most traffic laws, for example, specify that certain signals be met with certain types of responses. Laws governing the inciting to riot generally state that if the signs used to excite people possess signal responses, a sign user can be found guilty. The issue of pornography can be viewed in this perspective. Most statutes on pornography define some signs as being obscene, because legislators or community officials believe that those signs will produce predictable responses of moral decay and sex-related crimes. As long as people in positions of authority think that pornography produces detrimental responses in a signallike fashion, there will be statutes governing its use and dissemination.

A popular rock song of the early 1970s was entitled "Signs." Part of the chorus was: "Signs, signs, everywhere a sign. Do this, Don't do that. . . ." The song lamented the vast numbers of signals that attempt to regulate and direct people's behavior. Keep Out; Don't Touch; Stand Behind the Line; Out Only; the list is almost endless. Each signal tries to restrict behavior to only one particular action. No one will be arrested for dashing in the "Out Only" door of an airport. Yet courtesy and signal training keep most people from doing so. Behavior norms are often as strong as statutes with the force of law behind them.

In most instances of signal transmittal, there seems to be a distance between the initiator and the respondent. This distance tends to eliminate the most simple types of interaction. Most drivers are unlikely to contact the city traffic engineer and ask what the "Yield" sign at a particular intersection means. Most people don't question a property owner about why the "No Trespassing" sign was placed on the fence. Signal transmission implies action and does not allow for assumptions of interaction. Consequently, signalizing is a normative behavior rather than a communicative behavior.

When people respond to signals, their behavior is causally linear. A stimulus produces a predictable response. Such a sequential analysis denies the interaction and negotiation assumptions of communication. Hence it must be another part of the sign system that is employed for communication. In a symbolic interactionist's perspective, the use of *symbols* offers people the possibility of communication.

As people attempt to share meaning by means of communication, symbols become their tools of communication. Because symbols have a degree of ambiguity in their representation of sensory experiences, people may "bargain" over the symbols and begin to reach commonalities, or shared views, of a particular topic under discussion. Figure 2.3, a modification of Fig. 2.2, presents a schematic representation of how two people come together in communication. Figure 2.3 demonstrates that the linkage between two communicators is the symbols that both employ in communication. The bonds leading from the symbols to meaning are the strongest ones. One person's reality is most distant from the other person's, and those realities are filtered through the people. Symbols become arousers of meaning in individuals, who then will attempt to relate the meaning to their particular reality of the world. When the symbol, meaning, and reality do not seem correlated, a person will offer symbols back to the other person in an attempt to arouse more of a correlated meaning. Although English makes this explanation sound sequential, communication is not a linear sequence. Both communicators are continually interpreting and representing themselves to the other. Moreover, no single element shown in Fig. 2.3 causes the linkage to become active.

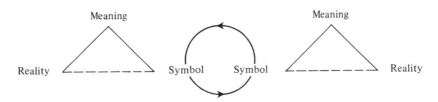

Figure 2.3

As communicators are linked by symbols, all of the aspects of the sign system (syntactics, semantics, and pragmatics) come into play by encouraging certain types of meanings to be aroused in the individual. The statement "I love snowstorms and blizzards" presents a communicator in a certain meaningful orientation. The meaning is changed if the syntax is inverted: "Snowstorms and blizzards love me." Semantically, the communicator has labeled events that might be quite different from your events and has offered a statement about the communicator's world view. A skier and a commuter in a large industrial city may have quite different views toward snow.

NONVERBAL BEHAVIOR AS SIGNS

Spoken and written language is not the only artificial sign system. Humans employ a number of sign systems, the most basic of which are the verbal and nonverbal sign systems. We argue, however, that what has typically been called "nonverbal communication," or body language, is inappropriate. Nonverbal signs are not necessarily communicative in the strict symbolic sense. Many nonverbal signs are signals in many contexts and possibly symbols in other contexts. In the heat of an argument, a person may extend the middle finger and then walk off. In American culture such a gesture can be interpreted in only one way. However, a young person who has just learned "the gesture" may use it in many situations, including a form of salutation to close friends. The test of a communicative event is whether or not the linkage is symbolic, with all its constituent implications. When a nonverbal behavior is interpreted as a symbol, it is communicative. Moreover, when a nonverbal behavior is linked to verbal behavior for a more complete interpretation, it is communicative.

Harrison notes that many writers have attempted to say what nonverbal communication is by categorizing nonverbally communicative phenomena.[18] He states that the categories have been as few as 3 and as many as 18. The categories presented by Knapp, however, appear to be adequate.[19] We will therefore use Knapp's seven categories to show what behaviors are typically considered to be nonverbal communication.

Kinesics, or body motion, includes gestures, hand signals, posture, facial expression, and the like. A smiling face and angry words give out discrepant cues and make interpretation more difficult, because the receiver does not know which symbol is the "correct" one.

Physical characteristics, such as body shape, odor, height, weight, and skin color, form Knapp's second category. Many personality myths are based on physical characteristics, e.g., jolly fat men and dumb blondes.

Touching behavior may be communicative. Many people believe that a handshake reveals a lot about a person. Aunts always hug and kiss at reunions to show family affection.

Paralanguage refers to voice qualities, inflection, and various nonverbal vocalizations. The intensity with which a person utters "damn" may "say" more than the word itself.

Proxemics is the study of social and personal space. Interest in this area has shown that people maintain certain distances for different types of interaction and arrange themselves in various ways, depending on the purpose of the event.

Artifacts is the category that deals with objects used for adornment. Glasses, wigs, medallions, jewelry, and cosmetics are typical artifacts. Clothes may say a great deal about the person wearing them. Artifacts are even used to label various groups of people, e.g., "hard hats," "long hairs," "white-collar workers."

Environmental factors, Knapp's last category, include lighting, interior decorating, colors, smells, noise, music, architecture, and the like. Stadiums are for yelling, whereas churches and synagogues are for praying. Certain decors suggest restfulness; others, restlessness.

Today, there is widespread interest in nonverbal communication, and it is indeed fascinating to talk about clothes making the person or certain gestures having different meanings in different cultures. However, the concern of communication scholars lies in the more substantive issues in nonverbal behavior. What behaviors facilitate communication? Which ones communicate? How is nonverbal communication integrated into the whole context of communication? According to the symbolic interactionist, a behavior communicates only to the degree that it becomes a symbol. From such a perspective, the answer to what is nonverbally communicative must be cast in terms of symbolic behavior. Many of the items in Knapp's categories do not meet the criterion of being a part of the symbolic and interpretative processes. Stadiums may be for yelling, but they do not communicate to people. Rather, they are facilitative; they serve as a context for a communicative event.

SUMMARY

In review, we have argued that whereas signals are like conditioned responses, symbols are the communicative signs employed in transactions. Both signals and symbols may be analyzed in terms of syntactic, semantic, and pragmatic relationships.

Despite all of the current interest in nonverbal communication, researchers have not come to terms with the issue of its place within the sign system.

Symbolic interactionism suggests that to the degree that a nonverbal behavior is symbolic, it is communicative.

In this chapter we have attempted to briefly review some primary concepts of the human sign system. In each of the chapters in Part III, we shall return to the ideas of language usage. The basic information provided here about symbolic processes will be applied and analyzed later in the text.

PROBLEMS AND ISSUES

1. Is there thought without language? This issue has been debated for years. We have implicitly leaned toward one answer in this chapter. Identify our position and then defend or attack that view.

2. A long-standing language controversy has existed between the empiricists (e.g., B. F. Skinner) and the rationalists (e.g., Noam Chomsky). The heart of the argument centers on whether or not language acquisition and behavior can be explained by means of reinforcement. Write a synopsis of one point of view and have a friend write a synopsis of the other point of view. Then engage in a discussion and attempt to determine which point of view appears the more reasonable.

3. Popular writers, such as Julian Fast (*Body Language*), have attempted to take research on nonverbal behavior and present prescriptive methods for reading and presenting nonverbal signs. Can you determine how effective these approaches are to understanding human communication?

NOTES

1. Ernest Becker, "From Animal to Human Reactivity," in *Social Psychology through Symbolic Interaction*, ed. Gregory P. Stone and Harvey A. Farberman (Waltham, Mass.: Ginn-Blaisdell, 1970), p. 99.

2. Charles W. Morris, *Signs, Language and Behavior* (New York: Prentice-Hall, 1946).

3. *Ibid.*, pp. 217–218.

4. Noam Chomsky, *Syntactic Structures* (The Hague: Mouton, 1957) and *Aspects of the Theory of Syntax* (Cambridge, Mass.: M.I.T. Press, 1965).

5. Peter Herriot, *An Introduction to the Psychology of Language* (London: Methuen, 1970), p. 58.

6. Ray L. Birdwhistell, *Kinesics and Context* (Philadelphia: University of Pennsylvania Press, 1970).

7. Edward T. Hall, *Silent Language* (Garden City, N.Y.: Doubleday, 1959);

Robert Sommer, *Personal Space* (Englewood Cliffs, N.J.: Prentice-Hall, 1969).

8. Alfred Korzybski, *Science and Sanity* (Lancaster, Pa.: Science Press, 1933).

9. C. K. Ogden and I. A. Richards, *The Meaning of Meaning,* 8th ed. (New York: Harcourt, Brace, and World, 1949).

10. William V. Haney, *Communication and Organizational Behavior,* rev. ed. (Homewood, Ill.: Richard D. Irwin, 1967), pp. 349–356.

11. Jerry Della Femina, *From Those Wonderful Folks Who Gave You Pearl Harbor* (New York: Pocket Books, 1971).

12. Roger Brown, *Words and Things* (paperbound edition, New York: Free Press, 1968).

13. For a fascinating account of some origin theories and a history of language, *see* Mario Pei, *The Story of Language,* rev. ed. (Philadelphia: Lippincott, 1965).

14. B. L. Whorf, *Language, Thought, and Reality,* ed. J. B. Carroll (New York: M.I.T. Press/Wiley, 1956), p. 212.

15. John B. Carroll, *Language and Thought* (Englewood Cliffs, N.J.: Prentice-Hall, 1964), pp. 107–108.

16. *Ibid.,* p. 109.

17. Haney, *op. cit.,* p. 59.

18. Randall P. Harrison, *Beyond Words: An Introduction to Nonverbal Communication* (Englewood Cliffs, N.J.; Prentice-Hall, 1974), pp. 27–29.

19. Mark L. Knapp, *Nonverbal Communication in Human Interaction* (New York: Holt, Rinehart and Winston, 1972), pp. 5–8.

Chapter 3

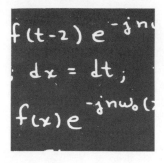

The Process of Self in Communication

INTRODUCTION

Having discussed the symbolic process, we now turn to a second important concept of symbolic interaction—self. Of central concern in this perspective, the self gives the human being the basis for action and the distinct character of interaction. For a symbolic interactionism perspective, we must define self, show how relationships are maintained, and offer a method of analyzing behavior that reveals self.

SELF IN PROCESS

The term "self" (as opposed to "personality," "self-concept," etc.) is preferred by symbol interactionists because it forces a view of the person as a whole, ever-changing entity. Moreover, the concept of self requires the presence of another person, because it is not structure but interaction that defines the self. This construct of self is based on three attributes of the self: holism, process, and interaction.

Interaction

A person's concept of self is derived from communication with others. William James states that "a man has as many social selves as there are individuals who recognize him and carry an image of him in their minds."[1] In other words, self is realized through interdependence with others. Writing about the self, Stone and Farberman underline James's point: "All conduct must be situated in a matrix of communication before analysis and explanation begin."[2] Taken together, these two ideas suggest that the self is developed in communication with others and that the self can be understood only as it is revealed in communication.

Process

The self as a process has been best described by Gordon Allport.[3] He notes that the self has been viewed in three alternative ways. The first is self as a "reactive being," a view taken by behavioral psychology. The person is reactive as a result of a history of conditioning. Such a view leads to a vocabulary or "reaction, response, reinforcement, reflex, respondent, reintegration . . . reference is backwards. What *has* been is more important than what *will* be."[4] The second alternative, seeing the self as "reactive in depth," is characterized by Freudian psychoanalysis. Here too the person is viewed as being constituted by past experience. According to this view, the *re-* compounds most aptly describe the person, e.g., repression, regression, recall, and resistance.

The first and second alternatives place the self in a historical perspective, but they avoid the existentialist question: "Who am I?" Allport states that the third alternative is the attempt to answer that more current question. Thus self is "being in the process of becoming."[5] In other words, self is a present phenomenon that is progressing or growing toward the future. The language of such a view is linked with *pro-* compounds, e.g., proaction, progress, program, production, and problem solving. Such a view forces one to say, "I am here, and that is where I will probably go."

Allport states that the process view of self is based on commitment and tentativeness. Commitment refers to deciding on a course of action, wagering that that is the way to grow. However, realizing that a wager is always governed by probability, the person is tentative about those commitments. New avenues for the person's becoming self may arise.

Two consequences of this commitment-tentative process are that a person never necessarily arrives at a final destination and that a person can change and yet not feel inconsistent about doing so. In summarizing his call for viewing self as a being in the process of becoming, Allport states:

> Most of all we need to surrender the models that would compress human personality into the routine homeostatic situation that we find in quasi-closed systems. Human personality [read] self is a wide-open system, responsive to tangible and intangible culture, on the look-out for new ideas, and capable of asking an altogether new type of question . . . "Who am I?"[6]

Holism

The notion that the self is holistic is based on a rejection of dualism and a statement about how "aspects" of the self relate. In earlier times, people believed that their thinking processes could not be held accountable for what their bodies did or were. Most people today, however, reject this dualism— the idea that mind and body are two separate operating entities. William James expanded the concept of holism. The whole, or self, is more than just mind and body. Self, he argued, is all that one claims to own: house, clothes, cars, work, bank accounts, and educational degrees.[7] A person is a single self comprising mind, body, and possessions.

In addition to being holistic, the self also has several aspects. Indeed, it has been argued that the self has separate, distinct parts. These parts of the self were labeled the *I* and *Me* by William James. The use of such terms suggests a mind duality—a person's "good" and "bad" selves. But the duality is not of this type. Rather, as James argued, the duality is one of "discriminated aspects and not separate things."[8] James suggested that when thinking about one's own self, a person thinks of the self as an object. Self-as-object can be explained as follows. If a stranger asked, "Who are you?" you would probably respond by stating your name. But if the person persisted and said, "But who are you *really?*" your answer would contain adjectives and nouns. You might say, "I am a student" or even "I am a symbolic interactionist." Your "self" as known is always an object, or what James termed the Me.

The I, by contrast, refers to the self as actor. Your answer to the question "Why are you doing that?" deals with your self as an actor, as a being-in-process.

A whole self is not possible without this duality of self-as-object—Me—and self-as-actor—I. Further, this duality is not merely one of parallel aspects. Indeed, "the I pushes into the Me."[9] The self is complete only when action and object are taken together.

The I appears to be the active aspect of self; the Me, the reflective. Suppose that you sell shoes in a department store and that you are also taking an interviewing-sales course. When the instructor says that the poorest opening of a sales interview is "May I help you?" you begin to reflect on how you open conversations with customers in the store. If you respect the instructor, you might think that perhaps your sales technique is not too good and that you should change. Your I opened sales in the past, but it is your Me that is now thinking of that previous action. To say that only actions or only reflections about action are self is to make self an incomplete or fragmented concept. To be whole, the self must include one's action (I) *and* one's thoughts about that action (Me).

Self Defined

Having described the assumptions underlying the construct of self, we can define the self as a *person's organization of accumulated experience, which provides the basis for personal action.* The self, then, is what a person has experienced and knows about one's self. This organized, experiential foundation encourages a person to behave in certain ways. Implicit in this definition is Kelley's idea that the self is acquired, not given.[10] The self is not static, but rather continuously gains new experiences, which in turn forces greater and greater organization of what the person is becoming.

DEVELOPMENT OF SELF

There are three areas in which the self and communication are vitally linked: development of self, self-disclosure, and ego states in communication analysis. As Stone points out, "A primary tenet of all symbolic interaction theory holds that the self is established, maintained, and altered in and through communication."[11] Stone's point is well taken; communication is not only the means by which self is developed, but also the expression of self. It is probably impossible to communicate without saying something about one's self. Even the most innocuous conversations—"How are you?" "Fine."—reveal something about the participants through their tones of voice, facial expressions, and who says what to whom. Such brief encounters as passing greetings on campus "say" which people you will treat as persons and which others you will treat as nonpersons or simply as objects in your environment. Although some expression of self pervades all communicative encounters, certain aspects offer direct bearing on the self.

In isolating one aspect of communication and self as the development of self, we want to reemphasize that the self is never developed; rather, it is always in the process of becoming. Development of self occurs as long as a person is alive. The development of self may be most rapid in childhood, but growth and change are lifelong processes; only their rates of speed change.

Labeling

One aspect of communication that is a part of the development of the self is labeling, the use of words to categorize another person as a particular type or thing. Rosenthal offers an excellent example, though not about people, of the effect of labeling.[12] He took a group of laboratory rats and divided them randomly into two groups. The cage of one group had a label that read "Maze Dull"; the other, "Maze Bright." Then Rosenthal's students in his experimental psychology course ran experiments on conditioning rats in maze running. Despite hundreds of trials, no rat in the "dull" group ran as fast as the slowest rat in the "bright" group. Why? Rosenthal suggests that the students reacted to the labels; they expected the rats in the bright group to do better, coaxed them, petted them, and handled them gently. If people can change the behavior of rats by thinking that one group is brighter than another, think of what happens when the recipient of a label is a thinking human being.

Children say, "Sticks and stones will break my bones, but names will never hurt me," but never when somebody is actually hurling a rock; rather, the words are a defense mechanism against the label. Names *can* really do harm. A bone can be mended, but what do you do with a self that has been labeled "stupid" again and again and again? Labels generally have to be attached many times before they take hold. But if a person really significant in another's life offers a label, it may "stick in one application."

First names and nicknames may also be used as labels in developing the self. Different "personalities" are associated with Chrissy, Chris, Christine; with Charlie, Chuck, Charles. Few people want or change their names to Hortense, Mortimer, Clarabelle, or Horace unless it is highly respected in the family.

Value/Significant Others

Another aspect of communication that works in developing the self is the value attached to utterances. A person's self-worth and independence are determined largely by the way others respond to that person's statement. The following conversation illustrates the idea of value attached to a person's utterance.

A: The U.S. has really solved racial discrimination.

B: I don't think so.

A: Oh sure, look at all the blacks in college, and public schooling can't be segregated.

B: Yea, but Southerners send all their white kids to private schools.

A: That's just in the South.

B: Maybe, but it's subtle in the rest of the schools. Don't schedule them in certain classes, and make them take a lot of P.E. and Vocational Ed.

A: Well, there are more blacks in business.

B: Not really, because there are more whites too. Our population has grown, so the proportions are the same, but the TV tells you more about the blacks to soothe them.

A: I don't like to say you're right, but I guess we haven't made much progress.

B: You bet I'm right.

We must assume that because A talks to B, B is important to A. B consistently denies any point A makes, unless it agrees with what B has said. Numerous such conversations, in which B is always labeling A's statements as insufficient or erroneous, will lead A to feel less worthy than B. Moreover, A will become dependent on B, beginning conversations with, "What do you think about such and such?" B will say something, and A and B will talk at great length about B's point of view being correct. If, however, B had wanted to help A develop a more positive self, B would have agreed with some of A's statements and then offered a point of view, with which A could either agree or disagree.

We all have certain people whom we use as standards. We seek out these people, offer our ideas, and await validation. These significant others become a large part of the tools we use to check our developing selves.

Language Impact

A third aspect of communication's role in the developing self is language impact. Language impact refers to the role of language as a means of both communicative linkage and also conveying an image of self. In Chapter 2, we said that language affects people and vice versa. One of language's effects is to mold a person's self-image in correspondence with the prevailing social order's view of people.

Miller and Swift have addressed this point in showing how language encourages females in American society to view themselves as second to males.[13] They argue that society (which is governed mostly by men) has used language as one device to build in women a self that is viewed as inferior. The male bias in language is exemplified by words such as hu*man, man*kind, and *man,* all of which are highly valued words which stress "man" to the exclusion of "woman." "Queen, dame, and madam have all acquired additional derogatory connotations without counterparts in king, lord, and sir."[14] Historians, most of whom are men, easily (if not unconsciously) group woman as a part of man's possessions. "Young people learn that intrepid pioneers crossed the country in covered wagons with their wives, children, and cattle; they do not learn that women themselves were intrepid pioneers rather than part of the baggage."[15]

To counteract the impact of language on the developing self, Miller and Swift recommend using "genkind" and "gen" as the group, or generic, word. "Gen," they suggest, would refer to both sexes and would also express "the warmth . . . of generous, gentle, and genuine."[16]

Language discriminates on the basis of not only sex, but also color. Indeed, Ossie Davis has called language a tyrant in racial discrimination.[17] Davis cites the use of the color terms of black and white; black has negative connotations, and white has positive and saintly connotations.

After an article had appeared in *Psychology Today* which forcefully demonstrated black-white connotations, the magazine challenged its readers to try reversing the bigotry of language by offering white negatives and black positives.[18] Although the readers came up with some reverses, two things were apparent. First, the lists were very short. Second, nearly all of the reverses had to be explained, for they were not common, e.g., Black Betsy (a baseball bat) or black gold (oil). One reader, arguing that the word "discrimination" goes beyond black and white, wrote: "Actually, we Chicanos are the ones with the real handicap. Try a brown list for size."[19]

Authority

A fourth aspect of communication's relation to the developing self is what Kelley has called authoritarianism.[20] Most people, Kelley argues, communicate with children from an authoritarian point of view. Although Americans live in a democracy and elect public officials, the sources of communication that impinge most on the developing self of the child are family, school, and religious body. He calls this small-scale tyranny (as opposed to the large-scale tyranny of a Hitler). Operating "on the growing edge of the personality of the young," the authoritarian communication becomes: "Do this. Do that."[21] The child is not allowed to choose or to make decisions. Rather, the developing self of the child is expected to obey the commands and learn that knowledge and volition are in the hands of another. When authoritarianism becomes the dominant form of communication, the developing self will become crippled and unhealthy, because its only experience has been in obeying another person's decisions.

Kelley offers a list of what the developing self should be. He states that a fully functioning self "thinks well of [oneself] . . . thinks well of others . . . sees [one's] stake in others . . . sees [oneself] as a part of a world in movement —in process of becoming— . . . sees the value of mistakes . . . develops and holds human values . . . knows no other way to live except in keeping with [those] values . . . is cast in a creative role."[22] This list of eight items for a healthy developing self is lodged in a social matrix that uses communication to hold it together.

SELF-DISCLOSURE

Although most (hopefully all) people have a concern with the continual development of self, generally a person's more immediate concern is how to establish and maintain relationships with others. Self-disclosure is a type of communication aimed directly at the issue of relationships. Stewart has stated that genuine self-disclosure simply means honestly "sharing with another some aspects of what makes you a person, aspects the other individual wouldn't be likely to recognize or understand without your help."[23] The essence of a relationship is the sharing of one's self with another. The goal of a relationship is to transform you and me to us. The "us" becomes an intimate contact wherein my*self* and your*self* take on a sharing or view of being linked. This is a situation in which a self appears more complete because it has the complementarity of another *self*. Another way of saying this is that as social beings, humans are never complete in isolation. In prison, a severe form of punishment is for a person to be put in isolation; in the elementary grades, a child's punishment may be to sit in a corner facing the wall. Similarly, American culture has always viewed the hermit as being eccentric and weird.

Any communication sets up a relationship, and people are trained to perceive different types of relationships. There are differences between acquaintances and friends, between friends and lovers. The level of relationship seems to be dictated by how much the participants actually know about each other. Hence self-disclosing communication is a means of establishing and maintaining deeper-level relationships.

Often people assume that self-disclosure means a revelation of intimate sexual detail and bizarre fantasies. But self-disclosure need not have such "X"-rated content to be a genuine sharing. For example, to tell you that Don Faules and Dennis Alexander were born in Colorado and Nevada, respectively, and that we are Westerners at heart is self-disclosing. It is not the content that makes communication self-disclosing; rather, it is the openness with which information is offered that truly reflects the giver.

Relationship Expressed

In communication analysis the content level can be separated from the relationship level. The content refers to the clarity of the idea expressed; the relationship defines how the communicators are linked. If someone says to you, "Move over, dammit" or "May I step in beside you?" the content, or the basic idea, expressed may be the same in both statements. However, the relationship is different; the first statement suggests superiority and disregard, whereas the second may indicate a caring peer relationship.

Often the relationship is communicated by nonverbal means. If two old cronies are in a bar laughing, slapping each other on the back, and addressing each other as "ya old sunovabitch," we know that the intent is friendship, not insults. In communication, the wink of an eye, a touch, or a smile may say more about the relationship than the content. Consequently, in self-disclosure the way in which something is said may be more meaningful than the words. *Time* reported an interesting example of nonverbal relationship beyond the content. An airline company that got a lot of business out of the "I'm Cheryl. Fly Me." advertising campaign is planning another, similar campaign. "The new ads feature National stewardesses looking seductively into the camera and breathing 'I'm going to *fly* you like you've never been flown before.' The film makers coach them 'to say it like you're standing there stark naked.' "[24] The content could be a business proposition, but the relationship indicates a proposition of a different sort. In short, the heart of self-disclosure is the relationship set up between people, not the content.

Few Instances of Disclosure

After surveying the research in self-disclosure from a communication perspective, Pearce and Sharp identified five generalizations about self-disclosing communication.[25] Relatively few communication interactions involve high levels of disclosure. Think back on all of the communicative situations you were in during the last 48 hours. Undoubtedly, most do not fall within the category of self-disclosure. In normal daily activities, few people demand self-disclosure. Moreover, most routine business transactions do not need a high degree of self-disclosure. The check-out clerk at the bookstore, the shoe salesperson, or the attendant at a ball game—one recognizes them as persons and speaks to them accordingly, but one does not generally expect an enduring relationship. On the other hand, a few business transactions *do* necessitate self-disclosure. In these transactions people become friends: "*My* stock broker," "*My* realtor," "*my* insurance person." These business people handle large amounts of individuals' money and important aspects of their future; people should know them as well as they know their clients. Still, most people do not get a new stock broker or buy a house every day.

Dyadic Occurrence

Self-disclosure usually occurs in dyads. Sharing a part of oneself with others involves a great deal of risk, and in risk situations one wants to be able to have as much opportunity for feedback as possible. Two-person—dyadic—communication maximizes the chances for feedback.

Our culture also seems to teach us that the more people added to communication, the more public the topic of conversation. Two-person conversations may be personal and intimate, but they become less so as the number of participants increases. For example, we have often noticed what we call the "after-class shuffle." A number of students will come up to an instructor after class, and there will be a lot of "Why don't you go ahead?" "No, I can wait, but you probably have to get to another class." After the shuffle is finally arranged, the first topic usually deals with the day's class discussion. Then a few students drift away. The next topic might be questions about the final course project. More students leave. When the two students who are left begin to move uneasily, it is time for the instructor to say, "Let's go back to my office and give each of you a chance in private." The students' relief is obvious. Each wants to share a part of his or her self with the instructor, but relationships on private matters are not held in groups.

Symmetrical Talk

In a dyad, self-disclosure is usually symmetrical. That is, if one person self-discloses, the other person will generally offer some self information in return.

A bond of a relationship is reciprocal feelings and sharing. If only one person gives and the other takes in a communication, the giver begins to feel uneasy. Returning to the "after-class-shuffle example, one student wants to talk in private with the instructor. Once they are seated and comfortable in the office, the student starts by saying, "I haven't been doing well this quarter, and I wanted to talk to you so you would know I'm not a poor student." After some easy talk the student says, "My fiancée and I have been having a rough time, and we have finally broken off our engagement. It has been more involving than my studies." For symmetry of this self-disclosure (although not aware of symmetry), a good communicating instructor might say, "I can see how you feel; you know, if my wife and I argue in the morning, my teaching is just plain lousy." Although the students' grade problem hasn't been solved, the student and the instructor are beginning to see each other in a human way. Symmetry of self-disclosure seems to be a demand of a relationship.

Positive Social Relationships

Self-disclosure occurs in the context of positive social relationships. This generalization of Pearce and Sharp seems to be a truism. People who are hostile or dislike each other are unlikely to engage in high amounts of self-disclosure. However, on close examination this generalization may reveal why people with whom a person has good relationships often find communication strained or difficult. Even those who have deep affection for another will be in conflict at times. When in conflict, the participants will not generally be self-disclosing. A lack of self-disclosing brings on a stagnation in the otherwise growing relationship. After a heated argument with a friend, your subsequent communication will be terse and more public until the argument has been resolved or forgotten. During this period of time your relationship will not be positive and hence you decrease self-disclosure.

Self-Disclosure Increases

Self-disclosure usually occurs incrementally. As two people begin to feel more comfortable with each other and find that their relationship is growing, they will engage in more self-disclosure. In a way, this is saying that it takes time to make friends. Most people, on meeting someone for the first time, feel somewhat ill at ease about engaging in a great deal of self-disclosure. If the person seems empathetic and reciprocal, self-disclosure is likely to increase. But initially in developing relationships, the revealing of one's complete self too quickly is seen as dangerous and risky. Stewart says that the risk is a natural one; people lock their cars and homes against intruders, and it is only natural to be on guard about that most prized possession—self.[26]

No one can tell someone else how or when to self-disclose. It is known, however, that a primary ingredient in a lasting, deep relationship is each person's open, honest, genuine sharing of self with the other. Sharing is risky business, and everyone gets hurt a few times, but to touch the humanness of another person is a most rewarding experience.

EGO STATES AS COMMUNICATION ANALYSIS

Up to this point, we have discussed the self as if it were directly revealed in communication. One method of communication analysis proposes that the person may display or reveal the self from different psychological positions. Eric Berne labeled this type of study "transactional analysis."[27] If you watch a person communicate over a period of time, you will note changes in his or her posture, verbalization, voice, and point of view. Berne says that these changes are manifestations of the individual's current *ego state*. An ego state is a collection of feelings and experiences that serves as a source of behavior. An ego state, then, reflects the self and also acts out the self. Analyzing a person's self in this way is called "structural analysis," and it is part of the broader concept of transactional analysis.

Types of Ego States

Each person has three main sources of behavior, or ego states—the Parent, Adult, and Child. The Parent ego state incorporates the feelings and behaviors learned from one's parents or other authority figures. When you are acting from your Parent ego state, your behavior may be loving and nurturing ("That was a good paper you wrote. Keep up the good work."). But your Parent may also be harsh and authoritarian ("Do as I say. I know what's best for you."). Parent-type communication may be based on clichés and therefore require little effort.

The Adult ego state is objective, analytical, and focused on the present. When you are acting from your Adult, you look for the facts, search for needed information, and make rational, intelligent decisions and judgments.

The Child ego state contains the feelings and behavior of the impulsive, fun-loving, self-centered, manipulative child that each of us once was. Your creativity, intuition, and spontaneity all stem from your Child ego state.

Every person has these three ego states, and every person's behavior and communication stem from his or her Parent, Adult, and Child ego states.

> When you are acting, thinking, feeling as you observed your parents to be doing, you are in your Parent ego state.
> When you are dealing with current reality, gathering facts, and computing objectively, you are in your Adult ego state.

When you are feeling and acting as you did when you were a child, you are in your Child ego state.[28]

In communication settings, certain nonverbal and verbal behaviors serve as clues to which ego state a person is in. The following list relies heavily on the work of Harris.[29]

Parent nonverbal: Furrowed brow, pursed lips, pointing finger, head-wagging, foot-tapping, hands on hip, sighing

Parent verbal: How many times have I told you; If I were you; Now what; Do it this way; Poor dear; Sonny; Honey; Disgusting; Maybe (when used to avoid a problem)

Adult nonverbal: Eye-to-eye contact, quizzical look, body alert, head tilted for listening

Adult verbal: Why; What; Where; When; Probable; Comparative; How; It appears; I think

Child nonverbal: Tears, pouting, temper, whining voice, shrugging shoulders, teasing, delight, laughter, giggling, hand raised for permission

Child verbal: I wish; I want; I dunno; I guess; Bigger, biggest; Better, best; Mine

The lists for Parent and Child behaviors are more recognizable and typical. This is because the Parent and Child are general models of behavior, whereas the Adult is more open and direct and less typical. No one state is preferable to the others. Each is appropriate at times. If one state *does* dominate a person, that person would be regarded as maladjusted by a social psychiatrist.

Alignment of Ego States

When analysis of an individual's personality—structural analysis—is broadened to focus on two persons interacting, as in dyadic communication, the process is called *transactional analysis*. Each person in the transaction is acting from his or her Parent, Adult, or Child ego state.

Figure 3.1 shows a typical diagram of a transaction. Person 1 and person 2 are always represented by their three ego states: Parent (P), Adult (A), and Child (C). Each arrow goes from the ego state of the message sender to the perceived ego state of the other person. In Fig. 3.1, for example, the communication is Adult/Adult. Person 1 is communicating from the Adult to the Adult in person 2. Similarly, person 2 is communicating from the Adult to the Adult in person 1.

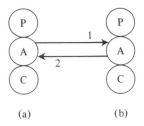

(a)   (b)

Fig. 3.1 A typical transaction: (a) person 1; (b) person 2.

Complementary transactions The transaction shown in Fig. 3.1 is complementary. That is, the message sent by person 1 from a particular ego state to a specific ego state in person 2 is responded to appropriately.

Figure 3.1 shows only one type of complementary transaction. Other types are shown in Fig. 3.2. As you can see, a complementary transaction need not involve only one ego state. Rather, what makes a transaction complementary is the fact that a message sent to an ego state is responded to from that ego state. The ego state reflected in the response was predicted. Thus any of the three ego states can take part in a complementary transaction. In fact, there are nine possible combinations (Parent/Parent, Parent/Adult, Parent/ Child, etc.).

Complementary transactions characterize productive communication, because each person is behaving according to the other's perceived ego state. The topic of communication may be national politics or gossip about Hollywood personalities; the communication will go smoothly as long as the transaction is complementary.

During a communication the type of complementary transaction may change, yet the communication will continue to go smoothly. We may call this *variability of transactions*. For example, consider the following exchanges between a high school student and a teacher.

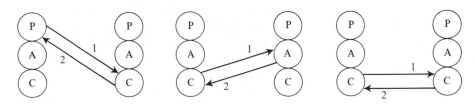

Fig. 3.2 Complementary transactions.

Student: I don't know why, but I never seem to get my homework
(Adult/Adult) completed.

Teacher: I'm not sure I can give you the answer. Have you tried setting
(Adult/Adult) up a study schedule?

Student: May I go to the bathroom?
(Child/Parent)

Teacher: Yes, but come straight back, hear me?
(Parent/Child)

Thus even though the transactions may vary, they are still complementary. In each case the response was sent from the predicted ego state. But sometimes this does not happen.

Crossed transactions If the lines of transaction intersect, the predicted response is not forthcoming, and therefore the communication will not go smoothly and will soon be broken off. Two types of crossed transactions are shown in Fig. 3.3.

A crossed transaction might occur if the high school student tries to relate to the teacher on an Adult/Adult level, but the teacher's response is Parent/Child. However, the transaction could become successful if either of the two people changed—for example, if the teacher responded from the Adult to the student's Adult or if the student responded from the Child to the teacher's Parent.

Complex transactions Both complementary and crossed transactions are straightforward. For both participants, only two ego states are involved. But some transactions are more complex, involving more than two ego states. Berne suggests that a transaction has both a social level (the surface, apparent one) and a psychological (hidden) level.

Figure 3.4 shows two types of complex transactions. In each case the solid lines represent the social level of the transaction; the dashed lines, the psychological level. The angular type of complex transaction occurs, says

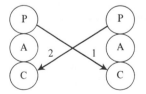 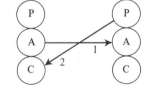

Fig. 3.3 Crossed transactions.

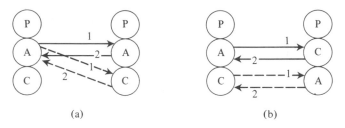

Fig. 3.4 Complex transactions: (a) angular; (b) duplex.

Berne, when, for example, a salesperson says, "This is best for you, but you can't afford it," and the client responds with, "I'll take it." What sounds like an Adult statement by the salesperson is actually an appeal to the client's petulant Child. As shown in Fig. 3.4(a), the client does in fact respond from the Child ego state. The second, or duplex, type of complex transaction is described by Berne as follows:

Cowboy: Come and see the barn.

  Visitor: I've loved barns ever since I was a little girl.

Here, what appears to be an Adult discussion of barns is really a Child transaction of sex play.[30]

Transitional transactions To us as symbolic interactionists, the primary importance of complex transactions lies in their *behavioral* aspects. We are interested not so much in whether transactional analysis reveals stable patterns of behavior, but rather in how these patterns change so that the communication, or transaction, can continue.

Crossed and complex transactions lead to a breakdown in communication. In these cases communication can continue, however, if the *type* of transaction changes. We call such transactions *transitional*. Transitional transactions are in effect "bargaining sessions." Person 1 sends a message to a particular ego state in person 2. Person 2 chooses to respond from a different ego state to a different ego state in person 1. If person 1 then responds from that ego state, the communication will continue; the transitional transaction evolved into a complementary transaction, as in Fig. 3.5(a). If, however, person 1 refuses to "bargain" and instead responds again from the first ego state, as in Fig. 3.5(b), the attempted transition (person 2's Adult/Adult transaction) will result in a crossed transaction, and the communication will therefore break down.

Generally occurring at the beginning of a communicative situation, a transitional transaction is a signal that at least one of the communicators wants to change the self-in-process aspect of the communication. Ideally, then,

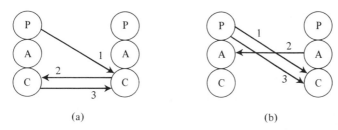

(a)   (b)

Fig. 3.5 Transitional transactions.

each participant should work toward accommodating the other's view of self
and other. Most of us have had occasion to think to ourselves, "I don't seem
to be on the same track as so and so." Even though the words seem to be
appropriate, the communication isn't going smoothly. That is the time to
check on the alignment of ego states and on whether there is a hidden psychological level operating in the communication.

Transitional transactions may also be used to make a change from one
transactional "set" to another. One or both communicators may wish to
change the ego states involved. The middle ground between one stable set
and another will usually include a transitional transaction. The following conversation and Fig. 3.6 illustrate this type of transition.

Husband (1): Will you find my new tennis racket, 'cause I can't.

Wife (2): It's in the trunk of the car, dear. I told you to bring it in.

Husband (3): I seem to be getting absentminded. I also misplace things at
work.

Wife (4): I can't help you solve being absentminded.

Husband (5): I know, but it's frustrating that I can't organize things so that
I can remember.

Wife (6): Answers to organization are not my strong suit, but you might
try a special memo pad designed for writing notes to yourself
about special projects.

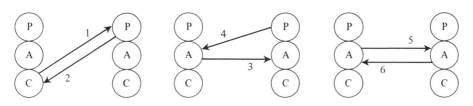

Fig. 3.6 Transition from one transactional set to another.

Although the wife didn't completely recognize her husband's switch of ego state, she was quick to gain the complementary set by the third exchange. With both in the Adult/Adult mode, the communication situation may go on smoothly, with the husband and wife discussing ways in which they may solve the husband's problems with organization and absentmindedness. They also could have stayed in the first phase—Child/Parent. The only one of the three phases they could not remain in was the transitional middle phase. If the wife had reacted in statement 4 as she did in statement 2, the transaction would have been crossed, and the communicative encounter would probably have broken off.

Performing transactional analysis of the ego states operating in a communication setting is a way to gain a better understanding of how people act and react in communicative situations. Implicit in the concept of transactional analysis—that an individual's personality is made up of three different parts—is the notion of the self in process, of the self changing in response to interaction with another self.

SUMMARY

Symbolic interactionism encourages a process approach to a developing person. In other words, a self must be observed as a person in the process of becoming. Such a self is both holistic and interactional; such a self acts and thinks about those actions, as well as becomes self through interaction with others.

Communication with significant others is the manner in which a person validates current concepts of self and thereby develops self. Thus self is shaped and continuously changed by the way a person is labeled, the value of others' statements, language impact, and authoritarian teaching. These four elements of communicating with others, though by no means an all-inclusive list, have dramatic effect on the developing self.

Self-disclosure is a means of sharing a genuine relationship. Self-disclosure is a seeking of contact with another person on a most intimate level without many societal demands. This type of communication is important to the healthy growth of self-development.

Transactional analysis is a method of analyzing communicative behavior in terms of the display of self. Every person's sources of behavior—the Parent, Adult, and Child ego states—come into play during a communicative transaction, and these ego states may either help or hinder communicative efforts.

The concepts of self in process, self-disclosure, and transactional analysis are all internal aspects of a communicator. An external factor in the communication process is role, the topic of Chapter 4.

PROBLEMS AND ISSUES

1. The rigorous behaviorist would say that "self" is not a viable concept because it requires speculation of nonobservable elements which therefore can never be known. Speculation of this type may be fun, say the behaviorists, but it is not rewarding because it doesn't explain human behavior. Defend either the behaviorists' position or ours—that studying self is a rewarding endeavor for communication.

2. According to Manis and Meltzer, symbolic interactionists see the self in one of three ways: "self as a dynamic process of viewing and responding to one's own behavior, . . . self as a structure of internalized roles, . . . self as a set of attitudes or evaluations."[31] Can you identify our point of view? Moreover, can you explain the implications of each of the three points of view?

3. The list of verbal and nonverbal cues for the three ego states (on p. 53) is not exhaustive. What items would you add to the list?

4. Observe a dyadic communicative transaction and then use transactional analysis to show the various transactional acts that the communication included.

NOTES

1. William James, "The Social Self," in Gregory P. Stone and Harvey A. Farberman, eds., *Social Psychology through Symbolic Interaction* (Waltham, Mass.: Ginn-Blaisdell, 1970), p. 374.

2. Stone and Farberman, *op. cit.,* p. 368.

3. Gordon Allport, "Psychological Models for Guidance," *Harvard Educational Review* **32** (1962): 373–381.

4. *Ibid.,* p. 375.

5. *Ibid.,* p. 377.

6. *Ibid.,* p. 380. It should be noted that this section on process is a review of Allport's essay.

7. James, *op. cit.,* p. 373.

8. *Ibid.,* p. 374.

9. Stone and Farberman, *op. cit.,* p. 369.

10. Earl C. Kelley, "The Fully Functioning Self," in *Bridges Not Walls,* 2d ed., ed. John Stewart (Reading, Mass.: Addison-Wesley, 1977), p. 107.

11. Gregory P. Stone, "Appearance and the Self," in Stone and Farberman, *op. cit.,* p. 394.

12. Robert Rosenthal, *Experimenter Effects in Behavioral Research* (New York: Appleton-Century-Crofts, 1966), pp. 158–165.

13. Casey Miller and Kate Swift, *Words and Women: New Language in New Times* (Garden City, N.Y.: Anchor Press/Doubleday, 1976).

14. *Ibid.*, p. 65.

15. Casey Miller and Kate Swift, "One Small Step for Genkind," *New York Times Magazine,* April 16, 1972, p. 36.

16. *Ibid.*, p. 106.

17. Ossie Davis, "The English Language Is My Enemy," *American Teacher* (April 1967): 14.

18. Paul Chance, "Reversing the Bigotry of Language," *Psychology Today* **7** (March 1974): 57.

19. *Ibid.*

20. Kelley, *op. cit.*, pp. 108–110.

21. *Ibid.,* p. 109.

22. *Ibid.*, pp. 115–117.

23. John Stewart, in Stewart, *op. cit.*, p. 172.

24. *Time Magazine,* June 24, 1974, p. 76.

25. W. Barnett Pearce and Stewart M. Sharp, "Self-Disclosing Communication," *Journal of Communication* **23** (December 1973): 416–421.

26. Stewart, *op. cit.*, p. 173.

27. Eric Berne, *Games People Play: The Psychology of Human Relationships* (New York: Grove Press, 1964). Berne has written several books on his concept of transactional analysis, but this is his most readable treatise for nontherapists.

28. Muriel James and Dorothy Jongeward, *Born to Win: Transactional Analysis with Gestalt Experiments* (Reading, Mass.: Addison-Wesley, 1971), p. 18.

29. Thomas A. Harris, *I'm OK—You're OK* (New York: Avon, 1967), pp. 90–92.

30. Both examples are paraphrased from Berne, *op. cit.*, pp. 33–34.

31. Jerome G. Manis and Bernard N. Meltzer, eds., *Symbolic Interaction: A Reader in Social Psychology* (Boston: Allyn and Bacon, 1967), p. 215.

Chapter 4

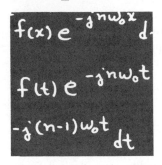

Role Behavior: Acquisition and Execution in Communication Acts

INTRODUCTION

Hundreds of people are marching, smashing store windows, and looting. Police watch with a feeling of disbelief and helplessness. After the assassination of Martin Luther King, this scene occurred in a number of major cities in the United States. Rioters looked on the police as representatives of a repressive system; others believed that the police were gutless wonders who refused to maintain law and order.

When the social system breaks down, one wonders what held it together at all. One policeman cannot control a large group that does not extend that right. The power of the police resides in the people and in their acceptance of policing authority; the police cannot shoot everybody or arrest everybody. What they stand for symbolically is more important than their physical strength. It is the symbolic relationships between individuals and between individual and society that guide behavior and maintain social stability.

Because of the pervasive influence of symbolic relationships, it is useful to have a term that describes how individuals orient and organize their behavior. Such a term is "role." Humans act toward one another on the basis of meaning acquired through social interaction. Out of this social interaction evolves a structure, or model, for behavior. The interaction may be experiential, such as an intern studying for a particular profession, or it may be vicarious, in that an individual may acquire a certain behavior from viewing models from everyday life or in the media. Role behavior can both facilitate and destroy communication outcomes, and as such constitutes an important concept for analysis. Knowledge of role behavior is essential to the communicator because it is this behavior that guides one's initiation and processing of messages.

In this chapter we first examine some general philosophical and theoretical notions about role behavior and its importance in organizing behavior, especially communication behavior. Next, becoming more specific about role referents, we explain key concepts within role theory that guide communication. This analysis is also designed to show the impact of communication on be-

61

havior patterns and thereby to demonstrate the relatedness between role concepts and communication. Finally, we present a specific application of role theory to communication behavior, to demonstrate the pragmatics of role theory.

THE CONCEPT OF ROLE

In our experience, most students react negatively to the term "role." Some common statements are: "He is just playing a role"; "I hate roles, I want to be myself"; and "Life is full of games and roles." Even if more neutral terms are used to point out that someone is "playing" a role, the connotation is that there is something phony about the behavior; it is contrived, and the person is deliberately trying to deceive others. When "role" is used in the theatrical sense, one person's behavior is used to portray another's. Here, however, we are using the term to describe individual behavior in society.

Individuals must be able to recognize and define social situations. People organize their perceptions of situations in terms of roles played by themselves and others. In this way individuals are able to initiate communication exchanges and accommodate to one another. For example, you may "play" the role of "friend" in a particular situation and view the action of others in terms of that role. Your "role" gives meaning to your behavior and the behavior of others and thereby defines the situation.

Role analysis may well help you discover why you are not perceived as an "authentic" person or why your perception of a role has molded undesirable behavior. In our view it is naive to assume that a "real" self exists apart from society or that authentic behavior is an objective sort of phenomenon that exists independently of those who perceive the behavior.

Necessity of Roles

Human interaction is often characterized as being mask against mask, image against image, and therefore destructive of honest and open relationships. Such criticism is directed at *how* role behavior is executed, not at whether role behavior should exist. Role does not refer to counterfeit acts, but to behaviors that maintain social stability by facilitating guidelines and predictability in human interaction.

Another frequent criticism occurs when individuals disagree about what the roles should be. For example, should members of the clergy be restricted to preaching from the pulpit, or do they have an obligation to march in demonstrations? Are women obligated to stay at home and care for a family, or do they have the option of pursuing a career while their husbands stay home? Should girls be permitted to play Little League baseball?

Regardless of the answers to these questions, guidelines for behavior must exist. Role behavior is negotiable, and redefinition of roles is usually commensurate with a changing value system. The most important point is that role behavior exists, and criticism of societal interpretations of a particular role is a criticism of the interpretations and not of role behavior per se. Thus, for example, nonconformists can be identified by their role behavior, and other nonconformists must learn how to behave like nonconformists. For example, Spates and Levin point out that beatniks and hippies shared not only many of the same leaders, but also dominant forms of rebellion. "Both shared the notion of use of drugs, sexual freedom, and 'hip' music and art. In addition, key hippies saw the beats as their cultural predecessors."[1]

Thus even though rebels may oppose the structure of society as it exists, some sort of structure is necessary; a universal "do your own thing" would not allow for coordinated effort, a necessary component of any group's survival. Humans are interdependent by the very nature of the environment. In other words, humans must rely on one another to cope with environmental pressures. Allegiance to only oneself seems as destructive as total compliance to roles dictated by others. Somewhere in between these two extremes is a position where accommodation takes place so that roles serve the participants involved.

Structural and Behavioral Concepts

The concept of role becomes more meaningful when it is placed in a more comprehensive framework. Sarbin does that when he writes:

> We regard a culture as an organization of learned behaviors and the products of behavior which are shared and transmitted. . . . Moreover, persons are always members of a society . . . and these societies are structured into positions or statuses or offices. The positions are collections of rights and duties designated by a single term, e.g., mother, village chief, teacher, etc. The actions of persons, then, are organized around these positions and comprise the roles. Role and position are conjoined. Roles are defined in terms of the actions performed by the person to validate his occupancy of the position. . . . In sum, all societies are organized around positions and the persons who occupy these positions perform specialized actions or roles. These roles are linked with the position and not with the person who is temporarily occupying the positions.[2]

It is important to note that the terms "position," "status," and "office" refer to structural concepts, whereas the term "role" refers to the behavior associated with a particular position, status, or office.

Role Defined

Simply stated, role is what an individual has to do in order to be accepted by others as an occupant of a given position, status, or office. It is through the learning process that one comes to expect certain behaviors to be associated with particular positions. These behaviors are conveyed by verbal and non-verbal cues, which places the communication process at the heart of any discussion of role enactment. According to Stone and Farberman, role is "those expectations mobilized by an identity through verbal and nonverbal communication in a specified social situation."[3] This definition stresses the notion that the individual must identify the situation and also his or her place in that situation. The part played by self in role enactment is thus critical to the selection of alternative behaviors.

Role and Self

In Chapter 3 we described the self as an organized collection of attitudes, opinions, and beliefs that individuals hold about themselves. It is through interaction with others that people come to see themselves as possessing certain qualities. In addition, particular qualities are associated with a given status or position, and the enactment of a role depends on the person's exhibiting those qualities. Sarbin and Allen assert that the self is coordinate with role, and "self-role congruence refers to the degree to which qualities of the self—traits, values, or beliefs—and requirements of the role exhibit fittingness or overlap."[4] The interplay of self and role results in the broader notion of "personality."

To enact a role most effectively, not only must others perceive the enactment as appropriate, but also self-perceptions should be congruent with role requirements. This does not mean that the qualities of self and role must match exactly or that individuals should come equipped to deal with each new role without experiencing anxiety. Nor are we overlooking the factor of deception; individuals *can* enact a role to the satisfaction of others without being satisfied with themselves. However, such activity places a strain on the individual, and the resultant long-term anxiety and tension are harmful to both the actor and the position.

Because one of the major purposes of communication is to socially confirm the existence and identity of humans, the relevance of self and role to communication is obvious. Sometimes a communicator must ensure the congruence between role and self, and such congruence is established by the messages directed at an individual. For example, when most individuals enter a new job and are required to take on new roles, they find it helpful when the people around them recognize and reinforce personal qualities that are demanded by those particular roles. A shipping clerk likes to be told that he is efficient. A hostess enjoys hearing that she is attractive and provides a congenial atmosphere for guests. Such messages can reduce the new incumbents' anxiety as well as increase their self-satisfaction. (This concept will be extended and applied in Part III of this text.)

ROLE REFERENTS AND KEY CONCEPTS

So far we have discussed the concept of role as a general guide to the analysis of behavior which, as such, cannot be used to account for all behavior. In this section, we get more specific, focusing on the various referents of the term "role."

Role can refer to: (1) the behavioral patterns of what an "actor" should do; (2) the actual behavior of the "actor" in a particular situation; (3) the individual's definition of his or her place in a situation; and (4) the patterns of acts made in response to others' acts. These various role referents (to expectations, behavior, perception, and organized responses) are all involved in the verbal and nonverbal aspects of communication.

Role theory contains a number of key concepts that can serve to guide communication behavior. All of these concepts influence what takes place between people—their communication behavior.

Role Enactment (Role Playing)

When using certain behaviors to carry out the rights and duties of a particular position, a person is engaged in role enactment. The actor and observers determine the quality of the behavior on the basis of verbal and nonverbal cues and decide if the actor is legitimately occupying that position. For example, several years ago one of the authors entered the hospital for some tests and was greeted by an intern who appeared to be pushing twelve years of age. The young "doctor" unwrapped a kit containing an injection needle and then proceeded to read aloud the directions for administering the test, murmuring to himself that the substance must be kept in the vein. Needless to say, the patient did not give the "doctor" rave reviews for his role performance.

If the mental and physical well-being of patients is important, such behavior by the doctor is significant. If other people perceive age to be related to a role, a youthful occupant of that position must take particular care to avoid appearing incompetent. Although one could describe the intern's behavior as authentic, it was not authentic for the position he held.

This distinction is critical in the execution of roles. It is not enough for teachers to care about their students; this concern must be communicated. It is not enough for parents to love their children; this love must be communicated. *Role enactment is a matter of understanding the requirements of a particular position and communicating that role to others.*

Role Taking

Role taking refers to projecting oneself into the position or viewpoint of another person. It means trying to walk in someone else's shoes and to see the world as that person sees it. Effective role execution requires engaging in the role-taking process. For each role there is a counterrole that the actor must understand in order to meet other people's expectations about the role. The actor defines the situation and behaves on the basis of predictions of the other person's behavior. This does not mean that the actor follows a rigid formula and is at the mercy of another. As Lindesmith and Strauss point out, one may emphathize and identify with another person's role without sympathizing with that position. One may even exploit the other person.[5] The focus in role taking, in short, is simply on understanding the point of view of another person. On the basis of that understanding one may or may not choose to accept the expectations held by others.

Simply stated, what you do is shaped by the expectations of others, and you know those expectations by role taking. However, the role-taking process is not always routine. Hewitt points out that because interactants may not agree on expectations, they may pretend to be what they are not or suspect others of doing the same. Situations of conflict and power complicate the role-taking process.[6]

Mutual and continuous role taking is very much a part of communication. When two people communicate, each predicts the response the other will make to a particular message or the meaning that will be attached to that message. Each participant selects from alternative symbols, and each performs the same behaviors in an out-of-phase sequence. In other words, a communicator must be both sender and receiver simultaneously. For example, in communicating with your instructor, you take that person's perspective and observe your conduct from his or her point of view. In that sense, then, you are both student and instructor. Thus, as we suggested in Chapter 1, both the initiator and respondent are responsible for selecting, sending, and interpreting messages.

The nature of role taking illustrates the difficulty of placing communication in an S-R model. How does one decide which behavior is stimulus and which is response? Where did the communication start and where did it end? How could cause and effect be identified in the communication situation? How much power is held by the initiator of a message? Furthermore, how does one "take" the role of another? Can one "feel" one's way into another person's point of view symbolically? In order to understand another's motives, values, and perceptions, one should first try to view that person's symbolic world. What do symbols, objects, events, and people mean to the other?

Rather than executing a preconceived role and "coming on strong," it might be advisable for a person to communicate with others to learn about their symbolic systems and what those systems mean to them. Every person links certain role behaviors with certain defined situations. For example, Phillipson points out that subcultures vary in their emphasis on the value of talk.[7] Fruitful exchange in these subcultures, therefore, would depend on different linkings of role enactment and counterrole.

Sillars writes: "Meaning, not reason, must be the key word in our psychology of communication. 'What does this man mean?' not 'Is he reasonable?' For the basis of all so-called reason is a value system. . . ."[8] This suggestion does not mean that "reason" will be excluded. Rather, Sillars is pointing to a functional relationship that should exist between individuals, one in which a role can be performed within certain limits and the meaning for those involved can be determined before outcomes are negotiated.

Role Sets

The behavioral relationships that exist between positions are known, collectively, as a role set. In other words, certain behaviors are expected of the participants holding particular positions. These expectations are determined by the rights and duties of the positions involved. Of course, not all behavior between individuals is prescribed; also, the nature of rights and duties varies considerably with the position involved. An individual comes to a situation with certain expectations (a role set), initiates communication based on that role set, and looks for behavior to validate the role set. For example, a customer in a store has preconceived ideas of how customers should behave and how salespersons should behave. The individual has defined in advance the general customer-salesperson relationship, although the specific behaviors of this relationship will vary with every instance.

Types of role sets According to Borden, Gregg, and Grove, there are two general kinds of role sets—*traditional* and *unique*.[9] Traditional role sets refer to institutionalized relationships, e.g., husband/wife, doctor/patient, lawyer/ client, and employer/employee. These traditional role sets provide general guides to behavior for the occupants of these rules, but they do not specify the wide range of behavior possible and the special expectations arising out of interaction. When individuals go beyond the general requirements of a role set, they are engaging in a unique role set or relationship. In other words, the relationship becomes refined such that it meets the requirements of not only a particular position, but also the individuals involved.

The traditional role set can be said to serve a *task*-maintenance function, whereas the unique role set serves a *person*-maintenance function. For example, the behavior between doctor and patient can vary greatly, depending on the intimacy of the association. Suppose you overheard the following conversation between doctor and patient: "Well, I can see that you're pretending to be sick again so you can get out of work." "Yes, and I thought that as long as I was pretending, I would pretend that you're a doctor." Such an interchange would not make sense in the framework of a traditional role set. However, the doctor and patient have developed a unique relationship, one in which "leg pulling" can take place and friendship can be displayed.

Sometimes the language of unique relationships misleads observers, and the communicators must be aware of this if they want others to draw valid conclusions about their behavior. If students attended a faculty meeting, for example, they might go away convinced that certain professors were under attack, when in reality games of friendship were being played. Because of the unique relationships involved, the participants engaged in behaviors not prescribed by traditional role sets. Communication, then, conveys both certain content and a relationship of a particular nature. Unique role sets are characterized by communication that reveals the level of intimacy in the relationship.

Communication in role sets Perhaps the criticism that role behavior is mask against mask and image against image is more valid when aimed at behavior that considers only traditional role sets. Communication arising out of general prescribed guidelines is somewhat impersonal and ritualized. Nevertheless, general guidelines serve to initiate the communication and to define the positions. If essential social functions are to be carried out, the position, as well as the person, must be maintained. Communication is essential to the establishment of unique role sets and person maintenance.

The rights and duties of individuals occupying positions are matters for negotiation, even though traditional guidelines may exist. Indeed, such guidelines may change as society changes. (Several traditional values that seem to be in transition will be discussed further in Chapter 11.) One such change is occurring in the employer/employee relationship. Some organizations are beginning to view their employees as individuals in their totality rather than as fillers of particular job descriptions. Such organizations obviously want to interact with their members on more than a traditional role-set level. Thus astute personnel directors, teachers, or work-crew supervisors will seek to develop unique-type work relationships. Similarly, today's emphasis on feelings and free expression can be effected by seeking unique relationships. Although certain feelings may be associated with traditional role sets, the most personal characteristics of individuals are elaborated only through unique role sets.

Traditional role sets help initiate communication and provide an important function by setting up general expectations of the participants. The amount of person maintenance necessary in a relationship and the level of intimacy, however, depend on the specific needs of the participants. Difficulty occurs when the same behavior is applied to all role sets. For example, the clerk who spills out intimate personal details to a customer or the executive whose spouse must make an appointment before they can talk are hardly meeting the needs of all the participants involved.

According to Toffler, people define their relationships with others in functional terms, and in a modern society this leads to limited interpersonal involvement.[10] But this is not necessarily bad, he asserts. "Total involvement" with everyone, Toffler says, really means that no one would have time to develop and nurture friendships. In other words, a person must be able to relate to the personalities (self and role) of many while spending more time on those relationships that are more demanding.

Whether or not a relationship is functional depends on the expectations of the participants that arise out of their respective value systems. If the participants in a traditional-type teacher/student or employer/employee role set are productive and satisfied when a certain level of involvement has been reached, that level of involvement is functional. In long-term role sets, however, a traditional role set by itself is probably inadequate to meet individual and person-maintenance needs.

Impact of time and situation The factors of time and duration of a relationship are important considerations for the communicator. It is dysfunctional for a communicator to rely entirely on either traditional role sets or "total involvement" with every person one encounters. The individual who maintains a traditional role set regardless of the conditions may even be a source of humor. For example, television's Archie Bunker continues to protect the virtue of his "little girl," although she is married and no longer living under his roof. Another target for the humorist is the individual who strives for *instant* unique relationships, *instant* trust, and *instant* disclosure of self. The young man who picks up a young woman for their first date is probably ill-advised to call her father "Dad!"

Another aspect of a situation is language. The language one may use in a unique relationship with one individual may be insulting to others. Nonetheless, the relationship is valid; the "insulting" language may even enhance the relationship and make it more meaningful to the participants.

The literature on therapeutic relationships provides insight into principles of communication which may be applied to everyday settings. However, several qualifications must be made. First, the "openness" of communication between therapist and client is a function of both traditional and unique role sets that have formed over time. There is intensive involvement on the part of both the therapist and client, and the level of intimacy is such that the client is willing to share any and all of his or her thoughts. Thus the climate of the therapeutic relationship is one of trust, acceptance, and willingness to become involved. The traditional role of the therapist implies that such a climate ought to exist from the outset, but it is only through communication over time that such attitudes become validated in a unique non-therapist-client relationship. In addition, the therapist is trained to handle both negative and positive forms of communication. In the nontherapeutic situation, however, the communicators must be aware of what kinds of messages each is capable of handling. It is both naive and destructive to assume that communication begins at the most intimate level in everyday settings.

Role Distance

"Role distance," according to Goffman, is the ability of individuals to separate themselves from role requirements while performing their roles.[11] Although the requirements for a role are being met, the individual is communicating qualities of self that indicate his or her humanness and that of others. Perhaps role distance can best be explained in terms of its antithesis, or stating what it is not. The individual who follows a traditional role set to the letter without deviation or humor and who embraces the role totally can be said to lack a sense of role distance. A corporate executive who becomes so involved in the role and so "businesslike" that no qualities of self show through is exhibiting this type of behavior. Such behavior can result in anxiety for those in the counterrole. The subordinates of this corporate executive may feel tied to rigid role behavior and limit their interaction to what is safe, namely, traditional subordinate behavior.

Indicating role distance is also a way of pointing out that one has a sense of perspective about the role. In other words, role and self are not the same, and one can execute a role with expertise without being that role only. Individuals who are inept at communicating role distance are also usually afraid to deviate from a role, fearing that they may lose the control accorded to the role. This malady is common among individuals who are executing a role for the first time.

For example, a young high school teacher was in charge of a "study hall" made up of several classes. The teacher had resolved to maintain strict order and clung to her role unremittingly. Her opportunity to show who was in charge came when she spotted a student moving his jaws and making a popping sound. "Do you have something in your mouth?" The room grew very quiet, and the student nodded sadly. "March right up here and put whatever is in your mouth on the desk!" Every eye was on the student as he walked to the front of the room, looked at the teacher with a slight trace of a smile, removed a dental plate, and with a flourish plopped it on the desk. Unfortunately the teacher refused to see the humor of this situation and grew even more rigid. Although she may have been dedicated to the students, to them she appeared to be cold and unapproachable. Her behavior defined the role of teacher so narrowly that her capacity to help others was severely restricted. She not only had defined the role in a questionable way, but was also unable to step back from her own definition and alter her behavior.

The concept of role distance serves several important purposes for the communicator. (1) It allows flexibility of interaction and preserves the human qualities of communication by relieving tension and putting others at ease. (2) A sense of perspective about role requirements allows the participants to convey a positive regard for each other, which in turn facilitates communication between them. (3) There is evidence to suggest that out-of-role behavior not only facilitates interpersonal attraction, but also enhances one's positive feelings about the task at hand.[12] (4) Open communication allows participants to execute their roles and at the same time indicate those qualities of self that show human understanding.

Role Conflict

Role conflict occurs when contradictory types of behavior are expected from a person who holds different positions or when contradictory types of behavior are expected within one role. To cope with a complex environment, individuals are expected to take part in multiple roles. However, some of the roles may require seemingly contradictory role enactments. For example, subordinates may expect their work supervisor to look out for their best interests; top management, however, may expect the supervisor to favor the interests of the organization.

One of the most dramatic examples of contradictory behavior demanded from a single position can be found in the sex role of women. Komarovsky points out that parents and professors pressure college women to achieve in academics, whereas other groups expect them to be nonintellectual and noncompetitive.[13] This conflict of role expectations may lead some women to "play dumb" on dates. Similarly, many women are brought up to believe that one day they will be wives and mothers, that they are going to college "to get a man."

> They may even identify themselves in terms of these roles—as someone's wife or someone's mother—and ignore their own capacities. [Such women] feel OK only when fulfilling their sexual roles as wives and mothers; they feel not-OK in vocational or other roles which challenge their nonsexual or personal potential.[14]

Conflict resolution Role conflict, of whatever type, needs to be resolved if effective communication is to take place. Sarbin has identified several categories of behavior employed to reduce the strain arising from role conflict.[15] Some of the more common forms of conflict resolution are: (1) separating roles in time or space, (2) placing priority on one role, (3) merging conflicting roles into a single new compromise role, (4) removing oneself from the situation, (5) directing attention only toward the role being enacted, and (6) changing beliefs so that the roles appear compatible or giving one role higher priority. These modes of behavior are designed to reduce an individual's tension, but more importantly they can sustain the contradictory expectations. A woman might play dumb on a date and appear nonthreatening to her male companion, but her communication pattern to him sustains the notion that she lacks intellectual capabilities.

Traditional roles can dominate and direct a person's behavior rather than facilitate it. When roles become destructive to the self, they should be changed. Initiators of a message must be aware of the expectations they communicate, and respondents must be aware of the expectations they have validated. One way to reduce role conflict without denying essential qualities of·the self is to redefine the role.

Role Redefinition

The various modes of conflict resolution also serve as types of role redefinition. Our main concern here is with contradictory expectations inherent within just one role.

Role redefinition occurs when a person rejects a role in whole or in part by restructuring his or her behavior. The success of role redefinition, which is usually aimed at the value system, is dependent on persuading others to drop certain expectations. For example, minority groups have questioned the application of the value "equality." If minority-group members are capable people, they can no longer be expected to fulfill only subservient roles.

A communicator must be aware not only of the traditional rights and duties of roles, but also of roles that are in transition. As values change to meet social needs, so do roles; both values and roles are matters of conventional choice.

Verbal and nonverbal cues Beliefs about who others are, their positions, and the rights and duties of those positions are conveyed both verbally and nonverbally, though not always consciously. Recently one of the authors invited a businessman to speak to a class on the communication problems in his organization. In his presentation the businessman referred to the "girls" in his office and the "girls" in the class. He then gave a knowing look and pointed out that "girls" tend to be emotional and require special handling. The women in the class interrupted his lecture to denounce his use of language and to point out that they resented the insults. The visitor was flustered and did his best to point out that he really loved women and added, "Sometimes I even call my wife a 'girl.' " This man was perplexed because of the reaction his language provoked.

This incident points up several role redefinitions. First, many women today are reluctant to accept a role that places them in a subservient position. Although some may regard the term "girl" as flattering to age, others react negatively to the notion that they are forever children. Indeed, it is interesting to note that at one time the word "girl" referred to "a young person of either sex."[16] Second, women have come to recognize that "emotion" rather than "objective fact" is the attribute that has been thrust on them.

But it is not only the role of women that is changing. The role of students has also undergone a redefinition. In this case students were not individuals who sat placidly while knowledge was dispensed and who were reluctant to express their feelings. Contemporary values are moving society toward the recognition of the whole person and the free exchange of ideas. Redefinition of roles is an attempt to align values and roles.

Why redefinition takes place   Role redefinition usually takes place because the participants in a relationship feel that inequities exist. These inequities are perceived in the discrepancy among qualities of self, role demands, and values. If an individual demonstrates qualities of self that fulfill the demands of a particular role and yet is denied that role on the basis of behavior ascribed to sex, age, or race, there is direct conflict with a value system based on an individual's right and obligation to reach full human potential. Many minority-group members have experienced the frustration of trying to achieve a role that is commensurate with the qualities of self.

Today, however, social values are changing, and there is a concomitant process of role redefinition. In the early days of television, for example, acting roles for minorities in other than subservient positions were almost nonexistent. Today, although social equity has not yet been achieved, it is not unusual to see black actors as detectives, executives, and lawyers on television programs and in commercials as home owners and middle-class parents concerned about laundry detergents and their children's eating habits.

Role redefinition can also occur in response to the discrepancy of power between role and counterrole. In the traditional coach/player role set, for example, a coach had virtually total control over the lives of athletes, and players did not protest or suggest another way of accomplishing a game objective. This discrepancy of power led to player associations, protests, and negotiated roles. Today, coaches must be able to "communicate" with their players. Even owners of professional clubs have felt the impact of this change. After the owner of the Oakland Athletics fired a player who made several errors during a World Series, he faced both player and public wrath.

Values of redefinition Redefinition of role can be productive for all participants. The traditional teacher/student role is an illustration of this. In the past, teachers were regarded as selectors and dispensors of knowledge; students, as listeners expected to meet the standards of conventional learning—information recall, achievement scores, and grades. A redefinition of the roles of teacher and student allows for a cooperative enterprise in which the focus is on a realistic learning environment for everyone. The teacher who is bound by the role of "knowing all" will engage in self-deception and awkward behaviors that are destructive to learning. The teacher in a cooperative environment is not reluctant to say, "I don't know." Without free interchange a teacher cannot assess how much learning is taking place.

Redefinition of the teacher/student role set has received increasing emphasis in educational literature. Postman and Weingartner write:

> We want to elicit from students the meanings that they have already stored up so that they may subject those meanings to a testing and verifying, reordering and reclassifying, modifying and extending process. In this process, the student is not a passive "recipient"; he becomes an active producer of knowledge.[17]

This does not leave the teacher with merely a passive role in exposing students to additional knowledge; rather, the teacher becomes a facilitator of knowledge. Through the "extending process," a teacher provides additional knowledge, alternative interpretations, and also maintains respect for the knowledge students possess.

When is redefinition appropriate? There is generally some lack of *fit* between the perceived qualities of self and the traditional roles one is expected to carry out. One of the factors making some roles bearable is the thought that they provide a transition to other, more desirable, positions. Possibilities for growth and advancement mean a great deal to employees who are expected to fulfill a secondary role, for example.

There are several conditions under which role redefinition seems especially appropriate: (1) when individuals are locked into a position of subservience, regardless of their individual qualities; (2) when the discrepancies between self and role are so great that an individual must act to perserve an identity; and (3) when adherence to a particular role is inconsistent with utilizing human resources and potential. Why not do away with roles altogether and avoid the pitfalls? Structure in human behavior is both inevitable and necessary. All of us find a certain amount of predictability useful in initiating and maintaining relationships. In order to complete cooperative efforts, a person needs to know who is going to do what and where she or he fits in the scheme. The challenge is to use the structure and not to let it dominate one's behavior.

Role behavior is not an action-reaction model of behavior, but rather a mutual causal process in which behavior is modified through a communication exchange. In role behavior there is a reciprocity in which needs are being met —a bargain is struck—and relationships are being defined and negotiated. All participants possess bargaining power by virtue of the resources they bring to the situation at hand. This is not meant to imply that individuals should refuse to follow all expectations they do not find to their liking. The "do your own thing" approach is antithetical to negotiation, and *how* one contends for power decides the stability of all relationships.

COMMUNICATION APPLICATIONS

"Role" is both an initiating factor in communication behavior and part of the formative process that creates new behaviors. As we stated earlier, symbolic interaction forms human conduct and is not merely a release of it. Mutual role taking is at the heart of communication and effective symbolic interaction. Again, an actor has to define and interpret meanings in light of the situation in which the interaction is taking place. This is, of course, both a blessing and a curse. The role concept adds stability, but it can also allow preconceived notions to prevail throughout interchange, which may inhibit the development of a unique or authentic relationship. However, this is not inherent in role behavior. It is the *communication* that allows the formation of human conduct and the negotiation of role relationships. The centrality of communication becomes apparent when one explores the various dimensions of role behavior.

Acquisition of Roles

Throughout our discussion we have used the term "role" to refer to a variety of behaviors. To subsume all behavior under "roles" and to claim predictability about what that behavior is going to be presents two problems. First, many positions in the social structure have a very general form, as do the expectations about those roles. For example, the role of "helper" sets up more general expectations than do "nurse," "priest," or "dentist." Second, few roles permit variations from the norm. Although the role concept may apply best to occupational analysis, roles also involve the complex organization of behavior through symbolic means and as such serve an orienting function for communicators.

One can acquire role behaviors through vicarious learning, as well as through direct experience. An individual can view various "actors" and receive patterns and indirect reinforcement for following or not following those patterns. Thus individuals are taught their roles through symbolic means and are reinforced for performing those roles adequately.

Masculine and feminine roles provide an excellent example of a symbolic field that conditions its recipients into role behavior. Children's books clearly point out the different behaviors Tom and Jane engage in. Jane rarely has a pet frog. Toys too are stereotyped by sex. The more "aggressive" toys are billed for the boys and are linked with potential occupations available for men in our society.

Movies also have aided in the acquisition and perpetuation of sex-role stereotypes. They have not only portrayed what a woman does and should do, but also what a woman has to offer. Advertising on television leaves little doubt about the concerns of men and women. Much to the consternation of those involved in the women's liberation movement, women are most frequently seen in the role of compulsive cleaners and happy homemakers.

In experimental studies, women generally were more willing to agress physically before a female than before a male experimenter. Researchers Larwood, Zalkind, and Legault reasoned that women were more aware of stepping beyond their usual role bounds before a male.[18] Their investigation of the effect of cross-sex behavior was made in a bank setting; both male and female tellers cashed checks for both male and female customers. Transaction times were longer for female customers than for male customers and were longer with male tellers than with female tellers. In other words, the impact of sex roles was greater in cross-sex dyads.

As we pointed out in Chapter 3, subtle forms of positioning in American society occur through the use of language. "He" is used as a universal pronoun. The leader of a group is referred to as "chairman," regardless of the person's sex. Such symbols have a decided impact on the acquisition of roles. But communicators do not come into a setting with a complete script. Much of the acquiring of a role takes place during the subsequent interaction.

Alteration of Roles

Changing circumstances can bring about role changes. For example, during World War II, housewives suddenly became factory workers, and expectations about the role of women were altered to fit immediate needs. Roles are also defined, perpetuated, and changed through communication. Language is shared behavior and as such requires validation from the participants involved. Both verbal and nonverbal language are associated with roles which will not function without counterroles. A friend described an incident in which a group was deciding on recruiting for a position. One member of the group said, "We must get a good man for the job." A woman in the group challenged the wording of the statement and asked why the job required a man. The group then rejected the language and also the counterrole it implied. One must be aware of the symbols of a particular role and willing to alter those symbols if roles are to be altered.

Becoming aware of communication behaviors that reinforce a role is not always easy. Exline, Gray, and Schuette suggest that sex differences in eye contact are a result of women's greater orientation toward affectionate and inclusive relationships with others, an interpretation consistent with theories of sex-role differences learned in the family.[19] Further evidence of the impact of roles on behavior is cited by Vinacke, who concludes that females are less competitive than males and more oriented toward cooperation.[20]

As roles change, both verbal and nonverbal behaviors change, and the reverse is also true; communicative behaviors can also change roles. Symbolic interaction emphasizes joint action between individuals and the formative nature of interaction patterns. Even those patterns occurring again and again between individuals must be formed or reformed, and one can be the user of symbols and not the victim of them. One can be aware of symbol use that implies a role or counterrole to which one does not subscribe.

Execution of Roles

Roles are executed through communication behavior, with verbal and nonverbal symbols attached to that particular role. Certain expectations are held by the initiator and respondent, respectively, in a role setting. Goffman asserts:

> Society is organized on the principle that any individual who possesses certain social characteristics has a moral right to expect that others will value and treat him in an appropriate way. Connected with this principle is a second, namely that an individual who implicitly or explicitly signifies that he has certain social characteristics ought in fact to be what he claims he is.[21]

This statement has several implications for those in the communication setting. The communicator should be aware of the "claim" he or she is making and if that "claim" is consistent with self and role. The respondent, in turn, must decide whether or not to honor the "claim." Certain rights and obligations are attached to roles, and one must remember that both self and role are important.

In certain circumstances, one is limiting what one is and what others can be. Role demands may be such that individuals have to adhere to defined obligations of that role. Critics may point out that individuals may become so "role-centered" as to lose themselves and their freedom as individuals. It is just as logical, however, to note that one can become so "self-centered" as to lose sight of the role and its function in society. A middle ground is needed. The holder of a particular role must both possess and communicate the qualities of that role. In honoring a claim, a respondent does so through communication behavior, e.g., listening to what an individual has to say.

The decade of the 1960s was one of communicative violence—riots, sit-ins, public obscenity, heckling, and burning. Students refused to accommodate to traditional expectations and instead attempted to redefine their roles. They wanted more influence over their educational destinies and refused to follow the normal channels of communication. In other words, they refused to play the counterrole to institutional expectations.

Such activity had both positive and negative effects. On the positive side, students were given more voice in their own affairs. They did get a hearing, and college administrators engaged in much self-examination. It is fair to say that students gained more influence in university affairs, and the goals of the university were reexamined. On the negative side, many people—both inside and outside the university—found the behavior shocking, and financial and community support for universities declined. In effect, those who had engaged in communicative violence crippled the very institutions that protected their right to free expression. State legislatures allocated less funds and passed laws some people considered repressive. In addition, the students' techniques of communication created suspicion and sometimes damaged their cause. For example, students were not always selective on issues. At one university a list of some 90 "demands" submitted to the administration included everything from more student representation in decision making to complaints about lumpy mashed potatoes in the cafeteria. Although students complained about not having a voice in the undeclared war in Southeast Asia, they shouted down those who did not agree with them.

The selection of communication means to deny a counterrole is extremely important. Communicative violence may get immediate action, but it may also produce detrimental outcomes and destroy what is sought.

Communication Analysis of Roles

Examination of communication behavior can serve to explain how one perceives one's role and also what one expects of others in the execution of particular roles. Two thousand students at Ohio University, for example, were interviewed and asked to describe the behavior of a "good" teacher. The behaviors were content-analyzed, and a frequency count resulted in the following categories:

1. Personal concern for students
2. Class atmosphere
3. Willingness to spend time out of class
4. Willingness to answer questions
5. Preparation and organization of lectures
6. Relates to students on their level

7. Testing procedures–preparing students

8. Knowledge of subject

9. Promptness-scheduling

10. Enthusiasm and interest in subject

11. Consideration for other pressures on students.

This list also reflects the rank ordering given to these categories by students at the University of Utah.

The categories/rankings have several implications for communication and role. Certain roles require particular communication behaviors, and those behaviors communicate the degree to which one is carrying out that role satisfactorily. Because of the overwhelming number of students who ranked "personal concern for students" as the most important category, for example, Linda Larsen, a student at the University of Utah, explored the communication aspects of that category. A selected sample of 50 students were asked to think of a teacher who showed a personal concern for students and to describe the behavior of that teacher. The descriptions were then content-analyzed, with special emphasis on the nonverbal cues those teachers used. The following rank-ordered categories were mentioned most frequently:

1. Taking time to listen

2. Eye contact—indicating attention in listening

3. Facial expression—smile

4. Tone of voice—did not convey judgment

5. Physical reinforcement—enthusiasm for ideas

6. Remembered students' names

7. Body movement and position—alert and interested

8. Attitude of acceptance—nodding and withholding judgments

9. Revealing part of self—not tied to role

10. Extra work for student—available for conferences.

Although such studies are not comprehensive, they do illustrate the symbolic cues associated with roles. In other words, verbal and nonverbal messages contain both content and relationship cues. A teacher who calls a student by name not only verifies the student's name (content), but also conveys the idea that the teacher cares enough to know the person's name (relationship).

Much of the most important communication in a relationship between individuals is nonverbal. Thus teachers who define their roles so narrowly that dissemination of subject matter overrides all other concerns may inhibit the learning process by "turning off" students who hold a different set of expectations. But earlier we advanced a model of communication based on mutual causation. Accordingly, teacher behavior is also affected by student behavior (counterroles also carry responsibility). Students can define their roles so narrowly that the teacher/student relationship is sterile and nonproductive.

The way in which roles are executed can help an observer determine how the executor views the functions of communication. For example, a bank president may view communication as primarily telling others what to do and therefore spend considerable time sending subordinates memos. This narrowly defined role has resulted in narrowing both the functions and forms of communication used. It is little wonder that such executives do not learn much about their subordinates and that those receiving a barrage of memos feel alienated.

Perceived roles can be determined by observing communication patterns. For example, people in power positions or those who perceive themselves to be in power positions in a group normally give the most opinions and suggestions for action, whereas those who perceive their role as subordinate ask questions or give information.[22] Such analysis may be used to break down the role barriers that inhibit free and open challenges to ideas.

Role Ambiguity

Individuals in groups and organizations often wonder what their roles are and where they fit in the scheme of things. These roles are discovered through the communication process. Problems of communication are often symptomatic of the uncertainty of not knowing where one stands or who one is in relation to others. In the organizational setting, for example, Jackson maintains that a major source of communication problems centers on individuals coming to common agreement about the social structure. In other words, individuals need to know what their roles are and where they stand in relation to others.[23] This assertion was confirmed by Smith, who asked members of the International Communication Association what the greatest communication research need was in their organization. Most of the respondents answered, "how to find out who's supposed to do what to whom in this organization."[24] This issue of role clarity in an organization is, according to Keller, closely related to employees' levels of satisfaction with their work. He found that role conflict is significantly related to low levels of satisfaction with supervision, pay, and opportunities for promotions.[25]

When a new member enters a group and seeks accommodation, his or her role-seeking behavior promotes various communication behaviors. Such behaviors are an important ingredient in the evolution of a group and the socialization of an individual into the group. Schein maintains, "until the person finds a role for himself in the group and until the group develops norms pertaining to goals, influence, and intimacy, he will be tense and will respond in various emotional ways."[26] Table 4.1 lists various searching and coping behaviors and points to the issues that must be solved when an individual enters a group.

When you have entered a group, you have probably experienced the problems and feelings described in Table 4.1. The table should help you realize what your responses may be reflecting. The person who fights a group's norms may not dislike the group at all, but may be simply trying to belong. Table 4.1 is equally relevant for groups that assimilate new members. For example, there is good reason for groups to hold orientation sessions for new members, because until individuals find their place, they tend to remain preoccupied with self and to engage in behaviors that detract from group effort.

Communication and Role Adjustment

We pointed out earlier that there is probably always some discrepancy between perception of qualities of self and the qualities demanded by a particular role. It is here that communication plays a vital function in reinforcing self-role congruence. For example, a person who believes that another has the right to enact a particular role can enhance the role competence and growth

Table 4.1 Problems in Entering a Group which Promotes Self-Oriented Behavior

Problems	Resulting Feelings	Coping Responses (Self-oriented)
1. *Identity* Who am I to be?	Frustration	1. *"Tough" responses* Fighting, controlling resisting authority
2. *Control and influence* Will I be able to control and influence others?	Tension	2. *"Tender" responses* Supporting, helping forming alliances, dependency
3. *Needs and goals* Will the group goals include my own needs?	Anxiety	3. *Withdrawal or denial responses* Passivity, indifference, overuse of "logic and reason"
4. *Acceptance and Intimacy* Will I be liked and accepted by the group? How close a group will we be?		

Edgar H. Schein, *Process Consultation: Its Role in Organization Development* (Reading, Mass.: Addison-Wesley, 1969), p. ?5. Reprinted by permission.

of that person via communication. An administrator who praises workers gives them confidence in their role execution, and as a result both the self and role are strengthened.

Potential Destructive Nature of Roles

Roles serve as both facilitators of and barriers to communication, but it is the participants who decide what their roles are to be and how they are to organize their behaviors. Stewart states: "I am trying to say that interpersonal communication happens between *persons,* not between roles or masks or stereotypes. Interpersonal communication can happen between you and me only when each of us recognizes and shares some of what makes us human beings *and* is aware of some of what makes the other person too."[27] This statement highlights the formative process of communication. Roles may initiate interaction, but they need not dominate them. Stewart is defining interpersonal communication as the "quality" of interchange between individuals. When one becomes tied to a role, the humanizing qualities of communication can become lost.

Objectification of people Individuals need a symbolic starting place for interaction, and roles provide that orientation. Communication exchanges must have a certain amount of efficiency if human affairs are to be conducted. Sometimes, however, the search for efficiency negates the human element. People become objects to be processed. Persons become nonpersons.

When entering a hospital, for example, a patient's clothes are removed, an identity-robbing act. Numbers become more important, for computer purposes, than names, and the patient becomes part of a system that identifies people by ailment—"the gall bladder in room 201." The patient is further objectified by physicians and interns who mill about and talk about "this case." After all, how can a gall bladder have feelings?

At a time when individuals are most sensitized to all cues, it seems ironic that some professional roles are not sensitive to human needs. Yamagata, a student at the University of Utah, interviewed patients to determine behaviors of hospital personnel that lowered credibility. Her report of some of the messages used by technicians gives one insight into the double meaning of most messages:

> These remarks ranged from statements like "hummm . . . I know that you've got one," when a technician had difficulty finding the blood pressure of a patient, to "I don't know," when a technician was in a hurry, and didn't have time to explain a test to a patient. Lack of confidence in hospital personnel also stemmed from such remarks as "gosh, I've never heard of your doctor before. What kind is he?" Since every patient would like to think that the doctor who will be treating her is the chief of staff, it is rather unnerving to think that his name is not recognized.[28]

This example points to a minimal amount of exchange between people as human beings. Instead, the emphasis has been placed on the processing of people.

The tendency of roles to obstruct human interchange increases as organizations or groups become larger. Some efficient way must be found to deal with large numbers of people, and in so doing people are likely to both execute roles without regard to human needs and forget the multiple functions of communication. The organization may become so efficient that mass alienation results, with few people really feeling themselves as belonging to a human enterprise. (This challenge confronting the organization will be discussed in Part III.)

Limiting communication functions   McCroskey, Larson, and Knapp point up the potential destructiveness of a role as it may occur in marriage:

> The potentially destructive thing about a marriage contract is that it may lead one or both parties to conclude that they are justified in doing things and saying things to the other person that they would never consider doing or saying to another in a less constrained two-person system. One or both parties may even arrive at the unstated conclusion that they "own the other" or that the other "belongs to them."[29]

During courtship, individuals are likely to accommodate to each other as human beings and to communicate their appreciation for acts that contribute to the relationship. Once the marriage contract enters the picture, however, the individuals tend to expect certain behaviors associated with a particular role and to ignore communication expressing appreciation. In this way, the concept of role has obscured the formative part communication plays in maintaining relationships.

Limiting efficient and responsible communication   Some traditional roles make interchange tortuous and unrewarding. Stein, writing about the gamesmanship between doctor and nurse, maintains:

> The physician finds himself trapped in a paradox. He fervently wants to give his patient the best possible medical care, and being open to the nurses' recommendation helps him accomplish this. On the other hand, accepting advice from non-physicians is highly threatening to his omnipotence.[30]

This paradox requires nurses and doctors to engage in a game rather than in open communication. Furthermore:

> The cardinal rule of the game is that open disagreement between the players must be avoided at all costs. Thus, the nurse must communicate her recommendations without appearing to be making a recommendation statement. The physician, in requesting a recommendation from a nurse, must do so without appearing to be asking for it.[31]

Such exchanges are not, of course, limited to the doctor-nurse roles, and they may provide material for humorous anecdotes. However, avoiding direct exchange and disagreement can have serious consequences, as found in a fascinating study conducted by Hofling et al.[32] These researchers created an experimental conflict in which: (1) a nurse was asked to give an excessive dose of medicine to a patient; (2) the medication order was transmitted by telephone, a procedure in violation of hospital policy; (3) the medication was "unauthorized"; and (4) the order was given by a voice unfamiliar to the nurse. Of the 22 subjects who took part in the study—12 from a municipal hospital and 10 from a private hospital—21 would have given the medication as ordered. One implication of this study is that strict adherence to roles may undermine the very integrity of those roles. In addition, as much attention must be paid to the rights and obligations of counterroles as to the rights and obligations of roles.

SUMMARY

Role behaviors are both necessary and desirable to a functioning society. By giving meaning to acts, roles help individuals accommodate to one another. The concepts of role, role referents, and key concepts of role are communication-dependent. Role behaviors require a reciprocity in which relationships are defined and negotiated. Questionable role relationships and behavior may require redefinition, but such action must be done without totally destroying the relationship.

Mutual role taking is the basis of communication and effective symbolic interaction. However, one must always consider the legitimacy of the role and what behaviors are the obligations and rights of a particular role. The concept of "role distance" allows a person to occupy a role without being dominated by role structure. Although roles are necessary, they should not lead to dehumanization of the participants, a concept we will explore in more detail in the next chapter.

PROBLEMS AND ISSUES

1. Are roles more destructive than beneficial to the communication process?
2. Can one really engage in "authentic" behavior?
3. What roles make you feel uncomfortable and why?
4. Is American culture dominated by structure and statuses?
5. Cite instances of inept role behavior. Why was the behavior inept?
6. What roles have narrowly defined limits of behavior?

7. What are some of the weaknesses of "role" as an explanation of human behavior?

8. Contrast old and contemporary motion picture films in terms of the traditional roles portrayed.

9. What changes have taken place in terms of assigned roles in our society? What role redefinitions are taking place?

10. Select several roles and analyze the nonverbal behaviors associated with each of these roles.

11. Did role behavior inhibit investigation of the Watergate scandal? In what ways?

12. Discuss the concept of role distance. Under what conditions is it beneficial? When might role distance produce harmful effects?

NOTES

1. James L. Spates and Jack Levin, "Beats, Hippies, the Hip Generation, and the American Middle Class: An Analysis of Values," *International Social Science Journal* **24** (1972): 331–332.

2. Theodore R. Sarbin, "Role Theory," in *Handbook of Social Psychology*, Vol. I, ed. Gardner Lindzey (Reading, Mass.: Addison-Wesley, 1954), p. 224.

3. Gregory Stone and Harvey Farberman, *Social Psychology through Symbolic Interaction* (Waltham, Mass.: Ginn-Blaisdell, 1970), p. 208.

4. Theodore R. Sarbin and Vernon L. Allen, "Role Theory," in *Handbook of Social Psychology*, Vol. I, 2d ed., ed. Gardner Lindzey and Elliot Aronson (Reading, Mass.: Addison-Wesley, 1968), p. 524.

5. Alfred R. Lindesmith and Anselm L. Strauss, *Social Psychology* (New York: Dryden, 1956), p. 387.

6. John P. Hewitt, *Self and Society: A Symbolic Interactionist Social Psychology* (Boston: Allyn and Bacon, 1976), pp. 112–126.

7. Gerry Phillipson, "Speaking 'Like a Man' in Teamsterville: Culture Patterns of Role Enactment in an Urban Neighborhood," *Quarterly Journal of Speech* **61** (February 1975): 13–22.

8. Malcolm D. Sillars, "Universities and Minority Students: A Problem in Communication." (A lecture at the University of Utah, July 28, 1971), p. 4.

9. George Borden, Richard Gregg, and Theodore Grove, *Speech Behavior and Human Interaction* (Englewood Cliffs, N.J.: Prentice-Hall, 1969), pp. 108–109.

10. Alvin Toffler, *Future Shock* (New York: Bantam, 1971), p. 98.

11. Erving Goffman, *Encounters* (Indianapolis: Bobbs-Merrill, 1961), pp. 85–162.

12. Donn Byrne *et al.*, "The Situational Facilitation of Interpersonal Attraction: A Three Factor Hypothesis," *Journal of Applied Social Psychology* **5** (March 1975): 1–15.

13. Mirra Komarovsky, "Cultural Contradictions and Sex Roles," *American Journal of Sociology* **52** (1946): 184–189.

14. Dorothy Jongeward and Dru Scott, *Women As Winners: Transactional Analysis for Personal Growth* (Reading, Mass.: Addison-Wesley, 1976), p. 76.

15. Sarbin and Allen, *op. cit.*, pp. 542–543.

16. Casey Miller and Kate Swift, *Words and Women: New Language in New Times* (Garden City, N.Y.: Anchor Press/Doubleday, 1976), p. 96.

17. Neil Postman and Charles Weingartner, *Teaching as a Subversive Activity* (New York: Delacorte, 1969), p. 62.

18. Laurie Larwood, David Zalkind, and Jeanne Legault, "The Bank Job: A Field Study of Sexually Discriminatory Performance on a Neutral-Role Task," *Journal of Applied Social Psychology* **5** (March 1975): 68–74.

19. Ralph Exline, David Gray, and Dorothy Schuette, "Visual Behavior in a Dyad as Affected by Interview Content and Sex of Respondent," *Journal of Personality and Social Psychology* **1** (1965): 201–209.

20. W. E. Vinacke, "Sex Roles in a Three-Person Game," *Sociometry* **22** (1959): 343–360.

21. Erving Goffman, *The Presentation of Self in Everyday Life* (Garden City, N.Y.: Doubleday, 1959), p. 13.

22. *See* Elihu Katz and Paul Lazarfeld, "Interpersonal Networks: Communicating within the Group," in *Foundations of Communicating Theory*, ed. Kenneth K. Sereno and C. David Mortensen (New York: Harper & Row, 1970), p. 336.

23. Jay Jackson, "The Organization and Its Communication Problem," in *Business and Industrial Communication*, ed. W. Charles Redding and George A. Sanborn (New York: Harper & Row, 1964), p. 124.

24. Clarence C. Smith, "Summary of Division IV Survey: Closing the Gap Between Communication Researchers and Practitioners" (mimeo.), 1972, p. 1.

25. Robert Keller, "Role Conflict and Ambiguity: Correlates with Job Satisfaction," *Personnel Psychology* **28** (Spring 1975): 57–64.

26. Edgar H. Schein, *Process Consultation: Its Role in Organization Development* (Reading, Mass.: Addison-Wesley, 1969), p. 37.

27. John Stewart, ed., *Bridges Not Walls* 2d ed. (Reading, Mass.: Addison-Wesley, 1977), p. 3.

28. Brenda Yamagata, "Communication Between Hospital Personnel and Patients" (manuscript, 1973), p. 5.

29. James McCroskey, Carl Larson, and Mark Knapp, *An Introduction to Interpersonal Communication* (Englewood Cliffs, N.J.: Prentice-Hall, 1971), p. 182. Reprinted by permission.

30. Leonard I. Stein, "The Doctor-Nurse Game," *American Journal of Nursing* **68** (January 1968): 103.

31. *Ibid.,* p. 102.

32. Charles K. Hofling *et al.,* "An Experimental Study in Nurse-Physician Relationships," *Journal of Nervous and Mental Disease* **143** (1966): 171–180.

Part III

Communication Purposes

In Parts I and II we explored central concepts of communication and symbolic interaction. Part III deals with the purposes of communication. In the broadest sense, chapters in this part answer the question: How do people use communication?

Chapters 5 and 6 look at the ways in which communication is used when people relate to one another. Chapter 5 focuses on how people use communication to recognize one another's reality and thereby generate mutual understanding. Chapter 6 studies how people regulate the actions of self and others through communicative behavior.

Chapters 7 and 8 explore communication purposes related to information and how people use ideas. Chapter 7 explains how information is sought and disseminated. Chapter 8 offers a view of how a person uses information to make decisions in various communication settings.

Chapter 5

Facilitation and Corroboration

INTRODUCTION

A customer entered a laundry shop, unaware that the other people in the shop were television actors who had planned an interesting day for anyone who came in. Someone asked the time of day. The clerk pointed to the wall clock, which indicated 5:00 P.M. (The time was actually 3:00 P.M.) Another person in the shop looked at his watch and verified the 5:00 P.M. time. The customer looked at his watch in disbelief. Then another person entered the shop, and the clerk asked him why he was arriving on a Saturday. (It was actually Friday.) The man replied by pointing out that he made his inspections on Saturdays during the spring. (It was really autumn.) A wall calendar indicated that it was both Saturday and a spring month. The effects on the unsuspecting customer were quite visible—confusion, frustration, and helplessness.

Differences between symbolic referents are seldom as discrepant as those occurring in this television production, but the outcomes can be much the same. People rely on others to confirm their reality and existence. This social confirmation is symbolic in nature. In the foregoing example the confirmation of time (a socially valued symbolic notion) was lacking, and an anchor to reality was loosened. Most people who see something unusual say, "Do you see what I see?" The desired response is a corroboration (validation) of the questioner's perception of the world. Because so much of "reality" is symbolic in nature, we assert that individuals rely heavily on *symbolic corroboration* of their reality and existence. Denial of that reality can lead to hostility as well as confusion. In addition, denying or ignoring another's reality is to question the worth of that individual.

A major purpose of communication is met when individuals facilitate (make easier) exchange that leads to an understanding of the world views of the participants. Symbolic corroboration of the existence and worth of individuals is an important part of the facilitative process. Of course, everyone has self-interests, and everyone has occasionally felt that the world would be a better place if one's self-interests prevailed. Through the facilitation process, individuals negotiate these interests and accommodate to others. Equally important, the facilitative process allows one to examine one's personal realities and interests in order to judge their reasonableness.

In Chapter 2, we argued that one's perception and interpretation of the environment depend on communication. This chapter suggests ways in which that knowledge can be put to use. The first section of this chapter explores the concept of symbolic corroboration to illustrate the significance of symbolic exchange and the functions performed by a seemingly simple everyday occurrence. Next we analyze the principles of facilitation and the factors that influence those principles. Finally, we show how facilitative principles can be applied to both interpersonal and group communication.

SYMBOLIC CORROBORATION

Reality Construction

What is reality? For most individuals, "reality" has three aspects—the outside "real" world, an inner private world, and a shared symbolic world of beliefs, experiences, and meanings generated and maintained through communication.[1] Knowledge of the first aspect of reality—the "real" world—is hard to come by, because it is always experienced through the filter of social reality. Moreover, our concern in this text is with symbolic reality—what is communicated, shared, and acted toward as though it were the real world. As such, symbolic reality is social reality, about which people *can* communicate.

How does one construct social reality? Social reality arises out of experiences that are shared and validated by other people. Experiences are shared with others through symbol systems (language, music, art, mathematics). A considerable portion of each person's reality is made up of linguistic constructions acquired and validated through the communication process. Therefore, only things that can be communicated can be validated and thus entered into social reality. It is for this reason—the impossibility of social validation—that hallucinatory experiences may be regarded as "unreal." Nonetheless, as Shibutani maintains, the nature of the sensation in the two types of experiences is similar.[2]

Individuals receive their reality from groups via symbol systems, and those symbol systems affect perceptual behaviors or what is seen. Individuals must verify what they have seen, and again cultural groups perform that function by providing validation. The problems involved in "getting outside" this reality are illustrated in the works of Castaneda, who attempts to "see" the world of don Juan, a Yaqui Indian, and to learn a new way of knowledge—an awesome task.[3]

What part is played by communication? The construction of reality is an active process. Individuals do not simply respond to what is "out there." Reality is created and defined. People define a situation and act toward it on the basis of their definition. In many cases the definition brings about conditions that confirm the definition. For example, if a man thinks that there are great differences between himself and someone else, he will not interact with that other. Because the two people do not interact, the man knows that there are great differences between them.

Communication allows one to make sense of the world. Interaction allows one to categorize people and the attributes of the people in that category. Society has provided the means of categorizing, and in that sense much of social reality is imposed. Individuals use such categories to make demands on the behavior of others and themselves.[4] Investigating how one becomes a symbolic leader or a celebrity, for example, Klapp stipulates that one becomes a symbol by seizing the cues offered by public response and then moving in the direction indicated.[5] A celebrity, in other words, must rise to the demands made on the symbol. For example, if the public responds to Joe Namath as a swinger, it is to his advantage—both financially as an endorser of products and as a celebrity—to be seen in the presence of beautiful women and to present a swinger image.

Berger and Luckmann suggest that even the reality of everyday life presents a world that is shared and confirmed by others; to exist, one must continually interact and communicate with others.[6] This capacity to communicate enables humans to construct a world and behave toward it. People "construct" in interactional contexts composed of real and imaginary rules, players, objects, others, and situations.

Watching children "play" can give one insight into this process. Denzin distinguishes three forms of play ranging along a continuum of rule-embeddedness.[7] *Playing-at-play* describes the free-floating interactions of the young child who creates for the moment. *Playing-at-a-game* refers to a young player who hits at a ball, yet has no firm knowledge of how a specific ball game is played. *Playing-a-game* describes the skilled player who works within rule-constructed boundaries of a particular game. Gaining experience with interaction, the child moves from playing-at-play to playing-at-games. To become players of games, individuals must be able to conceptualize the generalized other (collective attitudes of a group of individuals), so that the predicted behavior of others can be taken into account. Thus the critical variable in Denzin's scheme is *interactional experience.*

All forms of play involve variable degrees of pretense, and the same may be said about social reality. Players may pretend to be serious or seriously pretend not to be serious. How "real" are the activities of children and adults? What about children who decide to hold a birthday party for a cat, for example? Is this activity any different from a celebration in honor of Queen Wilhelmina's birthday? Which act is "real"?

Imagine yourself observing some children play "war." One child proclaims that anyone who is on the "good side" will be protected by a special uniform covered with magic powder. Would adults create that sort of reality? How about the "ghost shirt" of Indian braves or the "invincibility" of the Marine Corps uniform? Reality construction consists of interaction involving "actors," a setting, social objects which are acted on, a set of rules, and a set of relationships that orients people toward themselves and others.

Although individuals rely on socially valid and institutionally recommended standards of reality, there is no deterministic position whereby their given symbolic capacities "cause" humans to forever behave in certain ways. Cultural groups and realities change because of the formative process of communication. Behavior is determined by language, but language also allows one to form new behaviors.[8] In short, symbolic validation has considerable impact on how each of us approaches the communication act.

Confirmation Seeking

Individuals seek reality and confirmation of that reality through others. In order to maintain some stability, people look for symbolic signposts that tell them who they are and where they fit. If this is done at a subconscious level, the person may not be aware of social confirmation until it is removed. For example, calling an individual by name is a validation of who that person is. Of course, an individual is unlikely to respond to such validation by saying, "Yes, by thunder, that's who I am!" Nonetheless, most people welcome this type of validation.

The most pleasant experiences are socially confirming ones, e.g., interacting with people who think as you do or exposing yourself to ideas that agree with yours. Of course, individuals also seek out new ideas and may be willing to consider opposing ideas. Conversations between individuals are geared toward not only social validation, but also comparisons between realities. A critical point to be made here is that individuals are most likely to consider contrary ideas and engage in self-examination when the conditions are nonthreatening. Most people are willing to examine the realities of others as long as their own realities are recognized (corroborated) and they feel a sense of free choice.

All of us are necessarily protective of our world views; taken together, they represent stability. One cannot drift quickly from one reality to another and still have the world make sense. Humans rely heavily on symbolic constructions and corroboration to derive standards for reality. Harold Garfinkle asserts that the human imputes understanding to experience from "socially valid and institutionally recommended standards of 'preference.' With references to those standards he makes the crucial distinctions between appearances and reality, truth and falsity, triviality and importance, accident and essence, coincidence and cause."[9]

Individuals bring these symbolic values and beliefs to the communication situation. Although humans are not totally bound to them, some perceptions are more resistant to change than others. Moreover, individuals look for social confirmation in their interaction with others. At the very least, a person wants others to see how he or she looks at the world, whether or not they agree with that view. The corroborative process consists of seeing what the other person sees.

Self

Two key factors in self-development are stability and exploration. A person's self-concept needs to be both stable and open to new exploration and development. When stability and exploration are denied in the communication setting, the self is threatened and the response is highly predictable—avoidance of the threatening or unrewarding situation. Conversations that start with "You are totally wrong" are likely to provoke defensive reactions. The situation offers little stability or room for exploration.

The tendency toward preservation of self has an impact on the initiators of messages as well as on the respondents. It is through communication or symbolic interaction that one acquires, and is able to sustain, standards for reality. The more a person's thoughts are sustained, the more comfortable the person will feel. In a search for stability, it is not uncommon to seek control over another, thereby confirming the self. In addition, individuals not only tend to believe that they possess the truth, but also have a need to convince others. For example, many people justify their membership in a particular organization on the basis of the number of other people who hold membership or on the basis of status figures within that organization.

The corroboration process is necessary to facilitate interchange, but it can also inhibit that interchange if there is a lack of awareness of the impact that it has on human behavior. This impact is manifested in several ways. When one communicates with another who holds differing views, to listen might be thought of as a form of "selling out." An individual may not want to be reminded of inconsistent positions, because to admit to inconsistency is to deny stability of self. Efforts to maintain the self may take the form of striking out and getting control of others. One way to do this, of course, is to "write off" what others say with hasty evaluations. Another is to impute undesirable motives to others. This kind of self-delusion does not have to occur at a conscious, deliberative level. The human's propensity to make evaluative statements in response to most things is both culturally conditioned and a result of a symbol system that emphasizes judgments.

Reality Assumption

The full development of decisions about self, others, or ideas is dependent on all the pertinent data one can gather. Most people start with the basic assumption that others possess or should possess the same symbolic realities as themselves. But this assumption generates several barriers in the communication situation. The most obvious one, of course, is that people can talk past one another. In addition, people's tendency to oversimplify the communication process leads to a level of involvement insufficient to develop mutual understanding. All of this is complicated by the defense mechanisms used to preserve the symbolic self—passing immediate judgment, imputing motives, reacting with anger and frustration, rejecting without scrutiny.

The first step toward facilitation and understanding is based on acquiring an attitude that allows one to get properly involved without using communication-blocking mechanisms. Suppose, for example, that you were conversing with someone who had been placed in a mental institution. One would expect a different set of behaviors on your part. You would probably probe carefully to determine how the patient viewed the world—and you. You would probably not try to impose your views on that individual or become angry or defensive about observing a different reality. Moreover, you would probably exhibit patience and realize that adjustments would have to be made by the patient, not by you. The point to be made here is that all of us are out-patients of one sort or another! Individuals' realities differ, and they are likely to resist the imposition of other points of view.

PRINCIPLES OF FACILITATION

Conceptualizations of Humans

In order to utilize communication to facilitate human exchange, one must first recognize facilitation as a legitimate and desirable purpose. If one believes that humans have growth potential and inherent worth, the necessary effort required to communicate with others can take place. Without this basic philosophy, however, exchanges with others become hollow and meaningless. In short, one's views of humans are inextricably bound with how one communicates.[10] For example, if one believes in the inherent worth of humans, it follows that each human has something worth saying. Within this framework it becomes easier to make the commitment to listen to others and exchange ideas.

We are not advocating that you adopt techniques to make others "feel important" so you can exploit them. Any power concepts employed should imply shared power and negotiation. Nor are we suggesting that everyone lives in a Pollyanna world where individuals never try to satisfy their own needs for power and control. However, those situations in which individuals can be considered opponents are few when compared to human exchanges that rely on cooperation stemming from human interdependence. Even in the opponent situation, a certain level of understanding and cooperation may be needed for mutual gain.

In Chapter 6 we will develop the idea that the American value system places a premium on the ability to manipulate others and maintain control. When this is coupled with the tendency to assert and protect self, it is clearly difficult to engage in communication that facilitates understanding. For example, consider the following advertisement for a book:

> Learn the art of nonverbal communication and use it to *your advantage* in social, sexual and business relationships. Know the *real meaning* behind a gesture, a smile, a sitting position, an unusual walk. You'll be able to detect the difference between a courtship and flirtation, a truth and a lie, boredom and interest. *You'll boggle your opponent's mind by knowing his real attitudes, in spite of what he tells you.* (italics ours)

Power over others is a prime consideration in the foregoing advertisement. In addition, others are considered as opponents whose motives are suspect.

If you consider your fellow humans as opponents who possess base motives, the following discussion will not make much sense or help you facilitate understanding. On the other hand, if you conceive of a relationship in which participants wish to deal in mutual problem solving and mutual understanding, the factors involved in establishing that relationship should be of value to you.

Basic Hypotheses

Psychotherapy, perhaps more than any other setting, stresses the importance of interpersonal relationships. Clients are seeking help and support, and their development depends on what they perceive to be supporting and helpful— not only what makes an individual feel good, but also what helps the individual to perceive choices that lead to adjustment.

Because of the intensity of involvement, the therapeutic setting has important implications for everyday communication. One can gain insights into behavior that facilitates human exchange by viewing this special setting. Of course, these ideas do not constitute a formula or a license to tell others what to do. Instead, the ideas should lead you to engage in self-examination and view some of the available alternatives in interacting with others. The therapist whose work we will focus on is Carl Rogers.

Carl Rogers has asserted that the *quality* of the interpersonal encounter with the client is the most significant element in determining the effectiveness of therapy. His observations led him to advance some hypotheses about the basis of effectiveness in relationships.[11] Those hypotheses are as follows.

1. *Congruence*—being what you are without façade; meeting the client on a person-to-person basis; being the feelings and attitudes which flow in you at that moment.

2. *Empathy*—experiencing an accurate understanding of the other's private world and communicating that understanding.

3. *Positive regard*—a warm, positive, acceptant attitude toward what is in the client; prizing the client as a person.

4. *Unconditionality of regard*—positive feelings toward the client without reservations and without evaluations.

5. *The client's perception*—communicating the foregoing attitudes to the client.

Each of the hypotheses advanced by Rogers is important for those involved in the helping professions, e.g., counseling, social work, teaching. In addition, there are important implications for everyday communication behavior when individuals seek supportive behavior; everyone needs corroboration. Before looking at the hypotheses and their relationship to communication, however, we will consider the attitudes they represent in totality. An underlying assumption in this discussion is that people are in process and have the capacity for change and development. Free expression is fostered by creating a nonthreatening atmosphere, one in which a person is willing to compensate for error rather than retaliate because of it.

The therapeutic situation is in some ways unique, and Rogers's five hypotheses are not applicable to all situations. The therapist, with sustained interaction with an individual over a long period of time, may not be forced to make judgments about that individual; in many other settings, judgments *must* be made. A therapist is trained to determine how much open communication a client can tolerate. By contrast, common sense tells us that it may not always be functional to have "genuine positive regard" for others, e.g., captives toward their enemies during war. Furthermore, some situations pose difficult questions about the openness of information. *How much* information can rival business establishments share? *How open* should the communication be among physician, terminal patient, and family?

Our concern is with most everyday exchanges, but here too the use of the principles involves risk. Ironically, people are most open with those they trust, yet it is openness that builds trust. Too much communication openness can create suspicion or result in the loss of a job, promotion, or friends. Information can be used against the person who offers it. Situations may call for varying degrees of openness, and each situation demands a thoughtful decision.

Congruence Role distance allows a person to carry out the obligations of a role without dehumanizing personal exchange. A person-to-person communication exchange occurs when one is willing to disclose the self in a spontaneous, honest way. A reciprocity is involved, and such behaviors may elicit the same responses in others. A person who expects others to risk open and honest communication must take a similar risk.

Sometimes people are reluctant to speak out until they are sure they are everything they would like to be. In reality, however, the speaking out and subsequent interaction develop the self. The critical question is not *where* one is, but rather *whether* one is developing the self as fully as possible. For example, Martin Buber tells a story of a rabbi who on his death bed laments that in the world to come, he will not be asked why he wasn't Moses; he will be asked why he wasn't himself.[12]

Empathy A supportive climate is generated when one person makes an effort to understand another's view of reality and to communicate that understanding. This says, in effect, "I want to know more," "You are worth listening to," and "You exist." To understand where a person is coming from is not the same as agreeing with that person. However, it is a form of social confirmation that allows the person to deal in comparative judgments about his or her views and those of others. A nonthreatening situation allows for self-growth.

Positive regard An honest acceptance of others allows one to perceive meaning from their point of view. Although this may seem to be a simple matter, it is often hard to put into practice. Think for a moment of someone you particularly dislike and then ask: "Do I value that person as a human being who has something worth contributing? Can I allow that person to feel hostile toward me? Can I accept that person's views, even though they differ from mine? Do I listen carefully to what that person says, or do I tune out immediately?"

It is important to allow others to have their feelings. When individuals can allow themselves to accept the feelings that others have toward themselves, the process of communication is more likely to occur.

Unconditional regard Unconditional acceptance of others opens channels of communication and maximizes exchange. Unconditional regard tests an individual's capacity to accept others without condition.

This is probably one of the most difficult principles to follow. Most people tend to say, "I will talk with you *if* you have something to say, *if* your ideas coincide with mine, and *if* it is rewarding to me." Someone who senses this feeling is unlikely to communicate openly or fully. Individuals convey this conditional regard for others in making immediate evaluations of what others have said or done. This in turn cuts off the formative process of communication and leaves little chance for either participant to understand the other's private world.

Accepting others helps one to distinguish between the worth of others and the worth of their ideas. In most communication situations the challenge is to accept the individual and to make a distinction between where the participants are and where a negotiated outcome might lead them. The Rogerian therapeutic setting implies that adjustment will come on the part of the client if he or she is accepted as a human being with potential for self-evaluation. In interpersonal communication, all participants must make adjustments. If one accepts the worth of another and listens to what is being said without immediate evaluation, the speaker just may reevaluate a previously held belief or position. In other words, one accepts another so that the person will change and also because it permits change in oneself.

Perception of participants To achieve quality in interpersonal communication, the participants must not only maintain attitudes of acceptance, but also communicate those attitudes. Indeed, what is personalized communication to one individual may be threatening to another. Although the participants' perceptions ultimately decide what the relationship is and the personal level of communication, the process can be facilitated in various ways, and these alternatives are the topic of the following section.

Impact of Role

Role sets The concept of role has several implications for communication that facilitates understanding. The basic hypotheses just examined move an individual toward a unique role set with others. Traditional role sets orient and help initiate a person's behavior with others, but by themselves they rarely produce a satisfying relationship. Individuals have a need to be known as persons as well as role or counterrole occupants.

One of the authors had a conversation with a student who could see no value in studying the communication process. "Since I'm going to be a dentist, I see no need to communicate with people." "What are you going to say to your clients?" "I am going to say, 'Next!' " Although some professions rely less than others on human exchange, a role can be so narrowly defined that the human aspects are lost, as revealed by the would-be dentist. People become objects to be processed, and the quality of life is relegated to an assembly-line mentality.

Obviously, the level of involvement required in the therapist-client relationship cannot be attained with all persons. Nevertheless, one can (and should) meet others on a person-to-person basis, accept them, and listen to them. Such behavior does not detract from the obligations of a role and in fact enhances those roles which are designed to help people.

Degree of involvement Some people argue that lack of involvement with others enables one to execute a role. For example, some physicians avoid knowing their patients in order to be better able to face sickness and death. There is safety in treating others as objects. Some supervisors avoid listening to their subordinates' personal problems because they find it painful to do so, and besides they have personal problems of their own. Some teachers avoid personal exchanges with their students because a certain amount of social distance must be maintained and they would prefer to spend their energies on subject matter.

One of the problems of treating others as objects is the reciprocity involved. In other words, it is difficult to treat others as objects without becoming an object by virtue of the communication or noncommunication one receives in return. The other person is forced into playing a narrowly defined role, and the exchange becomes mask against mask and image against image. For example, upward communication in the organization is not facilitated when an employee's concerns do not seem to matter to the supervisor. If an individual has worth, his or her negative communication must be regarded as legitimate as positive communication. In accepting another person, one does not place conditions on what can be communicated. One does not say, "I will communicate with you—*if* it is not painful or *if* it does not force me beyond the narrow confines of traditional role behavior."

Redefining role In most of the helping professions, success can be defined only in terms of the success achieved by the client. Therefore, it may be necessary to redefine professional roles to include behaviors that facilitate self-development on the part of the client. If respect for others is to be part of a social ethic, such behavior should be the obligation of most roles, regardless of one's concept of the basic nature of human beings. The preservation of role and of positive human values are as important as the preservation of self.

If one looked on the basic premises of facilitation as obligations of a role or obligations attached to human interchange, would one be engaging in phony behavior? Such a question is not relevant when the major consideration is placed on the outcomes of exchange between humans. We contend that all participants gain when positive human values are nurtured and preserved through the process of communication.

Role expectations Implied role expectations may inhibit facilitative communication. For example, a supervisor probably perceives "knowing" as part of the qualities of the supervisory role. A subordinate is sensitive to position and is normally reluctant to complain or challenge company policy. Because part of the supervisor's role is to obtain upward communication and generate data for decision making, upward communication must be recognized and explored. The most socially acceptable way of challenging a policy is to ask questions.

However, because of the implied role of "knowing," a supervisor may pass immediate judgment in answering questions and not recognize the need for stimulating further exchange.

Sometimes role expectations are set up during the exchange. Suppose, for example, that a teacher says to a class, "Now, I am sure that all of you understand what you are to do. Are there any questions?" A role expectation is implied in the statements, and it is unlikely that students will want to question, because to do so would reflect their inadequate performance of a counter-role. When a superior asks if a subordinate understands, the pressure of the "knowing" part of a role is operative, and most subordinates would merely nod their heads, regardless of their level of understanding. In short, one must be sensitive to role redefinition and the techniques that facilitate feedback.

The Impact of Language

The study of general semantics has dealt with the relationships among reality, language, thought, and behavior. Alfred Korzybski, father of the general semantics movement, was concerned that the structure of language did not match the structure of reality.[13] He felt that because language is so powerful in determining behavior, it really decides one's reality and promotes false behavior. Although reality is a process consisting of change and differences, language tends to be static and categorical. Korzybski advocated a system based on three principles: (1) *nonidentity* (e.g., A is not A); (2) *nonallness* (e.g., A is not all A); and (3) *self-reflexiveness*.

1. The word is not the thing represented This statement seems rather obvious; one seldom sees an individual carrying the word "hammer" and trying to pound nails with it. Nevertheless, equally unrealistic behavior does take place. Certain words are not used in conversations because individuals react as though the words are the objects. Wendell Johnson notes one such instance:

> People acted toward the word syphilis very much as they did toward what it presumably represented. They sought to avoid not only syphilis but the word syphilis. Their behavior was remindful of the primitive word magic, in accordance with which it is naively assumed that by controlling the word, one controlled the thing it stands for.[14]

In order to accept others, one must get beyond the level of signal response to certain words. People who tune others out because of their use of obscenity, for example, have little chance of getting meaning-centered or of discovering the other's reality. In addition, one must discover what may create a signal response in others. An attack or perceived attack on a master symbol may pose an insurmountable barrier to fruitful communication.

The use of language categories allows one to divide up the world so as to make it more manageable. But language, by its very nature, stereotypes people, objects, and events. Whereas reality consists of an infinite number of unique parts, language contains a limited number of words, and consequently gradations are not represented in the language used. This is further complicated by grammatical structure and has promoted the phrase "tyranny of the word 'is.' " Consider, for example, the statement "He is stupid," which classifies an individual in a rather severe way. The verb *is* gives a finality to the statement and suggests that an attribute (stupidity) is possessed by the person being labeled. In reality, a reaction has been projected onto one individual by another.

This type of "is-ness" can cause people to believe that such categorical statements are indeed true, and even more damage might be done to the recipient of such judgments who comes to believe those projections of others. Generalized evaluations not only represent inaccurate symbol/referent relationships, but also promote an air of certainty, which creates defensive reactions in the communication setting.

2. Words cannot be used to say all there is to say about an object, person, or event Two basic assumptions prompt people to believe or act as if they have said all there is to say about something. The first assumption is that there is a close correspondence between language and reality; the second, the belief that facts are facts. The two assumptions are related in that whereas reality is a process, language is more static and is not flexible enough to meet all of the degrees of varying perceptions. Language categories are global in nature and imply to the user that he or she has said all that needs to be said.

Facts are for the most part social products. According to Wendell Johnson, "any given fact is (1) necessarily incomplete (since it is impossible to know all the fact about anything), (2) changeable, (3) a personal affair, and (4) useful to the degree to which others agree with you about it."[15] In other words, the public and private worlds of fact are quite different.

How do individuals get facts? Kenneth Boulding maintains that "we do not perceive our sense data raw; they are mediated through a highly learned process of interpretation and acceptance . . . there are no such things as 'facts.' There are only messages filtered through a changeable value system."[16] In other words, an individual's perceptual processes are controlled largely by his or her symbolic structure. Therefore, what one knows is limited by language and the inherent difficulties in the language itself.

When individuals use know-it-all or describe-it-all statements, they convey both certainty and superiority, which generates defensive behaviors in others. Most of the time, however, such behavior is not intentional; most individuals do not believe that they know everything or want to convey that impression.

Language is not the only source of allness. There are nonverbal allness traps as well. Sometimes nonverbal allness is conveyed by a tone of voice that says, "I have said everything that can be said about the subject." A body that stiffens after making a statement says, "The subject is closed."

Closely related to the notion of allness is the idea that objects, people, and events can be placed in distinct categories. In the desire to make categories and manage reality, individuals tend to ignore gradations and thereby limit the number of categories. Language tends to become bipolar in nature. William Haney says that "polarization occurs when one treats contraries as if they were contradictories; when one deals with a situation involving gradations and middle ground in strict, either-or, contradictory terms."[17]

Contradictories are authentic dichotomies in which one alternative must occur, but both cannot. For example, a person either is or is not over six feet tall. Contraries, on the other hand, involve middle ground and alternatives. To say that a person is either tall or short treats a contrary as if it were a contradictory. There is middle ground, and a number of people are neither tall nor short.

Although there are significant dichotomized decisions (e.g., "I get the job or I don't," "male or female"), problems occur when people are categorized according to convenience rather than fact. Are you a liberal or a conservative? Smart or stupid? Honest or dishonest? Linguistic simplification may help one to categorize quickly, but it inhibits the response to highly differentiated people, objects, and events. Individuals who have themselves or their ideas thrown into a rigid category are resentful, and the facilitative process is hampered. (It is also worth noting that one of the characteristics of the authoritarian personality is the need for strict categories and an intolerance of ambiguity.)[18] Those who desire to transact with others will develop both the language and attitudes that allow for gradations and ambiguity.

3. Words are used to talk about other words Individuals' knowledge about the world comes largely through words. Again, words rather than raw sensory data are experienced. Because of the illusive nature of "facts," individuals usually are not telling others words about "facts," but rather words about words. How much of your communication involves discussion of your direct experience? It is the human's capacity to use words to talk about words that permits abstract thought. In communicating with others, it is useful to distinguish between a word about a word and a word about a "fact." This does not mean that one's language should be limited to what can be verified by direct observable data. If that were the case, we, as the writers of this text, would be in difficulty. Abstractions allow one to project and think about what might be verified. Thus in communicating with others, individuals should be aware of how they are behaving toward the language.

One of the ways in which people confuse words about words and words about "facts" is called *reification*. John Condon explains that "the term reification is used to describe the tendency to think that because there are certain words there must necessarily be certain 'things' that correspond to them. To reify is to 'thingify.' "[19] ¡To say that "my *ego* made me do it," for example, is comparable to saying that "the *devil* made me do it." Similarly, individuals are sometimes inclined to behave toward abstractions as though they were concretes. People who believe that a "real self" or "true love" actually exists may be somewhat rigid in behavior and may also forget that abstractions are tentative and creations of the mind.

The Fixit Syndrome

Adherence to cultural values that revere mastery over others compels individuals to make immediate judgments, get others straightened out, and have the "right" answers. The assertion and maintenance of self are part of locating oneself in a social scheme for some stability and wanting to control the environment and others in it. Some theorists suggest that people are most satisfied when they have power over others.[20] Having the "right" answer can validate one's worth; when this is a cultural norm, people tend to bulldoze others and to ignore their points of view.

The various media support the notion of telling others what to do, always winning, and helping others by solving their problems. The comic strips "Mary Worth" and "Little Orphan Annie," for example, manage to both moralize and remind us to straighten others out by our good common sense. How many people in the old TV series "Dragnet" were set straight by the many lectures of the police sergeants? How many TV lawyers are always in control, and how often do their views prevail? The lawyer who loses is usually arrogant, dishonest, or mentally dull. One rarely sees compromise, negotiation, and cases settled out of court. It is more exciting to see a person who is in control and who executes his or her knowledge in a flawless fashion. Even those who advertise products are always certain about what others ought to consume.

We are not suggesting that the media *should* reflect the everyday world, only that in fact they do not. People resist those who are critical, moralizing, and given to lecturing others. People who rush in to fix things are usually operating on less knowledge than is needed and in turn suppressing the knowledge required for a sensible decision. In addition, joint decisions are not the result of one person's point of view.

The fixit syndrome manifests itself in several ways in human exchange. One of the most common is seen in the individual who believes that logic or truth is the cornerstone of the communication process. This person is quick to dispense a logical point of view and just as quick to evaluate the logic of another's position. This does not facilitate communication, because another's position is reasonable from that person's point of view. Also, individuals who respond with hostility or frustration are not likely to make much sense in terms of any logical standard.

The *first* question to be asked in any communication is: "What does this *person* mean?"; the second is: "Why does *that* seem reasonable to the speaker and not to me?" The participants' meanings must be understood before any negotiation and decision can be made. Criticisms or evaluations aimed at "fixing things" generally create combative behaviors that erode the quality of any relationship. A person who is confident and has a fully developed self has the capacity to examine the position of others. Reuel Howe maintains: "The purpose of communication is not to seduce or exploit persons but to bring them into responsible relation to the world of persons and things."[21]

It is difficult to write about the "fixit" posture without engaging in it. It is comparable to saying "never use the word never." Of course, there are times when one's role demands engaging in criticism and evaluation. Communication is situational by its very nature, and its application must be tempered by that fact. Alternatives for behavior help one engage in self-examination and think about what there is to be learned.

FACILITATIVE INTERPERSONAL COMMUNICATION

Earlier we argued that relationships must be developed over time, and one must come to feel safe in a relationship. This process has been charted by several theorists.[22] Our suggestions for developing productive relationships are not to be taken as a formula; the participants' perceptions are the deciding factor in defining a nonthreatening situation. Nevertheless, some approaches appear productive by virtue of empirical study and personal observation.

Generating Data

Principles of verbal conditioning provide several insights into freeing others for giving their opinions. Individuals are more likely to talk freely when their opinions are accepted. This acceptance may be demonstrated by rephrasing what the person has said, to his or her satisfaction. This process of reflection demonstrates a recognition of the other person's reality and aids one in withholding immediate judgment.

Consider the following statements:

"Now, here is what you are saying, etc."

"What I hear you saying is that, etc. Am I on the right track?"

In the first statement the listener has passed judgment, which can result in combative or defensive behavior on the part of the initiator of the message. The second statement leaves some freedom for the initiator and also permits vague communication to be clarified.

The same principle holds true for hostile communication or apparent disagreement. It is fruitful to recognize feelings as well as content. Consider the following example:

Initiator: You don't give a damn about anyone but yourself!

Respondent: You seem very upset.

On first glance, the respondent's words seem absurd. But what might some other alternatives produce? How about "Who cares?" or "Blow it out your ear!"? How often is communication terminated or a relationship soured because someone was unwilling to permit hostility in another? A statement of the obvious allows the initiator to explore his or her own feelings without becoming more defensive.

Another way of withholding immediate judgment and generating more opinions is to ask questions. A question indicates that the respondent has paid attention and wants to explore the communication further. The nonverbal behavior of the participants also affects opinion giving. The nod of a head, for example, says, "I am paying attention to you, and I understand what you are saying."

Both the length and the nature of a response can determine how much information is elicited from others. In addition to restating another's point of view before one's own and asking questions rather than giving immediate answers, the initial responses in a communication setting should provide short stimuli rather than lengthy speeches. Too lengthy a response indicates not search, but rather a different form of evaluation. The initiator may even feel that she or he is being manipulated.

Facilitative Feedback

Generating data for examination is only the first phase of transacting with others. If all the participants simply reflected what they heard, communication would indeed be a tortuous and unproductive process. The views of all must be known and shared if decisions are to be reached. Both the initiator and respondent are responsible for congruency and meeting each other on a person-to-person basis. Responses directed at others can allow them to exist as persons and at the same time allow for the maintenance of self. The following suggestions seem useful for most communication situations between peers or superiors-subordinates.

Descriptive feedback A person who elicits as much feedback from another as feasible is free to utilize that feedback for decisions about self and subsequent behavior. The person who responds to communication should be skillful and mature enough to facilitate free choice for others. When evaluative language is used, individuals feel a need to protect the self, and defensive behaviors are generated. Evaluative language is avoided by describing one's reactions and feelings about the statement without judging the other person. A useful contrast is provided by Thomas Gordon in his discussion of the "I" message, with further elaboration by the Social Seminar Training Center.[23]

> Most of the messages we send to people about their behavior are "you messages"—messages that are directed at the other person and have a high probability of putting them down, making them feel guilty, making them feel their needs are not important, and generally making them resist change. "I" messages, on the other hand, allow a person who is affected by the behavior of another to express the impact it has on him and, at the same time, leave the responsibility for modifying the behavior with the person who demonstrated that particular behavior. An "I" message consists of three parts: (1) the specific behavior, (2) the resulting feeling you experienced, and (3) the tangible effect on you.[24]

The "you" message can consist of commands, accusations, name calling, statements that give solutions, or even threats. The following examples contrast the two approaches.

"You message": You are really domineering!

"I message": When you interrupt before I finish speaking (specific behavior), I feel upset (resulting feeling), and I feel as though I shouldn't be talking with you (effect).

"You message": You should just forget that plan!

"I message": When I hear a plan about overtime pay (specific behavior), I get disturbed (resulting feeling) because it caused a lot of headaches for the company in the past (effect).

Descriptive feedback in the form of "I" messages allows others to decide necessary changes in behavior. Because that decision has been left to another, the message conveyed says, "I don't need to evaluate you, because you are capable of evaluating yourself and adjusting to the situation."

Specific feedback To tell someone that he or she makes you angry or uneasy is so general that it does not allow the other person to adjust his or her behavior. In addition, it may stimulate more defensive behaviors. A more useful approach is to specify the behavior that makes you angry or uneasy. For example, "Just now when we were discussing the issue, you did not mention anyone's ideas, and I felt bulldozed into accepting your ideas or face ridicule." In the group setting, specific statements are necessary so that referents can be identified and explored. Note the contrast in the following statements:

"Some people in this group don't seem to be interested in the proposal."

"John, when you said, 'The proposal is OK, I guess,' what did you mean?"

Useful feedback Feedback should serve the needs of *all* participants in a communication setting; each participant should gain from the exchange. Destructive or tasteless feedback serves no useful function. Thus feedback should facilitate exchange rather than inhibit it, as when feedback is used to "tell someone off," "straighten someone out," or "manipulate another to accept one's point of view." An individual must be willing to state his or her understanding and acceptance of another's feelings, as well as make known private experiences and feelings. When part of the person comes through each role, person-maintenance needs, e.g., to know, to feel a sense of identity, and to feel a sense of control over what might happen to oneself, can be met.

In addition to serving all participants, useful feedback is of a form that can be used. For example, to talk about physical or mental capacities that cannot be changed can produce destructive behavior in others and therefore does not constitute useful feedback. Sometimes such feedback is unintentional. For example, a teacher may compare a student with his or her brother or sister. The unstated message is that the student should be as good a scholar or athlete as the sibling was. A less subtle maneuver is to compare a student to his or her classmates: "Jane behaves in this way, and I am sure that you can too." It is important to deal directly with the person involved and his or her capacities.

"Now" feedback Feedback directed at behavior in the immediate setting is generally the most effective in facilitating communication. An emphasis on the present allows an individual to examine his or her behavior and achieve an awareness of it. Little purpose is served by saying, "You always do that" or "You never have liked my ideas." Such statements create a defensive atmosphere, and as a result the immediate behavior is likely to be neglected.

In most cases feedback can be utilized to best advantage when it is given soon after the behavior occurs. However, the *readiness* factor—to give feedback and to receive it—needs to be considered too. Individuals are ready to give feedback when they can frame it so as to meet the needs of all participants. If an immediate reaction provokes hostility or frustration, the person was not ready to give feedback. Therefore, if one thinks that the response will be destructive, even if couched in neutral terms, it would be best to delay responding. Even though one should try to react as spontaneously as possible to a conversation, nonthinking responses are not the same as spontaneous exchange.

Role-free feedback Many people tend to adhere to unstated behaviors associated with counterroles. For example, when a superior asks whether a subordinate understands, all the pressure is on the latter to indicate understanding. More helpful are the kinds of exchanges that allow for the comparison of referents, e.g., by having one's feedback played back. For example, saying

"What do you understand?" or "As you see it, what am I saying?" allows the participants to compare and adjust their perceptions.

FACILITATIVE COMMUNICATION IN THE GROUP SETTING

Maintaining Self

No matter what the group setting, it is the *communication* employed that decides *how* people will live with one another and with themselves. Behaviors intensify when one interacts in a group. An individual seeks corroboration not only from one person, but from the larger entity—the group—as well; a group situation is potentially far more threatening because the self must be maintained in view of several peers or superiors.

In any type of group—social, work, study, decision making—several members may be searching to determine just where they fit in the group, and therefore a number of realities must be accommodated. Because the various participants have different perceptions, disagreements about any given communication event are likely to arise. Facilitative communication does not remove all disagreements and in fact may increase them. However, disagreements may be the mark of a healthy atmosphere, simply because disagreement is allowed to exist. The critical point is how one disagrees and still allows for the free flow of ideas and negotiated outcomes.

Climate

Any decision-making group needs as much input as possible, and therefore unless the atmosphere is nonthreatening, people will tend to be cautious and to maintain a low level of involvement. A group's climate can be affected by both verbal and nonverbal behavior. For example, nonverbal behavior may convey rejection and thereby damage group climate even if a speaker's words suggest otherwise.

Many people believe that nonverbal behaviors are not as easily controlled as verbal behaviors and that therefore they reveal one's real motives. Consequently, when an individual says that he or she will listen, but the words are spoken with a tone of superiority, it is as though a ritual were taking place rather than a person-to-person exchange. Similarly, what might be thought of as good humor in one context may appear to be a put-down to a serious participant in a group setting—"Ho! Ho! Ho! So you're going to try out *that* idea again!"

There are several questions a participant might consider in regard to the effect of nonverbal behaviors on group climate: Do I attend to everyone in the group? Whom do I interrupt? Do I speak to everyone in the group or only to certain people? Do I always sit next to those who support my views? How assertive is the tone of my voice?

Provocative Behaviors

Most people find it difficult to separate themselves from their ideas. Unfortunately, one's symbolic reality is very much a part of one's self, and few people enjoy being attacked. Therefore, to attack one's ideas is to attack one's self. Those behaviors that challenge the self are the antithesis of supportive behavior.

After considerable observation of and interviews with group participants, Lee identified several behaviors almost certain to provoke hostility.[25] Some of the more common behaviors are listed below.

1. Labeling people or calling them names
2. Interrupting others as they are about to make a point
3. Anticipating an argument with a counterargument
4. Implying an ulterior motive
5. Contradicting others
6. Listening with an air of incredulity
7. Using laughter to derogate ideas
8. Conveying a mood of dismissal.

Perhaps nothing is as irritating as being *directly contradicted*—especially in a group setting. There is something absolute about the words "That's not so!" The recipient is made to feel ignorant or deceitful. The only response possible seems to be a defensive counterattack to preserve the self. A contradiction or immediate rejection has a ring of finality and allness that rules out the exploration necessary for an examination of issues.

In most cases, the individual who contradicts has no desire to rule out further discussion or to provoke animosity. Responsible communicators, therefore, will become sensitive to the impact of their behavior on others and will also report the impact of others' behavior on them.

Enhancing Group Process

Consensus One form of decision making that facilitates human exchange is "decision by consensus," which Schein describes as follows:

> It is a state of affairs where communications have been sufficiently open, and the group climate has been sufficiently supportive, to make everyone in the group feel that he has had his fair chance to influence the decision.[26]

Schein asserts that this approach produces a psychological state which stimulates a person to say:

> "I understand what most of you would like to do. I personally would not do that, but I feel that you understand what my alternative would be. I have had sufficient opportunity to sway you to my point of view but clearly have not been able to do so. Therefore, I will gladly go along with what most of you wish to do."[27]

It is important that individuals have a hearing and so perceive in both interpersonal and group settings. This hearing should take place within a supportive climate that allows for maximum input. This is not to say, however, that a person should go along with the group no matter what! Schein's description should not be pushed beyond its logical limits. It is obvious that some matters of decision are more important than others. Deciding when to maintain a minority viewpoint and do one's best to disrupt the majority opinion is a *personal* decision.

Value of nonthreatening behavior Throughout the text we have maintained that certain basic human values are important to sustain in any communication setting. For example, the kind of communication one uses reflects one's perception of the inherent worth of the human being. A person validates the worth of others by being open and according them a full hearing. It is equally important to remember that humans are interdependent. In addition, there is value in getting as much input from group members as possible. Therefore, behaviors that detract from this goal weaken the group product, and everyone loses.

Gibb asserts that "as a person becomes more and more defensive, he becomes less and less able to perceive accurately the motives, the values, and the emotions of the sender."[28] Thus behaviors that create defensive reactions produce a vicious cycle. If the role-taking phase of one person is disturbed, the role taking of the other person is also affected. In other words, if I create defensiveness in you, your behavior will tend to create defensiveness in me. The communication in such an exchange becomes confused, motives are unclear, and the likelihood of cooperation is lessened.

After working for eight years with recordings of various discussions, Gibb concluded that certain behaviors foster defensive climates, whereas others help preserve supportive climates. A contrast of the communication behaviors that generate these two climates is given in Table 5.1.[29] Our descriptions are noted in parentheses.

There are no clear-cut behaviors that *always* result in a supportive or defensive climate; people's perceptions differ. However, certain behaviors are consistently more productive than others, and those behaviors should serve as a guide to supportive group climates.

Table 5.1 Behaviors Leading to Defensive or Supportive Climates

Defensive Climates	Supportive Climates
1. Evaluation (judging)	1. Description (seeking information and description)
2. Control (directing and controlling responses)	2. Problem orientation (mutual problem solving)
3. Strategy (hidden stratagems)	3. Spontaneity (free expression)
4. Neutrality (indifference)	4. Empathy (identifying with problems and feelings)
5. Superiority (communicating superiority in position, power, etc.)	5. Equality (mutual trust and respect)
6. Certainty (knowing the answers)	6. Provisionalism (communicating the spirit of inquiry and investigation)

Alternative Communication Behaviors

Evaluation-description Many of the difficulties in communication stem from two sources—a *misunderstanding* or an *intolerance* of what was said. An immediate evaluation or direct contradiction may be the result of the communicators talking past one another. Before making a judgment, the participants should explore the referents for each person's conclusions. Frequently they will find that they have been talking from different experiences. Similarly, a person shows tolerance for another's point of view by describing and reflecting what has been said. Of course, one need not agree with every idea that comes along, but an awareness of the symbolic process should illustrate that others are not stupid just because they see things differently.

Control-problem orientation Controlling-type behaviors produce defensiveness because they deny (by threatening) a person's ego assertion. If a group seeks consensus, everyone should have an equal opportunity to influence decisions.

Controlling behaviors are not always conscious. The person who says, "No! This shouldn't be discussed now." probably means, "I don't think this should be discussed now, because, etc." However, the first statement denies others an opportunity to make a decision, and therefore it is likely to generate combative responses.

Some individuals simply try to wear others down by continually pressing a point. This type of behavior too can be interpreted as a form of control. Controlling statements can be avoided if the participants become problem-centered and conscious of contributing to the solution. The term "contributing" is significant if one is to believe and convey the attitude of mutual problem solving.

Strategy-spontaneity Open, free discussion leaves no room for a hidden agenda. When individuals seem to be working from a script, others feel manipulated. One can be spontaneous by listening carefully to what others say and responding specifically to what is said. General, oblique comments may convey unwillingness to recognize a particular opinion and to instead direct the interchange toward certain self-interests.

Each communication interchange is unique, and although certain symbolic behaviors seem routine, each exchange requires a reformulation, at the very least. The importance of spontaneity suggests that an open, honest exchange is more facilitative than a polished, articulate communication performance.

Neutrality-empathy Everyone wants to be cared about as a human being. Communicators convey that care by recognizing the problems and feelings of other people. Compare the following exchanges.

Worker: How are we expected to make this deadline with no help?!

Supervisor 1: I just do what I am told.

Supervisor 2: This is a tough situation. You must feel frustrated.

Supervisor 1 remains neutral and aloof, passing the buck and cutting off further exchange. Supervisor 2, by contrast, takes some individual responsibility; by opening the door for further exchange, this individual is in a position to negotiate the problems of the worker and the organization. When one recognizes the feelings of others, the message says, "Your feelings are important because you are important."

Superiority-equality Communication restricted to role behavior tends to convey superiority and neutrality. There is little question about people's awareness of status differences. Nonetheless, individuals can meet on a person-to-person basis, e.g., by knowing the other person's name and by recognizing the other's unique qualities.

In a group setting, for example, the contributions of all should be recognized. If one member of a group is particularly powerful, the group as a whole should take care to prevent forfeiture of the information necessary for decision making. Accordingly, the person authorized to make the final decision might refrain from saying anything until others have spoken. This would overcome people's tendency to react to the role and to try to please the status figure. In addition, individuals not in power positions may well feel that unless they support the power figures, their contributions will be unwelcome.

Such feelings can be prevented by honestly believing that others have worthwhile contributions and listening to those contributions.

Certainty-provisionalism A supportive climate is marked by the absence of immediate evaluation. It is helpful to communicate to others the fact that one is willing to listen and investigate before making judgments. The process of reflecting and describing what others have said communicates the spirit of inquiry.

Even though participants may not feel superiority or certainty, they may nonetheless convey those qualities to others. For example, to give a speech without recognizing or making reference to others' views may be interpreted as certainty on the part of the speaker. Similarly, nonverbal behaviors may convey certainty. You might find it interesting to examine each of Gibb's factors appearing under the defensive and supportive categories in Table 5.1 and then assign nonverbal behaviors for each.

Listening Behavior

Perhaps no one is more supportive than a good listener, and nothing facilitates human transaction better than listening does. A good listener conveys the message that the initiator of a message has something worth saying. Listening abilities and attitudes help one generate and properly evaluate data. However, individuals' capacity to listen varies widely, and poor listening is difficult to detect in oneself. When an individual speaks, others operate as a correction device. This type of correction is not always operative when one listens, especially when what is heard is not reflected back for correction and adjustment. Of course, when one thinks one understands, there does not seem to be any reason to seek adjustment.

Listening, just as speaking does, requires attention and development if one is to use the skills competently, and listening, just as speaking is, is easy if one does not care about the results. In our view, however, listening skills are part of the facilitative process. On the following pages we discuss briefly some basic questions.[30]

What inhibits good listening? Studies have shown that a person can comprehend speech as rapid as 400 words per minute. Most actual speaking rates, however, are about 125 words per minute. Therefore, individuals have time for lapses and excursions into thoughts other than those presented by the speaker. In addition, since a person's span of concentrated attention is short, it is not uncommon for one to suddenly realize that he or she has not been listening. But finding it embarrassing to admit, most people will try to bluff it out. *The discrepancy between speaking and listening rates inhibits listening.*

Haney devised an interesting puzzle that gives insight into some of the factors involved in listening.[31] Solve the puzzle below.

• • •

• • •

• • •

Objective: Draw through all nine dots.

Restrictions: 1. Start with your pencil on any one of the dots.

2. Draw four straight lines without removing your pencil from the page.

3. You may cross over lines, but you may not repeat them, i.e., trace back on them.

Answer: Immediately after completing the exercise, turn to p. 122.

While looking at the answer, keep the following principle in mind: *Listeners tend to believe that meaning is in the message.* Most people are bound by a square and add that restriction, although it does not appear in the directions. *Listeners are bound by all manner of symbolic constructions as a result of language experience and cultural norms.*

The most predictable factor in communication is a certain level of misunderstanding. The reaction to this misunderstanding is critical to the relationships between people. Suppose, for example, that you did not solve the puzzle above and that you imputed motives to the person who gave the directions. This is common in communication settings, and one often hears remarks such as "He doesn't like me" or "She was just trying to show me up!" Conversely, the person who gave the directions might say, "He just doesn't pay attention" or "My lectures are great; the students just don't understand" or "These workers are lazy and just don't care anymore." The first measure of success in communication is the amount of shared meaning that is taking place, and an awareness of the symbolic pitfalls should enable one to compensate for error rather than to retaliate or impute motives.

Listeners are likely to make immediate judgments from their own symbolic worlds. The differences in witnesses' observations at the scene of a crime are well documented in fact and in an abundance of television detective dramas.[32] Part of the problem stems from the human tendency to confuse observation and inference; one may infer something rather than actually observe it. One interesting way to test this principle is to conduct an experiment in the serial transmission of information. Five people pass a verbal message through a chain (A → B → C → D → E) without the benefit of open-channel communication. After listening to the original message, person A passes it on to person

B, who repeats the message heard to person C, etc. Each person hears the message once and is not permitted to ask questions.

The following sample message has been submitted to a number of student groups.

> Every year at State University, the eagles in front of the Psi Gamma Fraternity house were mysteriously painted during the night. Whenever this happened, it cost the Psi Gams from $75 to $100 to have the eagles cleaned. The Psi Gams complained to the university administrators, and were promised by the university president, now retired, that if ever any students were caught painting the eagles, they would be expelled from school.

When this sample message has been used, three highly predictable outcomes have occurred. (1) There is a loss of detail, and the listener tends to compress the message to a more manageable length. (2) Listeners tend to magnify one theme and expand on one set of details, e.g., expanding on the feelings of the fraternity members and emphasizing the penalty for painting the eagles. (3) The details are assimilated into a meaningful framework for the listener. Thus most groups say that this event takes place during homecoming; when else would eagles be painted?

This exercise has been used at three different universities. Each time the color of paint has been added to the story, and each time that color has corresponded to the school colors of the university. When the exercise has been given to nonuniversity groups, color has not been mentioned.

Good listening is thwarted by the fact that listeners tend to listen in order to reply rather than to understand. This is especially true when there is disagreement. People concentrate so much on the protection of self that they bypass one another in their search for understanding. The assertion of self can cause one to concentrate on making an argument and a judgment rather than on listening for common ground.

What distinguishes a good listener? The following list of suggestions, though not all-inclusive, does offer some ways to facilitate human exchange.

1. The most important single factor in listening to others is being motivated to listen. According to Charles Kelly, studies

> strongly indicate that when persons know that their listening comprehension is being tested, differences between individuals are primarily matters of general mental ability; when they do not know their listening performance is being tested, differences are due to personality differences (including motivation to listen), as well as general mental ability. Of these two kinds of research situations, the latter is more representative of realistic listening events.[33]

Although one may not be able to alter general mental ability, one *can* improve listening skills by being motivated to listen. In making a firm initial commitment to listen, a person accepts that others have something worth saying.

In addition to being motivated to listen, a person must be *ready* to do so—mentally and physically. Thus, for example, one should shut out distractions. The individual who tries to engage in several tasks while listening not only impairs the listening process, but also conveys an attitude of indifference to what is being said.

The importance of motivation to good listening cannot be overstated. A significant portion of most professionals' time is spent in the listening process, and it requires a high level of energy and patience.

2. A good listener determines the reason for listening. Some of the most popular social models of listening are dysfunctional for most situations. For example, the television lawyer listens for errors, irrelevancies, admissions, and then triumphs—to the delight of the courtroom audience. In this context, the emphasis is on analytical skills and the determination of witnesses' real motives. In most real-life social situations, however, the participants are not hostile witnesses, and therefore to regard others as opponents erects barriers to communication.

When individuals limit their listening to recall and analysis, others perceive those behaviors as a predisposition to judge rather than to listen. Listening, then, involves two complementary procedures. First, one must obtain an understanding of the speaker's symbolic behavior from the speaker's point of view. What do the speaker's words mean to the speaker? In order to answer this question, the listener must become involved in such a way as to allow the other person his or her symbolic reality. Second, one must use one's analytical skills to determine the best way of reaching understanding or negotiation.

3. Good listeners give the speaker a complete hearing. They do not interrupt by saying, "I know just what you mean" or "That happened to me and this is what I did" or "Here is what you are trying to say." Instead, good listeners treat each individual's thoughts as unique and worthwhile; they do not make prejudgments.

4. Good listeners are meaning-centered rather than message-centered. They ask: What do the speaker's words mean to that individual?

5. Good listeners distinguish observations from inferences. They ask themselves what they are inferring from messages.

6. Good listeners restate thoughts to the satisfaction of the speaker.

7. Good listeners remain open and do not impute motives to the speaker.

8. Good listeners look for main ideas and major themes.

9. Good listeners are aware of "signal words" that trigger emotional reac-

tions in themselves. They avoid striking out at a speaker from their own symbolic world.

10. Good listeners avoid the pretense of attention, and they try to create a supportive atmosphere.

11. Good listeners respond to the feeling as well as to the content of a message.

Leadership Behavior

If one listens to others, engages in supportive behaviors, and practices the suggested feedback principles, how does one exert leadership? All of these practices seem antithetical to the popular image of the person who takes charge, motivates followers, and tells it like it is. In fact, a number of leadership styles seem to produce results. In addition, leadership characteristics are determined by the relationship between leader and followers, and these characteristics vary according to the expectations in the relationship. The characteristics of the leader of the Hell's Angels are most likely quite different from those of the leader of the Harper Valley PTA.

Our purpose here is not to compare the merits of leadership styles, but rather to compare the communication behavior of two general types of leaders. What behaviors produce the most satisfactory goals? What behaviors allow for personal growth? What behaviors produce a feeling of satisfaction about how the goals were accomplished?

James Sargent and Gerald Miller conducted an experimental study that examined 12 hypothesized differences between certain communication behaviors of autocratic and democratic group leaders.[34] The distinctions they found are shown in Table 5.2. After drawing up a set of hypotheses based on these distinctions, the researchers analyzed discussions of groups with autocratic and democratic leaders. The results of 11 hypotheses are shown in Fig. 5.1.

The first hypothesis, which does not appear in Fig. 5.1, was that autocratic leaders would engage in a significantly greater amount of communication with their groups than democratic leaders would. This prediction was accurate, but not quite to the point of statistical significance. Three hypotheses that dealt with social-emotional (supportive) statements demonstrated that democratic leaders do make more supportive statements, but again the results were not statistically significant. The hypothesis that authoritarian leaders utter more negative reactions was substantiated, as were the hypotheses that autocratic leaders attempt more answers, ask fewer questions, do not encourage as much participation, and generate fewer alternatives. The last hypothesis was that democratic leaders make a higher ratio of statements relating the dis-

Table 5.2 Characteristic Differences between Autocratic and Democratic Leaders

Autocratic Leader	Democratic Leader
1. A concern for efficient group productivity.	1. A concern that each group member has an opportunity to influence decisions in accordance with his abilities and desires.
2. A concern for achieving his own personal outcomes.	2. A concern for the evaluation of relevant alternatives.
3. A concern that his views are represented or understood in discussions.	3. A concern that the group reach their own decision rather than merely reinforce the leader's preferred decision.
4. A concern for control of the major communications interactions of the group.	4. A concern to stimulate thinking by posing choices and alternatives.
5. A concern for control of the knowledge necessary to achieve the goals.	5. A greater concern for group maintenance than group productivity.
6. A concern for fast action if he deems it necessary.	6. A concern for helping the group to clarify group goals.
	7. A concern for positive affective relations within the group.

James Sargent and Gerald Miller, "Some Differences in Certain Behaviors of Autocratic and Democratic Leaders," *Journal of Communication* **21** (September 1971), p. 245. Reprinted by permission.

cussion to the overall group purpose or objectives than autocratic leaders do. Although the "Group purpose index" in Fig. 5.1 indicates some movement in the predicted direction, the results were not statistically significant.

This study demonstrated that communication differences do exist between autocratic and democratic leaders. Moreover, the way in which one perceives leadership and the leader's role in the group setting have a direct impact on facilitative communication behavior.

SUMMARY

In this chapter we have examined the impact of symbolic corroboration on human behavior, set forth some basic principles of facilitation as well as some factors that impinge on that process, and applied the principles to interpersonal and group communication. Human beings have a desire for free exchange and

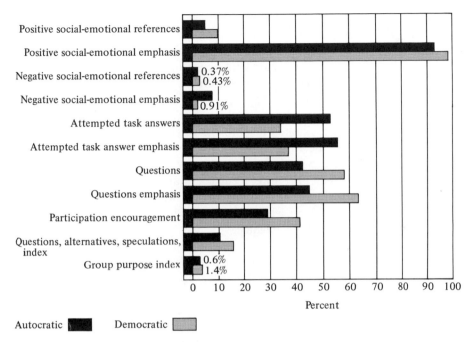

Positive social-emotional references

Positive social-emotional emphasis

Negative social-emotional references 0.37% 0.43%

Negative social-emotional emphasis 0.91%

Attempted task answers

Attempted task answer emphasis

Questions

Questions emphasis

Participation encouragement

Questions, alternatives, speculations, index

Group purpose index 0.6% 1.4%

0 10 20 30 40 50 60 70 80 90 100

Percent

Autocratic ▮   Democratic ▢

Fig. 5.1 Breakdown of autocratic and democratic leaders' communication behavior. (James Sargent and Gerald Miller, "Some Differences in Certain Communication Behaviors of Autocratic and Democratic Leaders," *Journal of Communication* **21**, September 1971, p. 235. Reprinted by permission.)

for recognition of their symbolic worlds. Thus communication, the act of exchange, is a two-part process, and each participant alternately initiates and responds to messages. In addition, communicators experience not only themselves in the process of exchange, but also the other participants and their experiencing of the exchange.

But in order for a free, open exchange to occur, the communication must be facilitated. Communication must occur in a nonthreatening environment. A primary goal of communication is mutual problem solving and understanding. Toward that end, participants need to focus on "quality" in interpersonal encounters. They need to be accepting of others and their views and, more importantly, to communicate that acceptance. This type of attitude can be achieved only when communicators meet on a person-to-person basis, not on a role-dominated, impersonal basis.

In addition to attitude, language itself is a factor that can either facilitate or inhibit the free flow of communication. Words are symbols; they represent something else—a person, object, or idea. Thus communication is facilitated to the extent that the participants are able to get beyond the word to what it represents. Similarly, words, because they are representations, are limited. As a symbol, a word cannot encompass all of the shades of meaning inherent in a perception of a given person, object, or event, or in the variety of perceptions experienced by numerous individuals. A third limitation of language is that in the very act of perception, a person's inference may become an observation. Thus a "fact" (observation) may be based on the unverifiable perception that may nonetheless be labeled a "fact."

Despite the factors impinging on the communication process, free and open exchange can be facilitated at both the interpersonal and group levels. These facilitators take the form of various communication behaviors. Communication is facilitated when participants know that their opinions will be listened to and respected. Therefore, feedback is an important facilitative element. Rephrasing, to the speakers' satisfaction, what has been said, asking questions, emphasizing the present—all are ways in which interpersonal communication becomes a quality exchange.

Because of the greater number of participants involved, communication in a group setting is more complicated than dyadic interpersonal communication, and therefore facilitation is even more crucial. A communicator in a group setting must work to maintain self and thus seeks corroboration from not only individuals within the group, but also the group as a whole.

A second factor in group communication is the group's climate. Communication is facilitated to the extent that group members feel comfortable in the group. But if participants perceive the group's climate as hostile or threatening, they will hesitate to offer their views, and thus communication within the group and the attainment of maximum input will be inhibited.

Even though there are pitfalls inherent in the group setting, communication can be facilitated. Members can avoid provoking others. The group can strive to achieve a supportive climate and arrive at decisions through consensus. Perhaps most important, the group members can improve their listening behavior. For it is good listening, more than any other behavior, that facilitates communication—at both the interpersonal and group levels.

PROBLEMS AND ISSUES

Answer to puzzle on page 116.

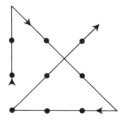

1. Create an illustrative experiment in which Gibb's defensive and supportive behaviors are used. Measure the results in terms of amount of communication and types of responses.

2. Record a group discussion and categorize supportive and nonsupportive behaviors. Can you get agreement among several observers?

3. Construct a message to use in the experiment about the serial transmission of information with several groups. What does this tell you about observation-inference confusion?

4. Are the principles of facilitation realistic? What are the barriers to such an approach?

5. Use the principles of facilitation in the following exchanges.

   Student: This class is really boring.
   Teacher:

   Friend: You are phony!
   Friend:

   Employee: Do you think we will get a union?
   Supervisor:

6. When have you used "you" messages instead of "I" messages? Describe how you could have proceeded differently.

7. The following tasks are suggested by Haney:

TASK 1

As quickly as possible, list the opposites of

Clean_____   _____
Strong_____   _____
Young_____   _____
Brave_____   _____
Beautiful_____ _____

TASK 2

Fill in the appropriate gradational terms between "opposite" words listed below, beginning with the center column (a) and proceeding to columns (b) and (c) only after completing (a).

	(b)	(a)	(c)	
clean	_____	_____	_____	dirty
strong	_____	_____	_____	weak
young	_____	_____	_____	old
brave	_____	_____	_____	cowardly
beautiful	_____	_____	_____	ugly[35]

Why was task 2 more difficult than task 1? Discuss.

NOTES

1. For a discussion of objective and subjective reality, *see* Alfred R. Lindesmith, Anselm L. Strauss, and Norman K. Denzin, *Social Psychology,* 4th ed. (Hinsdale, Ill.: Dryden, 1975), pp. 94–96.

2. Tomatsu Shibutani, *Improvised News* (Indianapolis: Bobbs-Merrill, 1966), pp. 120–171.

3. Carlos Castaneda, *A Separate Reality* (New York: Simon & Schuster, 1971). *See also The Teachings of Don Juan: A Yaqui Way of Knowledge* (New York: Ballantine, 1968), *Second Journal to Ixtlan* (New York: Simon & Schuster, 1972).

4. For a description of this process, *see* Erving Goffman, *Stigma* (Englewood Cliffs, N.J.: Prentice-Hall, 1963).

5. Orrin E. Klapp, *Symbolic Leaders* (Chicago: Aldine, 1964).

6. Peter L. Berger and Thomas Luckmann, *The Social Construction of Reality* (Garden City, N.Y.: Doubleday, 1966).

7. For a summary of classical and contemporary theories, *see* Norman K. Denzin, "Play, Games and Interaction: The Contexts of Childhood Socialization," *Sociological Quarterly* **16** (Autumn 1975): 458–478.

8. For discussion, *see* Gregory Stone and Harvey Farberman, *Social Psychology through Symbolic Interaction* (Waltham, Mass.: Ginn-Blaisdell, 1970), pp. 72–75.

9. Harold Garfinkel, "Conditions of Successful Degradation Ceremonies," *Symbolic Interaction,* ed. Jerome Manis and Bernard Meltzer (Boston: Allyn and Bacon, 1967), p. 205.

10. For a discussion of concepts of humans, *see* Gordon W. Allport, "The Historical Background of Modern Social Psychology," in *Handbook of Social Psychology,* Vol. I, 2d ed., ed. Gardner Lindzey and Elliot Aronson (Reading, Mass.: Addison-Wesley, 1969), pp. 10–15; Edward Zigler and Irwin Child, "Socialization," in Vol. III, pp. 470–471.

11. Carl R. Rogers, "The Interpersonal Relationship: The Core of Guidance," *Harvard Educational Review* **32** (Fall 1962): 416–429.

12. Martin Buber, *Hasidism and Modern Man* (New York: Harper & Row, 1958), p. 138.

13. Alfred Korzybski, *Science and Sanity,* 4th ed. (Lakeville, Conn.: International Non-Aristotelian Library, 1973), pp. xl–xlii.

14. Wendell Johnson, *People in Quandaries* (New York: Harper, 1946), p. 172.

15. *Ibid.,* p. 94.

16. Kenneth Boulding, *The Image* (Ann Arbor: University of Michigan Press, 1961), p. 14.

17. William Haney, *Communication and Organization Behavior* 2d ed. (Homewood, Ill.: Richard D. Irwin, 1967), p. 306.

18. For a brief summary of authoritarian personality, *see* Mark Abrahamson, *Interpersonal Accommodation* (New York: Van Nostrand Reinhold, 1966), pp. 100–101.

19. John Condon, *Semantics and Communication* (New York: Macmillan, 1966), p. 44.

20. *See* Mauk Mulder, "The Power Variable in Communication Experiments," *Human Relations* **13** (1960): 241–256.

21. Reuel Howe, *The Miracle of Dialogue* (New York: Seabury Press, 1963), p. 56.

22. *See* Irwin Altman and D. Taylor, *Social Penetration: The Development of Interpersonal Relationships* (New York: Holt, Rinehart and Winston, 1973); D. Taylor, "Some Aspects of the Development of Interpersonal Relationships: Social Penetration Processes," *Journal of Social Psychology* **75** (1968): 79–90.

23. Thomas Gordon, *Parent Effectiveness Training* (New York: Wyden, 1970).

24. Unpublished material from The Social Seminar Training Center, Bethesda, Maryland, 1975.

25. Irving J. Lee, *How to Talk with People* (New York: Harper & Brothers, 1952), pp. 26–46.

26. Reprinted by special permission from *Process Consultation: Its Role in Organization Development,* p. 56, by Edgar Schein, Addison-Wesley Publishing Company, Inc., Reading, Massachusetts. Copyright © 1969. All rights reserved.

27. *Ibid.*

28. Jack R. Gibb, "Defensive Communication," *Journal of Commnication* **11** (September 1961): 141–142.

29. *Ibid.,* p. 143.

30. For more extensive study, *see* Sam Duker, *Listening: Readings* (New York: Scarecrow Press, 1966) and *Listening Bibliography* (Metuchen, N.J.: Scarecrow Press, 1968).

31. Haney, *op. cit.,* pp. 407–408.

32. For some classic studies, *see* A. H. Hastorf and H. Cantril, "They Saw a Game: A Case Study," *Journal of Abnormal Social Psychology* **49** (1954): 129–132; M. C. Otto, "Testimony and Human Nature," *Journal of Criminal Law and Criminology* **9** (1919): 98–104.

33. Charles Kelly, "Empathic Listening," *Small Group Communication,* ed. Robert Cathcart and Larry Samovar (Dubuque, Iowa: William C. Brown, 1970), p. 255. Reprinted by permission.

34. James Sargent and Gerald Miller, "Some Differences in Certain Communication Behaviors of Autocratic and Democratic Leaders," *Journal of Communication* **21** (September 1971): 233–252.

35. Haney, *op. cit.,* p. 312. Reprinted by permission.

Chapter 6

Regulation
of Behavior

INTRODUCTION

One of the fundamental propositions advanced in Chapter 1 was that *one's perception and interpretation of the environment depend on communication.* It follows, therefore, that anyone who is able to withhold, alter, or selectively disseminate information is in a position to exercise power over others. A communicator who structures another's reality and limits choices exerts a measure of control over that person.

The complexities involved in discussing regulation of communication behavior are revealed in some important questions. What happens in this regulatory process? How can one exert influence over another? Should such influence be exercised and if so, under what conditions? How can one become aware of controlling others or of being controlled? Are there responsibilities involved in regulating the behavior of others?

This chapter examines the social process of regulation and the legitimate use of those processes. Having examined facilitation and corroboration—two purposes and results of communication that may develop interpersonal understanding—we are ready to focus on another purpose of communication— "controlling" the behavior of self and others. Our discussion is divided into four main sections. First, we explore the nature of regulation, so that this function of communication can be compared to other such functions. Second, we investigate various sources of symbolic behaviors that regulate individuals, in order to facilitate recognition of and ability to cope with controlling forces in the environment. Next, we develop a regulatory paradigm from the symbolic interaction approach to motivation, a useful approach to the practice of persuasion. Finally, we examine some significant issues involved in the regulation of others.

Although a number of implications for persuasion are given throughout the chapter, we do not offer a set of prescriptions. Rather, our major concern is with the theoretical and philosophical issues and with their implications for the communicator.

THE NATURE OF REGULATION

Definition

Regulation can be defined as *symbolic processes that induce change or maintain stability in self and others*. We regard "regulation" as an inclusive term incorporating various forms of social influence—persuasion, education, and propaganda. The title of this chapter could have been "Control of Behavior," "Persuasion," or "Social Influence." Because individuals are not passive in the communication process and because they have a great deal to say about what messages mean, the term "control" may be construed in an absolute sense. In other words, individuals receive both multiple and contradictory messages and must decide what roles or counterroles they are going to play. Therefore, "regulation" seems more accurate than the terms "control of behavior," "persuasion," or "social influence" in describing what occurs.

The term "persuasion," for example, is normally reserved for a narrow range of activities—politics, advertising, selling, etc. Although we are concerned about those activities in this chapter, we also consider a broader range of symbolic behaviors than are subsumed under the category "persuasion." Similarly, we feel that "social influence," as it is typically defined, does not cover the full spectrum of symbolic interaction. For example, King defines social influence as "the process by which the behavior of an individual or collection of individuals induces change in the state of another individual or collection of individuals."[1] We too are concerned with change, but also with the process that maintains stability and organizes behavior. In addition, our concerns are with the "self" and others.

Everyone is familiar with the external regulating influence of communication: "Shut the door," "Don't walk on grass," "No left turn." Communication is also internalized to provide self-regulation. Perhaps you have witnessed a child who reached for an object and said, "No! No!" The child internalized the original parental admonition to provide self-control and may later use this form of self-control to exert control over others.

Relationship to Facilitation

In our discussion in Chapter 5 of facilitative processes, perhaps you wondered whether the efforts to facilitate understanding and achieve quality in communication are antithetical to the regulation of others. Do people engage in facilitative behavior in order to eventually get their own way? Is "facilitation" just a more polite term for "seduction"? In the final analysis, is all symbolic behavior a matter of persuading others? Our answers differ from those given by people who maintain that the "humanist" approach to communication is nonadaptive and self-oriented.[2]

In our view, facilitation is a prelude to negotiation, and therefore achievement of mutual understanding would seem to be a highly complementary part of the regulatory process. An individual who comes to know another and is willing to look at that person's needs will also be in a better position to present choices that fulfill those needs. Of equal importance is the concept of self-regulation. By engaging in facilitative behavior, individuals are able to examine their own motives and beliefs, which may be in need of modification.

Necessity of Regulation

The concepts of facilitation and regulation can only exist together and make sense when they are placed in proper perspective. Should humans be allowed to do what they want, without restraint or regulation? If the concept of self-actualization is pushed to the extreme and all restraints are lifted, the philosophy becomes one of letting each individual become what he or she *can* become. Thus, as in a statement attributed to Bandura, "Hitler is an example of self-actualization."[3]

But human interdependence makes regulation and negotiation a necessity. The words "complete freedom" may be attractive, but they also screen out the realities that hold a civilization together and ensure continuity. As Spates and Levin point out, "the literature is full of reports about the sudden dissolution of hippie clans because a key leader unexpectedly 'split' (left), garbage was not taken out, rent was not collected, and so on."[4] In other words, one's "complete freedom" may have repercussions on the freedom of others, and to that extent behavior must be regulated, as indicated by the following statistics:

1. By United Nations' count, imminent starvation and bankruptcy now face no fewer than 32 nations.
2. In Bangladesh alone 100,000 have died in the last six weeks and the government says a million more will die by the end of the year unless they get emergency aid.
3. Death rates are climbing in Central America, Africa and India, as well as elsewhere in developing countries—reversing trends of 20 years.
4. Food prices are soaring around the world—increases in the U.S. now expected to amount to nearly 15 percent for the year, far above the forecasts.
5. Food reserves are depleted.[5]

Should people have complete freedom to reproduce, consume resources, and spend?

As we noted in Chapter 5, a number of ideas about facilitation have come from people concerned with the therapeutic setting. But even here individuals must eventually learn a proper balance between "complete freedom" and rigid restraints. Maslow observes as follows.

What has to be repeated again and again—is that the healthy person is not only expressive. He must be expressive when he wishes to be. He must be able to let himself go. He must be able to drop controls, inhibitions, defenses when he deems this desirable. But equally he must have the ability to control himself, to delay his pleasures, to be polite, to avoid hurting, to keep his mouth shut, and to rein his impulses.[6]

An individual may arrive at a sense of self and self-control in the therapeutic setting. What is sometimes forgotten, however, is that the individual is also learning to adapt to an environment bounded by constraints. Although a therapist may not tell a client how to behave, success can occur only if the client is able to adapt to a world of norms and certain values. In that sense there is regulation, and the client will also regulate others by his or her behavior. The therapist is a representative of the environment, which is also the locus of the coping behaviors a client learns.

A Negotiation Perspective

There are good reasons for people's willingness to be regulated. Individuals conform to groups because of social, economic, security, or other advantages that would not exist without the group. An exchange is made; an individual may give up certain freedoms in order to gain others. But when groups or individuals no longer represent advantages, they lose their regulatory powers.

Of course, regulatory behaviors are not necessarily destructive, and the regulation of behavior entails a price, as illustrated in the following anecdote. A very rich man had 50 books that contained all the wisdom of the world. However, he was quite concerned about his son's ability to handle the family fortune. He told his son that if the 50 books of wisdom could be reduced to 10 volumes, the son could expect to receive $25 million at the reading of the will. The son completed the task, but his father was still uncertain. He then challenged his son to reduce the ten volumes to one for $50 million. Much to his surprise, the young man succeeded. However, being very rich and somewhat salty (the old man was on his deathbed after all those revisions), he told his son that he could have the entire family fortune of $100 million if he could reduce all the wisdom of the world into one sentence. "There is no such thing as a free lunch!" the son wrote. The old man read the sentence, signed over the fortune, and died with a smile on his face.

Society is based on human contracts and exchanges, and it is naive to believe that humans are completely free from the restraints imposed by their societal groupings and alliances. All of us are regulated and by necessity strike a bargain (explicitly or implicitly) with other individuals, organizations, and the state. As participants, we all attempt to satisfy our needs and achieve the most we can from the bargain.

SOURCES OF REGULATION

An individual's behavior is regulated by a broad range of symbolic behaviors. A person is born into a group-filled culture bounded by a linguistic system. In this sense, therefore, "culture," "groups," and "language" are overlapping categories; members of a group operate within a cultural framework and acquire linguistic behavior that in turn affects their own behavior—especially their perceptual behavior.

Language

Within such a culture/group/language framework, children learn what language is reinforced and therefore considered acceptable. They learn not only "correct" usage, but also what to think. Gradually, children internalize language and form linguistically categorized ways of thinking and seeing. As individuals acquire new linguistic categories from persons outside the family, they modify their thinking patterns. Language, then, is not the vehicle of thought; rather, it *is* the thought.

Language as reality Despite the importance of language as a source of regulation, some questions remain. Is there nonlinguistic thought? Where do new ideas come from? In most cases, however, *what* one thinks is a given from the group; *how* one thinks is influenced by the culture.

The concepts of time, space, motion, and causality vary across cultures, along with available linguistic categories. Language in various groups is not a reproduction of the world, but rather is the world. People see "reality" as they are, and they approach the world according to their linguistic framework, which is imposed on what is out there. The linguistic categories that exist are decided by the needs of the group.

Language and self-regulation Lindesmith and Strauss maintain that self-regulation is not really different from social control. They give the following example of the internalized conversation of an individual who is thinking about robbing a bank.

Phase One	*Phase Two*
I could use that money.	But it's stealing
So what! Everyone steals if they have a chance to.	You know it isn't so.
I could get a new car.	No. Better be honest!
No chance of getting caught.	Dishonest.
Banks make lots of money; they won't feel it.	Isn't right to take it; isn't theirs either.[7]

This hypothetical conversation with self may not occur at all, or it may take place quite differently if the person's linguistic categories are different.

Groups

In noting the influence of "the group" on human behavior, we have not distinguished between two important types of groups—reference and membership groups. The term "membership group" suggests that an individual may be physically present within the group, but not necessarily involved psychologically. By contrast, a "reference group" emphasizes the psychological factor. (The most obvious example of a reference group exerting control over others is the family.) Thus an individual may use the group as a standard in defining a situation and/or aspire to the values of the group and seek acceptance.[8]

Conformity But the concept of group influence does not form a rigid, static source of regulatory influence. Rather, changes in behavior or belief toward the views of a group can take place as a result of real or imagined pressures. Changes can be a matter of compliance with group demands or actual private acceptance of group perceptions.

People conform to groups for a variety of reasons, but probably the most important one is that groups fulfill personal needs. In that sense all of us are conformers, and the term should therefore be considered descriptive rather than derogatory. Individuals may meet the expectations of a group so that the group will survive and continue to meet its members' needs. The group is also important to the validation of self. Who one is and where one fits depend a great deal on the confirmation bestowed by groups. In short, the group serves as a guide to "reality" and to evaluation of self and others.

Effects of group pressure A classic study of the effects of group pressure was carried out by Asch, who used a group of people, all but one of whom were confederates, or "shills." The experimenter presented the group with two or three lines of different lengths and asked the subjects to say which line matched a comparison line. Judgments were made sequentially, and usually the planted subjects (confederates) went first. The focus of the study was whether the naive subject would go along with the obviously incorrect answers made by the group of confederates. Approximately one-third of the subjects complied with the incorrect answers.

What is of greater significance for our purposes, however, is the individual differences found and the conditions under which people were more likely to change. Those findings are summarized below.

1. Individuals who remained independent could be classed as (a) confident and outspoken, (b) independent and withdrawn, and (c) independent with considerable doubt and tension.

2. Those who yielded to group pressure were placed in several categories. (a) Some experienced distortion of perception and were not aware that their estimates had been displaced or distorted by the majority. (b) Most submitting subjects experienced distortion of judgment in which there was primary doubt and lack of confidence. (c) One group experienced distortion of action and although they did not feel that they were wrong, they submitted rather than appear different from others.

3. The presence of someone who thinks like the naive subject increases his or her ability to withstand group pressure.

4. When a "planted ally" withdraws support from a naive subject, the full effect of group pressure tends to be restored.

5. The late arrival of a "true partner" modifies the effect of group pressure, but not completely so.

6. The presence of a "compromise partner," or one who makes estimates between the truth and majority position, reduces the frequency of errors for the naive subject, but not significantly.

7. Majority effects appeared in full force with a majority of three. Larger majorities did not produce more pronounced effects.

8. The majority effect grows stronger as the situation diminishes in clarity. If the stimulus to be judged is ambiguous, naive subjects not only go along, but feel little conflict in doing so.[9]

But Asch's studies did not investigate a number of variables that might be operative in the social situation. For example, individuals might respond more to significant others, and one's level of expertise, as well as the stimulus being judged, might make a difference. However, other studies have indicated that group pressure is even stronger when individuals are actually functioning as members of a group rather than as a member of an aggregate (a simple collection of people with no bonds among them).[10]

Some implications These findings have some important implications for not only regulators, but also those who are regulated by others. For example, a communicator might think about the following:

1. The group may be used as a medium for change. It may be much more effective to work through a group than to approach others individually.

2. To change an individual in any significant way, it may be necessary to change a group or separate that individual from a supporting group.

3. People react very differently to group pressure.

4. To keep an ally on a particular issue, it may be necessary to communicate support on a regular basis.

5. If an individual does not speak out on an issue, a withdrawn supporter may go along with the majority.

6. Individuals should ask the most questions when communication is ambiguous.

7. Social influences can be used to enhance rather than distort individual integrity. Groups can encourage their members to express independent judgments so that group consensus is meaningful.

Examples of the potency of group influence range from World War II studies demonstrating that individuals could be induced to eat less desirable cuts of meat (kidneys, etc.) to studies of the impact of brainwashing on the American soldier.[11] Although each study specifies particular conditions and variables, the impact of group support and language behavior is clearly evident. Three of the major group sources of regulation are one's family, peer group or subculture, and the larger community. Included within the larger community are the mass media.

Mass Media

There is considerable disagreement about how much impact the media really have and whether the major influence on people's attitudes and beliefs should be credited to interpersonal communication.[12] Our concern is more with *how* the impact occurs rather than with its extent. We contend that the characteristics of the media and the conditions under which they operate make them a potent regulating force.

Pervasiveness In the average home in the United States, the television is on for approximately six and one-quarter hours every day. In addition, many people are exposed to newspapers, radios, magazines, and films. Vast audiences receive messages that continually reinforce selected behaviors.

Social modeling The media provide, on a large-scale basis, social models and the consequences of particular behaviors. Individuals engage in vicarious learning (learning without direct reinforcement or direct experience) by observing others in the media and the consequences of their behavior.

Bandura's "Bobo doll" experiments provide an excellent example of social modeling.[13] Preschool children watched an adult pummel an inflatable plastic doll. The adult also attached labels to her behavior, e.g., "sock him in the nose!" When the children were left alone with the doll, they mimicked the adult's actions and verbal behavior (see Fig. 6.1). Moreover, there was no significant difference between those who witnessed the act in real life and those

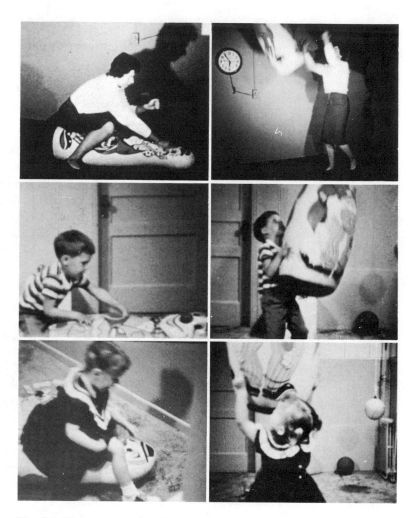

Fig. 6.1 The process of social modeling in the "Bobo doll" experiment. (Photograph courtesy Albert J. Bandura)

who watched it on a television screen. This finding suggests that by providing a social model, the media change or reinforce what is learned.

Atkin reports a study in which a sample of fourth and fifth graders viewed a video tape program containing a currently aired acne cream commercial in which preadolescents applied the preparation; another sample saw an irrelevant commercial.[14] Questionnaire results revealed that the group exposed to the acne commercial differed from the control group in that the students expressed significantly greater concern about blemishes, were significantly

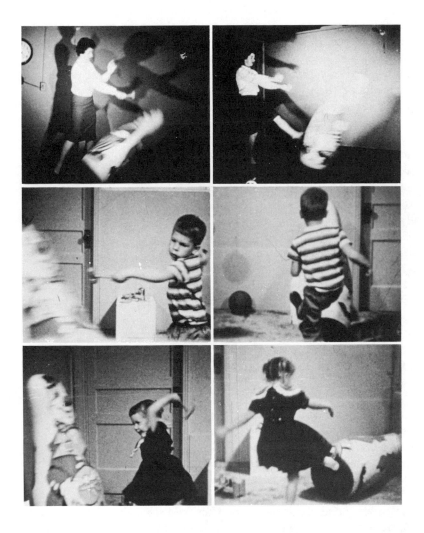

more likely to believe in the utility of skin cream over regular soap, and were significantly more likely to say that they would buy the product for their personal use.

Atkin also presents data indicating that advertisements generate themes in addition to specific brand preferences. In other words, the underlying theme is consumption behavior, and the media produce a cumulative impression of "eating cereal," "playing games," or "using shampoo."

Legitimacy and reality The impact of the modeling process goes beyond providing guides for individuals' behavior. The media may also present collective and institutionally sanctioned violence as part of the social model. Some researchers are concerned about not only the cause, but also the meaning, of violence in the media. They are concerned about a number of symbolic functions (including fear of victimization and the cultivation of a sense of risk and power) the media perform.[15]

Television news and programing constitute a large portion of one's reality and set the boundaries of behavior. The behavior is not just visual; symbols attached to the behavior filter into a society that uses them to describe, evaluate, and adjust behavior. Because some of these changes occur over a period of time, they are difficult to detect with traditional approaches to the study of human behavior. At what point, for example, did it become socially acceptable to discuss breast cancer in explicit terms and demonstrate self-examination graphically in television programing? At what point will the same be true for venereal disease?

Earlier we pointed out that the media express what roles are played by whom and the qualities attached to those roles. Although changes may occur in a society prior to their being displayed in the media, the media themselves give a legitimacy and reality to what may be happening. For example, when minority-group members are presented as holding status positions in the larger society or using products for the same reasons that nonminorities use those products, majority-group members tend to view these individuals as being less different. Of course, role stereotypes can be maintained, as well as broken down, by the media.

Symbolic events Events and the consequent symbols attached to them can regulate behaviors, even though those events may differ in character. For example, during the 1960s students engaged in a variety of activities ranging from barricading buildings to destroying them. The most dramatic of these incidents appeared on national television news. During the Kent State and Cambodia disorders, a group of Utah students marched quietly into an administration building and sat on the floor. They held signs, but did not disrupt the ongoing activities in the building. But these students represented a symbol of confrontation. They were taken to jail, and community reaction was immediate; there was a widespread belief that a "student riot" had taken place "just like on TV." Administrators felt that they had combatted the terrible forces of the time. Events had been equated, and the symbol attached to the events had regulated behavior.

The mass media also regulate behavior by the events they choose to publicize. Alternatives and complete details are limited by the time allotted to a news broadcast. Television, for example, is an action-oriented visual medium, and broadcasters tend to emphasize a particular event or the most action-packed part of that event. During the "police-student confrontations" at the Democrats' 1968 Chicago convention, the news media sought action. Some of their members were even accused of staging confrontation and action. If this accusation was accurate, some of those in the news industry not only selected the alternatives for the viewer, but also created them.

Communication advantages The emphasis on action and events has given television an immediacy and credibility not enjoyed by the other mass media. In addition to appearing as an objective source, television is comparable to a number of popular arts in that it injects a flavor of entertainment in whatever it does. Therefore, an "exposure factor" is operating when social models and ideas are presented on TV. Television viewers may expose themselves to a variety of contrary ideas in television programing because they expect entertainment and do not perceive ulterior motives. For example, you may be much more favorably disposed toward hearing Joan Baez sing than toward hearing her give a political speech, even though both instances may involve exposure to some different ideas.

"Comic strip rhetoric" is another medium that mixes entertainment and social messages, but its effectiveness and impact are open to question. Little Orphan Annie promotes the righteousness of capitalism along with elements of adventure. When a comic strip detective asks: "Are parole boards motivated by sociological stupidity, bribery, or just an inferiority complex that puts them on a level with the murderer?" the readers receive an argument, as well as their daily dose of suspense.

Mass exposure does not necessarily result in control, however. Individuals are not passive objects that absorb everything they are exposed to. Nevertheless, when mass exposure is coupled with an entertainment factor, the media have considerable opportunity to mold public opinion.

Repetition too influences what people remember and what symbols are available for processing. Indeed, the factor of repetition may account for product sales more than any of the arguments attached to the advertisements for those products. Multiple symbolic cues enhance the processing of information, and television and film are especially suited to give both auditory and visual cues that enhance the receiver's recall and belief of the products being advertised.

Television commentators interpret events for those who are not close to the event; therefore, a type of electronic dependence can occur during a crisis situation. News reporters become more than reporters, because the audience's searching-type behaviors bestow considerable credibility on familiar sources of information. For example, night after night during the Vietnam war, newscasters gave the "body count" on the number of enemy killed, a number always significantly higher than the number of South Vietnamese and Americans killed. Willingly or not, the reporters broadcast the misleading, highly inflated numbers given them by Pentagon and South Vietnamese officials anxious to maintain American support for the war.

In brief, although the impact of the media in creating behaviors has not been fully determined, they have considerable opportunities for changing others. The media (1) possess immediacy and thereby credibility; (2) have great opportunity to achieve receiver exposure to messages via perceived entertainment with absence of ulterior motive; (3) achieve mass exposure; (4) use repetition of messages; (5) use multiple symbolic cues; and (6) become primary sources of information.

An example The series of debates between the presidential and vice-presidential candidates in the fall of 1976 illustrates the impact of a mass medium —television—on behavior. Close to 100 million people—nearly one-half of the American population—were estimated to have watched the first debate. Thus the very pervasiveness of the medium was an important element in the significance the debates assumed in the campaign.

The stakes were enormous for both candidates. President Ford, widely regarded as the underdog when he proposed the debates during his acceptance speech as the Republican candidate, hoped to overcome that handicap in front of a vast national audience by appearing "presidential." For Carter, who during the primaries had emerged from the oblivion of "Jimmy who?", the debates offered a challenge as well as an opportunity—to convince the voters that his "presidentialness" was better than the incumbent's.

The factor of "appearing presidential" was in fact a matter of trying to live up to the social model suggested by "The President of the United States." Did Carter's apparent nervousness during the first debate detract from the image of how a president should appear? Was Robert Dole's sharp wit and hope to have a "fun evening" in keeping with the seriousness and high purpose a vice-president should demonstrate?

Political candidates generally speak at rallies to the "party faithful," to those predisposed to vote in a certain way. But in the debates each candidate was forced to address not only his own supporters, but also those of the other man, third-party candidates, as well as a large bloc of uncommitted and undecided voters. Especially for this last group, a candidate who seemed to "come across well" might as a result appear more "presidential," thus supporting the legitimacy of his candidacy.

The widespread publicity surrounding the debates elevated them to perhaps the single most important element in the campaign. Indeed, for many people, the debates *were* the campaign; the two events were equated. But the content of the debates was not controlled by the two candidates. Rather, the content was controlled by media representatives, the three-member panels of questioners. Occasionally the candidates tried to sidestep certain questions in order to get in a point, but then this too became a point of contention.

Although some may object that the debates were nothing more than a media event staged by and for television, they are nonetheless important for that very reason. Perhaps a media event was the decisive element in the presidential election of 1976.

Symbols

In Chapter 2, we asserted that: (1) language is a group product (individuals use group language for identity and social confirmation); (2) language involves shared behavior (the meaning of something depends on how individuals respond or behave toward it and one another); and (3) language is organized behavior (the use of linguistic categories helps one see a stable, orderly world). Thus symbols, of which language is an example, regulate behavior by their impact on people's perception and consequent judgment.

Expectation of self and others Symbols can regulate a person's behavior toward others as well as toward self. Some individuals go through life trying to live down labels, whereas others try to live up to labels that do not seem to fit. In both cases the symbol process has had a profound effect on the person's self-concept.

The impact of symbols on behavior has been dramatically demonstrated in studies of self-fulfilling prophecies, or of one person's expectation for another person's behavior making that behavior become reality. Rosenthal and Jacobson, for example, extended this principle into the classroom.[16] They devised a test, to be given in a school system, that would supposedly identify students who would "bloom" or "spurt" in intellectual capacity, and then teachers were given the names of those children who, according to the test, would show dramatic intellectual growth. The names of these children, however, had actually been chosen at random. The only difference between the special students and the ordinary students was in the labels suggested to the teacher.

Following up on the "test results" a year later, the researchers found that their hypotheses had been confirmed. Those who were expected to bloom intellectually bloomed more than those who were not. Labels and expectations had impact on both teacher and students. Favorable labels seem to generate other favorable labels.

> The children from whom intellectual growth was expected were described as significantly more likely to succeed in the future, as more interesting, as showing greater intellectual curiosity, and as happier. . . .
> The advantage of having been expected to bloom was evident for these younger children in total IQ, verbal IQ, and reasoning IQ. The control-group children of these grades gained well in IQ, 19 percent of them gaining twenty or more total IQ points. The "special" children, however, showed 47 percent of their number gaining twenty or more total IQ points.[17]

There is also evidence that labeling produces more than a cognitive realization of favorability or unfavorability toward others; it leads to changes in nonverbal behavior as well. For example, Chaikin, Sigler, and Derlega examined the nonverbal behavior of tutors after they had been told their pupils' IQ's. "Tutors expecting a superior performance leaned forward more, leaned backward less, looked their pupils in the eye more, nodded their heads up and down more and smiled more."[18] In other words, positive nonverbal reinforcement may occur without the person's awareness of such behavior.

Social sanctions Symbols also regulate behavior by producing negative bias or detachment. If one's conscience is an internalized regulator of behavior, how can a person then do violence to others? First, one can redefine the act in terms of high moral principles. This occurs frequently during war; God becomes part of the symbolization of war. For example, a popular song during World War II was "Praise the Lord and Pass the Ammunition!"

Similarly, social sanctions for violence can exist in the terminology applied to inhuman acts. If one would not behave in certain ways toward other humans, the object of violence must be changed or the action altered. The object can be changed by dehumanizing or belittling it. During World War II the enemy was referred to not as "Japanese" or "German," but as "Japs," "Nips," "Huns," and "Krauts." More recently, the Vietnamese enemy was a "gook."

News coverage and film reinforce the dehumanization of the enemy. "Body counts" are less person-oriented than "number of *people* killed." Pictures of high-flying bombers depersonalize the effect of their missions. Descriptions of "guerrillas" able to survive in the jungle on a handful of rice suggest subhuman animals rather than men and women.

These types of behaviors create a distance between oneself and the other, in addition to belittling and dehumanizing. Thus to "waste" others is more impersonal and more sanitized than to "kill." "I just do what I'm told" or "It's just part of the system" help one displace or diffuse individual responsibility.

Master symbols Master symbols regulate behavior by subordinating other considerations. A master symbol is a norm or a value that supercedes other symbols. If one attacks or evokes a master symbol, the response is likely to be intense—and unthinking.

Weaver has described master symbols as "God terms" and "devil terms"; a God term is an unchallengeable label requiring sacrifice or obedience, whereas a devil term is one of repulsion.[19] Examples of God terms might be "progress," "protection of environment," "free enterprise," "clean government," and "fiscal responsibility." God terms are not limited to the political arena, however. Educators refer endlessly to "meaningful experience" and "authenticity."

By contrast, some devil terms are "communist," "the establishment," "the system," "phony," and "Watergate."

Master symbols represent broad categories which are appealing because they simplify the world. It feels comfortable to be right and quickly so. Behaviors can be defined or redefined by the use of God and devil terms. Master symbols are created for their effect on others, and their use represents attempts to sustain attention to certain symbols that represent everything good or everything bad. Master symbols are used in all areas of society—from advertising to government. In addition to stemming from linguistic cues, master-symbol behavior can also be elicited by nonverbal messages and cues.

Nonverbal messages and cues Just as individuals have been taught to respond to certain linguistic symbols, they also learn how to respond to artifacts that convey expectations. The television show "Candid Camera" often uses this principle. One such segment that illustrated the control exerted by symbols and signs examined just how far a "phony" dentist could go with a client. All the artifacts associated with a dental office were there—the white coat, diplomas on the wall, and sparkling equipment. When the "dentist" (actually an actress) surprised the client by lathering his face for a shave, she simply explained that both she and the method were new. When the client asked why he had felt nothing when his teeth were being cleaned, the "dentist" said that another new method had been used. Although the client grumbled a great deal, he willingly submitted to some strange procedures.

Individuals rely on nonverbal messages and cues to guide their behavior. Perhaps this is why people have such a fear of "quackery" and why illicit behavior of those in trusted positions is so repugnant. The "clerical collar" or the "uniform of the police" become master symbols, and people submit to the authority and expectations they perceive in such symbols.

REGULATORY PARADIGMS: A SYMBOLIC INTERACTION PERSPECTIVE

So far we have considered some of the major sources that regulate human behavior—linguistic categories, groups, the mass media, and symbols—whether socially sanctioned linguistic symbols or nonverbal cues and behaviors. Whatever their source, regulatory factors set up perceptual expectations, sanction certain behaviors, and elicit particular behaviors.

These regulatory behaviors can also be viewed as patterns or groups of behaviors. Furthermore, they can be placed in the context of a symbolic interaction perspective.

Sources of regulatory behavior explain the *how* of human behavior; the study of motivation seeks to reveal *why* people behave in certain ways. Implicit in the concept of motivation is the assumption that if one could determine the general forces, drives, or urges that shape a person's behavior, one could also intervene and exert some measure of control over that person. Thus the typical approach in psychology and sociology has been to relate behavior to a particular drive and to then explain the behavior in terms of a particular motivation. In other words, the behavior occurs *because* of the motivation, e.g., "John bought a red sports car because of its *macho* image. His motivation was sex!"

Thus the typical motivational scheme centers on inner drives and states and equates motive and motivation. Motives are thought to *cause* behavior, as in "He did it because of a mother fixation"; "She did it because of a drive to be secure." This type of reasoning is reflected in commonly applied schemes of motivation.

Typical Motivational Schemes

Inner drives Traditional motivational schemes focus on inner drives and states. According to Maslow's schema, for example, each individual has a hierarchy of needs ranging from the lowest-level physiological needs to the highest-order need for self-actualization.[20] Because these needs form a hierarchy, says Maslow, lower-level needs must be met before higher-level needs can be satisfied. Thus only those needs not yet satisfied can influence a person's behavior.

Herzberg, by contrast, advances a two-factor model of motivation based on the work setting.[21] One of the major categories is what Herzberg calls maintenance, or hygiene, factors, e.g., work conditions, job security, etc.; although they are necessary for the individual, they do not serve as motivators, e.g., achievement, recognition, etc. In other words, Herzberg's basic premise is that although in many cases employees have satisfied some needs (inner forces), they demand a different set of primary motivators.

Both the Maslow and Herzberg models center on regulatory forces. As shown in Fig. 6.2, the three lowest levels of needs in the Maslow model form the category labeled "hygiene" factors by Herzberg.

Causation Other motivational systems are based on the notion that a primary human drive is "consistency." Consistency theories—also known as balance, congruity, symmetry, and dissonance theories—stress that all humans seek equilibrium, or balance.[22] Consistency theories rest on three basic assumptions: (1) humans seek a state of equilibrium; (2) inconsistency produces tension; and (3) humans will act to relieve the tension. By extension, communicators may either create inconsistency or alleviate it in order to regulate others. A brief look at some popular motivational paradigms reveals that the traditional view is "inner forces, drives, or urges" *causing* people to behave in certain ways.

MASLOW'S NEED HIERARCHY	HERZBERG'S TWO-FACTOR MODEL
↑ SELF-ACTUALIZATION: Becoming all that one can become	MOTIVATIONAL FACTORS
↑ ESTEEM: Self-esteem and esteem from others	Achievement Work itself Recognition Growth potential Advancement Responsibility
↑ BELONGINGNESS AND LOVE: Affection, acceptance, friendship	MAINTENANCE OR HYGIENE FACTORS
↑ SAFETY: Security, protection from harm	Interpersonal relations peers, supervisors, subordinates Company policy Job security
↑ PHYSIOLOGICAL: Hunger, thirst, sex	Work conditions Salary Personal life

Fig. 6.2 Comparison of the Maslow and Herzberg models of human motivation.

Symbolic Interaction and Motivation

To the symbolic interactionist, *communication* is at the heart of human action. Some symbolic interactionists distinguish between "motivation" and "motives." Hewitt, for example, explains: "Motivation refers to those internal states of the organism that govern its impulsive responses to various stimuli; motives, in contrast, consist of statements people make about their conduct or the conduct of others."[23]

If you are hungry (physiological state) and someone places a menu in front of you, you will probably respond to the thought of food. We could say that your motivational state (hunger) determined your impulsive response to a stimulus (menu). But the state of hunger by itself does not determine your conduct or how you will satisfy your impulsive response. Now, however, suppose you were asked why you requested a banana split. It is not enough to say that you were hungry, because you could have ordered many things other than the banana split. If you said, "I deserve a banana split because I have been on a diet" or "Banana splits give me energy," you are giving motives, or explaining your conduct.

The term "motive" refers to what people say about their conduct. Motivation can refer to physiological states or to previous conditioning toward the environment. A person can respond to stimuli at a preconscious or barely conscious level. For example, if you drive over the same route to work every day, you are probably conditioned to the traffic signals and barely remember them unless something unusual happens. One cannot see the impulses in another person. Motives, however, are observable in everyday communication. Our interest as symbolic interactionists is not in biological needs or psychic forces, but rather in the actions people engage in and their explanations of those actions.

What are motives? Motives are available verbalizations that are socially appropriate. People give reasons for their behavior by using the available linguistic structure, and they also perceive reasons via this linguistic structure. Motives, which can be given before, during, or after action, are therefore not causal factors. Viewed in this way, motives shed light on an individual's action and perspective, but they do not explain causes of behavior.

Motives and motivation For the sake of discussion, let us assume that sexual impulse is a state (motivation) that sensitizes you to particular aspects of your environment. Motivation might determine your impulsive response to stimuli, but such a state would not determine your conduct. How you decide to deal with sexual impulse and what you say about it would reveal your motives. In other words, a sexual impulse may initiate action, but it cannot explain what actions are taken; the variations in sexual behavior should tell us that much more is involved than impulse. Instead, individuals learn lines of conduct and ways of explaining that conduct.

When are motives used? What situations require a verbalization of motives? Why are some motives verbalized and others ignored? How are motives linked to action? In response to these questions, the symbolic interactionist would assert that: (1) when actions are deviant, they require an answer. The function of a motive is to satisfy a challenger.[24] (2) An actor will select those motives that have currency in the social circle of the challenger.[25] (3) Motivated acts are characterized by choice, control, and an agenda. Activities involving habitual behavior and physiological functioning do not fit in this category. Individuals make choices on the basis of their understanding or conception of who they are. They decide who they are in interaction with others through mutual identification.[26]

How do people acquire motives? Individuals act with certain consequences, and verbal judgments become a very real part of those consequences. Qualities of acts receive social approval or disapproval. Mills states: "Rather than fixed elements 'in' an individual, motives are the terms with which interpretation of conduct *by social actors* proceeds."[27] Thus motives can change as approved vocabulary changes.

This scheme suggests that people are not born *with* motives; rather, they are born *into* motives (linguistic categories). Therefore, motives may change as one's group affiliations change. Symbolic interaction forms human conduct and is not merely a release of "ids," "egos," "drives," "attitudes," etc.

Motive talk and lying How does the symbolic interaction scheme find the "real" motives for behavior? Do people conceal their motives from others and themselves? There is no value in equating verbal rationalizations and lying, because one is looking for "understanding" rather than "causation." Motives are not causes of behavior or forces behind the behavior. "All we can infer and empirically check is another verbalization of the agent's which we believe was orienting and controlling behavior at the time the act was performed."[28] The symbolic interactionist is concerned with the action of people and how they view this action. People may act on motives they deny publicly, but this discrepancy occurs between kinds of motives, not between motive and motivation.

Implications for the Communicator

The advantage of the symbolic interaction approach is that one does not have to impute motives to others. Instead, the focus is on action and the meaning of the action for the participants.

Motives require discovery Motives are not fixed elements "inside" people. A communicator who wishes to appeal to certain motives must first discover the defining process of the other person. In other words, the communicator must know what motives are linked with what perceived consequences. For example, suppose that your neighbor wants you to vote for Smedley in the primary elections. Discovering that you like "winners" and that the motive of winning is linked with pleasant consequences, your neighbor might devise a strategy centered on Smedley's ability to win in a final election, urging you to vote for Smedley for that reason, even though a primary opponent may be more qualified.

Although individuals may hold certain motives in common, they may assign different priorities to those motives. The communicator, therefore, must be aware of such differences, and this awareness can be facilitated through an examination of verbalizations. Furthermore, any values in transition should be noted in the reasons given for behavior or anticipated behavior.

Motives provide justification If motives are accepted justifications for past, present, or future acts, persuasion must be based on providing individuals with justifications for behavior that are meaningful to them. Toward this end, the communicator might find it helpful to understand the reference group of the individual to determine what motives (verbalizations) are operative. Verbalizations are necessary for present, future, and past acts; it is comfortable to act on "right" motives. The commercial that links its product with "you deserve a break today" provides justification for a present act. The literature that tells you how wise you were to buy a particular car provides justification for past behavior and sets up future justification.

McGuire has experimented with various procedures designed to "immunize" a person against persuasion.[29] He has found that the most effective way to do so is to first threaten a person's belief and then provide arguments that the belief is correct after all. When the individual hears arguments later that oppose the belief, he or she is able to resist them.

Motives provide action linkages If individuals select motives on the basis of who they are, it is important to symbolically confirm who they are. For example, if members of an organization believe that they are "professionals" and that "professionals" behave in certain ways, desired behaviors must be linked to "professional" behavior. "Professional" may even become a God term—a master symbol.

Groups have vocabularies of motives. A person's reference group provides and supports motives in accord with an individual's lines of conduct and self-concept. This twofold role—to provide and to support—suggests why a group may be attractive to both new and old members.

Motives are contextual Each situation is a "separate world," and motives that might be appropriate in one situation might be unacceptable and rejected in another. Self-interest may be more prevalent in one situation than in another. The communicator may use the motives that are understood and accepted in a setting or may challenge the compartmentalization of motives and try to introduce a different vocabulary of behavior.

The communicator who wishes to persuade must decide what motives will be legitimized. For example, in a business setting it might be useless to talk about adopting a policy because it would "serve God"; conversely, a comparable reaction might occur if religious leaders were asked to do something so their organization could make a profit. Similarly, whereas a presidential candidate might wage an effective campaign with the slogan "America can be saved," a candidate for local office might be ridiculed for using that same slogan.

Motives can be created In order to determine what makes people buy certain products or ideas, we can examine "buying" vocabularies. In some cases such vocabularies must be created. For example, if a person decides that only lazy people purchase instant cake mixes, someone else might point out that those who use such products have time to "develop themselves" in other activities or "meet additional family needs." These motives may provide justification for using the product.

To the extent that verbalizations are not a part of one's existing norms, the media have the capacity to create motives. First, there is the aspect of convincing the public that people of accomplishment and distinction present "elegant dinners" at which "fine wine" is served. The activities associated with "elegant dinners" and "drinking wine" become reasons for buying a particular product. Even if the consumers do not remember the name of a particular brand of wine, their wine consumption may increase, as well as the chances of the particular product's being purchased.

Motives neutralize the impact of behavior Individuals learn to give "accounts" of their behavior in order to protect self-identity. Two forms of accounts are *excuses* and *justifications*. Excuses place the blame for untoward conduct on someone or something other than the person being held accountable, e.g., "I was late because my car had a flat." Justifications provide a flexible means of judging acts.[30] When people use "justifications," they accept responsibility for an act, but deny that the act constitutes untoward behavior and instead plead special circumstances, e.g., "I took the car, but no one was injured."

The accounts used in the vocabulary of motives are relevant in regulating the behavior of other people. A professional poker player, for example, might provide an "easy money," losing amateur with a face-saving excuse for staying in the game: "Your luck [external force] is really running against you right now."

Justifications for behaviors become quite important when, for instance, lawyers seek to influence juries. People not only judge the acts, but also attribute motives to the actors, and these attributions have an impact on the final outcome. Hocking reports a study in which subjects were asked to visualize two women—one very attractive and the other quite plain—in a bar.[31] Both were "propositioned" and both complied. When asked to decide which woman was the more immoral, the subjects so rated the attractive woman. Reasoning that she would have more opportunity than the plain woman, the subjects rejected her justification for behavior.

What happens when motives are in conflict? As we noted earlier, social sanctions can provide justifications for behavior that in other circumstances might not be tolerated. Furthermore, the vocabulary of the justification can either dehumanize the object of the action or sanitize the action.

Motives can follow behavior In the self-persuasion setting, an individual acts first and then seeks out the motive. The reaction may be one of wonder: "Why did I do that?"[32] In other words, attitudes and motives do not necessarily precede action, but behavior may often precede attitude formation.[33] Therefore, for people who wish to regulate others in some way, behavior is presumed to be an important determinant of success.

Communication behavior can also be used as a form of action that generates further action. For example, the advertising agency that has potential customers write in 25 words or less why they like a particular product is generating beliefs that may have persuasive impact at a later time. In addition, individuals look on their symbolic behavior as a creative act.[34] People tend to put great stock in their own words; they are possessions and their use fashions the self.

The impact of communication behavior on opinion change has been illustrated by studies on forced compliance.[35] When individuals are required to argue a position that contradicts their initial beliefs, several factors affect how much opinion change occurs. Change is most likely to occur when the individual is active, improvises, develops arguments, is satisfied with his or her speaking performance, and receives reinforcement from an audience. Again, the words—the arguments—become possessions to be accepted by the self.

SOME FUNDAMENTAL ISSUES

Having considered what regulation is, sources of regulatory behavior, and a variety of regulatory paradigms, we can now turn to some basic issues of regulation.

Values

Central values in American society place the communicator in a power-conscious position. The ability to manipulate others is admired in our society, and the line between manipulation and exploitation is indeed thin.

The way in which communication is to be used depends largely on values and the orientation toward others that they provide. Earlier we noted that values consist of both norms and ideals. In this discussion we are concerned primarily with the ideals that guide communication behavior. Clyde Kluckhohn stipulates that "a value may be defined as that aspect of motivation which is referable to standards, personal or cultural, that do not arise solely out of an immediate situation and the satisfaction of needs and primary drives."[36] In other words, values are criteria, or standards, by which people may select behavior, in spite of their personal desires.

Florence Kluckhohn has identified a limited number of questions to which people of all cultures seek answers. The answer to each question constitutes a value orientation, and the answers form an orientation profile of individuals within a particular culture. The Kluckhohn profile is not one of just first-order choices, but rather a rank-ordering of choices within a postulated range of choices. The questions are listed below, and our conclusions about the dominant American orientations are given in parentheses.

1. "What is the character of innate human nature?" (evil but perfectible)
2. "What is the relation of man to nature?" (mastery over nature)
3. "What is the temporal focus of human life?" (future time)
4. "What is the modality of human activity?" (doing)
5. "What is the modality of man's relationship to other men?" (individualism)[37]

These general value orientations have impact on why and how one communicates. For example, how much of your communication is focused on what you are going to do at some future time?

The general guidelines for behavior are not always clear or consistent. For example, Williams has characterized dominant value themes in American society that we believe may pose conflict. Two such value themes are:

> [1] American culture is organized around the attempt at active mastery rather than passive acceptance. Into this dimension fall the low tolerance of frustration; the refusal to accept ascetic renunciation; the positive encouragement of desire; the stress on power; the approval of ego-assertion, and so on. . . .
> [2] In interpersonal relations, the weight of the value system is on the side of "horizontal" rather than "vertical" emphases: peer-relations, not super-ordinate-subordinate relations; equality rather than hierarchy.[38]

On the one hand, an individual is supposed to be assertive, but on the other is advised to believe in equality.

A recurring theme in most general value schemes is the individual's mastery over the environment through ego assertion and manipulation. It is little wonder that many students entering a course in communication want to know how to persuade others, win friends, influence people, etc. Nor is it surprising that although models of communication often include a message sender and a receiver, individuals rarely project themselves into the role of receiver. After all, most people want to be in the power position of being the sender of a message!

When individualism is examined in an economic context, it is easy to see how manipulation of others is not only stimulated, but also reinforced. For example, Fitzpatrick points out the traditional central value in American economic life has been individualism and doing everything possible to foster individual self-fulfillment.[39] Thus an individual's mastery of the environment through material gain was a sign of not only ability, but moral virtue as well. The common good was served best when each individual pursued personal development.

Communicators should be aware of the power component in communication and the cultural value placed on the use of that power. If individuals communicate to improve their position and compete in a society that reveres competition, manipulation—whether conscious or unconscious, open or subtle —will be used.

The Basic Nature of Humans

Do human beings have an inherent basic nature? If they do, is that nature "good" or "bad"? Furthermore, are humans responsible for their own conduct?

Those who believe in human "self-actualization" assert that intrinsic growth tendencies lead people to try and realize their full potential. This view subordinates regulatory behavior and instead emphasizes the facilitative process. An extreme position of the self-actualization theme is that persuasion by its very nature is exploitive because one person's will is being imposed on another. By contrast, people who believe that humans must be socialized in order to serve the common good favor manipulation, i.e., protecting people against themselves.

Is there an inner human? According to Skinner, a mystic belief in an autonomous inner being has led people to believe that they are free; consequently, they ignore controlling elements in the environment. Skinner challenges these sacred concepts of freedom and dignity.[40] One's beliefs about the basic nature of humans—and indeed if there is a basic nature—influence how one proceeds in regulating self and others and in answering the following questions. Are motives innate, are they learned, or do they even exist? Is there too much manipulation or not enough?

Confronting Issues—Some Guidelines

Communication is a potent force and it touches everyone. We believe that it is better to advance some principles—though they may be difficult to apply in some areas—than to ignore issues relevant to regulation and exploitation. Eventually everyone must construct a personal set of ethical guidelines. We offer the principles not as a formula, but as ideas to be considered. Situational contingencies militate against a universal ethic.

For example, should warring nations deal honestly with each other when a loss of strategy might imperil the survival of one? But just because one cannot make absolute judgments doesn't free one from having to make some judgments.

The following principles, directed at most everyday settings, are personal. As such, they have their limitations and are offered only as guidelines to be used for self-examination and not for imposition on others. In applying guidelines, the essential point is not whether or not someone is ethical, but rather what that person means and how a process of negotiation might be undertaken. In addition, the principles are interdependent; that is, none of them can stand alone.

Mutual gain Responsible regulation occurs when an individual exercises control over another in nonaversive ways so as to achieve mutual gain. "Mutual gain" will rarely mean "equal gain"; although the later is the ideal in bargaining, it is unrealistic in most situations. Instead, it is more realistic to look at equitable gains as determined by the participants. Jacobson, for example, points out that in power relationships, "if we want or need certain things, material or nonmaterial, that another person possesses, we are dependent upon that person in proportion to the strength of our desires for those things."[41] Most social situations involve the participants' interdependence; there cannot be a seller without a buyer, and groups cannot function without the support of their members. If individuals are given the right to negotiate, there will be mutual gain.

Informed and willing consent The methods employed to regulate others should be based on informed and willing consent. A gun pointed at the head is a powerful persuader, but the action requested is performed without willing consent. In the late 1950s many people were concerned about subliminal advertising, a technique of persuasion in which the recipients are unaware of being the targets of communication. Subliminal advertising often took place in movies. An image was flashed on a screen below the viewers' threshold of conscious awareness, and they were thereby induced to buy a particular product. Although the effectiveness of such approaches has been questioned and the conditions under which individuals act toward subliminal stimuli are said to be limited, laws were proposed to prohibit this kind of persuasion, because there was no informed consent.[42] (Vance Packard called attention to techniques that may work in this way on the "unconscious" of the consumer.[43])

Unfortunately, methods of controlling others cannot always be labeled "right" or "wrong"; many activities fit into an ethical gray area. If the language categories given individuals at birth program them to think in certain ways, have those individuals been regulated by informed and willing consent? In this case the best one can hope for is a system that allows one to become free of it and judge its qualities. In other words, individuals must be able to rid themselves of their Parent and Child ego states (see Chapter 3) in order to have free and mature choice.

Individuals *do* have informed consent, in that most realize the purpose of advertising and packaging; furthermore, the right to put forth the best possible case for one's product or idea is part of a system of free choice. Individuals can be persuaded, but they are not passive receptacles for every technique that may be devised.

Alternatives Responsible regulation permits alternative courses of action. In an advocacy system, an individual has the opportunity to hear various alternatives on issues and then choose the strongest case. In the free marketplace of ideas, individuals may be bombarded with messages from various groups, advertising agencies, and other individuals, but they also have alternatives for action.

Power over others can be exerted by limiting the number of or disallowing any alternatives. For example, an authoritarian leader in a group may announce a decision *before* the group has an opportunity to generate alternatives. Such an action is irresponsible in two ways. First, it reduces the probability of generating alternatives; second, it may prevent that leader from being persuaded. Persuasion is an important element in decision making. Humans need to understand others' points of view in order to make judgments about their own views.

The reciprocity of communication does not mean that one should be immunized against persuasive effects, only that one should be able to recognize the forces at work and choose among the persuasive messages. Often a person must be able to generate alternatives or search them out in other settings. For example, the wise consumer does not buy on impulse, but instead examines products in a number of settings to determine the best buy.

Legitimate appeals Responsible communicators utilize appeals that make for free, informed, and responsible choice. This principle is particularly difficult to apply, since some appeals are not based on evidence, yet may produce action beneficial to all.

The context in which the appeals take place may in fact be part of an expectation. For example, one of our colleagues was reminded that the candidate he supported had not produced on several campaign promises. Our friend replied, "Oh well, you can't hold him to that. After all, that was just campaign oratory!" Are ethical considerations different for the political speech and thereby situational? Do individuals expect hyperbole and half-truths in advertising and if so, does this make such appeals legitimate?

Winston Churchill was well known for his inspirational speeches to the British people, who were being bombed unmercifully during World War II. How accurate are the voices of governments when they try to calm their people during a crisis? Purity of intent may nonetheless entail unethical strategies when an absolute standard is applied. When one is trying to present the best case possible, ideas will be designed for maximum impact, and this may lead to distortion.

Although an absolute standard cannot be applied, several questions can serve as a guide to the participants in a communication situation. Is the appeal based on sound evidence and reasoning? Is the appeal labeled as "proof" when in reality it is a feeling of the communicator? Is a distinction made between the idea itself and the modifications used to receive acceptance from others?

Values are created and maintained through communication Responsible communicators recognize the impact their behaviors have on societal values and norms. Earlier we stressed that one cannot play a role without a willing counterrole player. What individuals do with symbolic behavior and the kind of symbolic behavior they accept are two factors serving to either change or perpetuate human values. For example, if one expects campaign communication to be distorted, such distortion will be preserved. If distortion and manipulation are both practiced and expected, that behavior becomes a part of group norms. Shostrom writes:

> The manipulator is legion. He is all of us, consciously, subconsciously or unconsciously employing all the phoney tricks we absorb between the cradle and grave to conceal the actual and vital nature of ourselves and our fellow man into things to be controlled.[44]

Although some people decry any kind of manipulative behavior, their strong objecting to such activity is in itself an attempt to persuade.[45] Control or manipulation in itself is not necessarily destructive, nor does it have to subvert or ignore the values of others. Manipulation based on human values of mutuality and freedom of choice is both necessary and desirable in a democratic society. Belief in the inherent worth of humans does not invalidate the need for controls for the protection of all. Certain norms and rules are required to sustain social order, and although they require some forfeiture of individual freedom, they also provide protection for all. Such norms and rules are desirable to the extent that they are based on human values that allow for maximum freedom and respect for the individual.

The culture-individual conditioning is mutual. Although government and legal agencies provide a level of protection through the controls they impose, large areas of freedom exist to be filled by individual responsibility. How that responsibility is carried out has a great deal to do with what the norms will be. Whenever one engages in exploitive behavior or endorses it in others, the principle of protection for all is weakened, and basic human values decline.

The Watergate scandal shocked the nation because of the violation of both laws and human values in high levels of government. However, this event was an extension of a system and not apart from it. Even after considerable evidence had been presented, some people maintained that the activities uncovered were just part of political life and that the people caught should not be penalized. This is a surprising view of what might be allowable in politics, but it should not be any more surprising than endorsing any other activities which, although they may be within the law, nonetheless exploit others, weaken positive human values, and thereby increase exploitation.[46]

SUMMARY

Regulation of one's own and others' behavior can be accomplished through communication. Such regulation, attained through persuasion, education, and propaganda, is both necessary and of potential benefit to the participants.

Some primary sources of regulation are groups, mass media, and symbols. Groups and the larger culture, for example, provide the linguistic structure, the framework through which one views and interprets the world. The regulatory impact of the mass media, by contrast, stems in part from their very pervasiveness. The social modeling the media provide also lend legitimacy and reality to certain behaviors.

Symbols, whether created through mass media or linguistic categories, are another source of regulatory behavior. They set up expectations of self and others, provide social sanctions, and convey norms and values. Thus they also serve as motivators, which are conveyed through the communication process. In this way, symbolic interaction rather than "motivation" can be used as the basis for explaining human behavior.

With symbolic interaction—and thus the communicator—at the heart of the regulatory process, several important issues emerge. In discussing these issues—pertaining to values, basic human nature, and guidelines for confronting everyday communication events—our concern has been with the consequences of regulation.[47]

Even though regulation is inevitable, it can nonetheless be conducted for the common good. Accordingly: (1) regulation should be exercised in non-aversive ways to facilitate mutual gain. (2) Regulatory methods should be based on the participants' informed, willing consent. (3) The system should allow for alternative courses of action. (4) Communication appeals should permit free, informed, and responsible choice. (5) Each individual should engage in behaviors that reinforce the best in societal values and norms.

PROBLEMS AND ISSUES

1. You work for a firm that sells appliances. Your employer informs buyers that they have 90 days in which to pay for the appliance before interest is charged, tells members of the company that most three-month combinations have 91 or 92 days and that probably two-thirds of the purchasers will be late and thus be charged interest, and estimates how much extra money the company can make by using this method. Is the employer's action ethical?

2. Examine entertainment media (e.g., songs, cartoons, films, television shows, etc.) and discuss any social messages that might be conveyed. What values are reinforced or advocated?

3. Examine language as a regulator. Submit a social problem for analysis to college students with different majors and analyze the language categories for differences among the students.

4. Compose a list of current "God" and "devil" terms.

5. Using Maslow's motivational scheme, analyze current television commercials and contrast with the symbolic interaction perspective.

6. Utilize Herzberg's scheme and analyze an organization's communication program. Use the symbolic interaction perspective and contrast.

7. Evaluate the statement: "People see what they want to see and hear what they want to hear."

8. Do the media affect or reflect a society?

9. What symbols have you used to change the object of a questionable action, or how have you described an action in order to sanitize it?

10. Examine the summary of social psychological findings presented by Philip Zimbardo and Ebbe Ebbesen and discuss the ethical implications of each. (See footnote 47 for source.)

NOTES

1. Stephen W. King, *Communication and Social Influence* (Reading, Mass.: Addison-Wesley, 1975), p. 6.

2. *See* Roderick Hart and Don Burks, "Rhetorical Sensitivity and Social Interaction," *Speech Monographs* **39** (1972): 75–91. For further explanation, *see* Alan Sillars, "Expression and Control in Human Interaction: Perspective on Humanistic Psychology," *Western Speech* **38** (Fall 1974): 269–277.

3. Edwin Kiester, Jr., and David Cudhea, "Albert Bandura: A Very Modern Model," *Human Behavior* **3** (September 1974): 27.

4. James Spates and Jack Levin, "Beats, Hippies, the Hip Generation and the American Middle Class: An Analysis of Values," *International Social Science Journal* **24** (1972): 327.

5. James McCartney, "Thousands Die as World Food Situation Reaches Crisis," *Salt Lake Tribune*, December 10, 1974.

6. Abraham Maslow, *Motivation and Personality*, 2d ed. (New York: Harper & Row, 1970), p. 137.

7. Alfred R. Lindesmith and Anselm L. Strauss, *Social Psychology* (New York: Dryden, 1956), p. 419.

8. *See* T. Shibutani, "Reference Groups as Perspectives, *"American Journal of Sociology* **60** (1955): 562–569; M. Sherif, "The Concept of Reference Groups in Human Relations," *Group Relations at the Crossroads,* ed. M. Sherif and M. O. Wilson (New York: Harper, 1953), pp. 203–231.

9. S. E. Asch, "Effects of Group Pressure upon the Modification and Distortion of Judgments," in *Groups, Leadership, and Men,* ed. Harold Guetzknow (Pittsburgh: Carnegie Press, Carnegie-Mellon University, 1951), pp. 183–189.

10. *See* Morton Deutsch and Harold B. Gerard, "A Study of Normative and Informational Social Influences upon Individual Judgment," *Journal of Abnormal and Social Psychology* **51** (1955): 629–636.

11. For example, *see* Edgar Schein, Inge Schneier, and Curtis Baker, *Coercive Persuasion; A Socio-Psychological Analysis of the "Brainwashing" of American Civilian Prisoners by the Chinese Communists* (New York: Norton, 1961); Charles A. Kiesler and Sara B. Kiesler, *Conformity* (Reading, Mass.: Addison-Wesley, 1969).

12. *See* James C. McCroskey, Carl E. Larson, and Mark L. Knapp, *An Introduction to Interpersonal Communication* (Englewood Cliffs, N.J.: Prentice-Hall, 1971), pp. 235–236.

13. Kiester and Cudhea, *op. cit.,* pp. 29–30.

14. Charles K. Atkin, "Television Advertising and Children's Observational Modeling." Paper presented to the International Communication Association, Portland, Oregon, April 1976.

15. *See* George Gerbner, "Scenario for Violence," *Human Behavior* **4** (October 1975): 64–69; a symposium of eleven studies in *Journal of Communication* (Autumn 1975); and George Gerbner and Larry Gross, "Living with Television: The Violence Profile," *Journal of Communication* (Spring 1976): 173–194.

16. Robert Rosenthal and Lenore Jacobson, *Pygmalion in the Classroom* (New York: Holt, Rinehart and Winston, 1968).

17. *Ibid.,* pp. 108, 176. Reprinted by permission.

18. Alan Chaikin, Edward Sigler, and Valerian Derlega, "Leaning Toward the Bright," *Human Behavior* **3** (December 1974): 35.

19. Richard M. Weaver, *The Ethics of Rhetoric* (Chicago: Henry Regenery, 1953), pp. 211–214.

20. Abraham H. Maslow, *Motivation and Personality* (New York: Harper and Brothers, 1954).

21. Frederick Herzberg, B. Mausner, and B. Snyderman, *The Motivation to Work* (New York: Wiley, 1959). For a critique, *see* Robert J. House and Lawrence A. Wigdor, "Herzberg's Dual-Factor Theory of Job Satisfaction and Motivation: A Review of the Evidence and a Criticism," *Personnel Psychology* **20** (1967): 369–389.

22. For further analysis, *see* Shel Feldman, ed., *Cognitive Consistency* (New York: Academic Press, 1966); Robert P. Abelson *et al., Theories of Cognitive Consistency: A Sourcebook* (Chicago: Rand McNally, 1968).

23. John P. Hewitt, *Self and Society: A Symbolic Interactionist Social Psychology* (Boston: Allyn and Bacon, 1976), pp. 127–128.

24. For specific analysis, *see* Marvin B. Scott and Stanford M. Lyman, "Ac-

counts," in *Readings in Social Psychology*, 2d ed., ed. Alfred R. Lindesmith, Anselm L. Strauss, and Norman K. Denzin (Hinsdale, Ill.: Dryden Press, 1975), pp. 146–168.

25. *See* C. Wright Mills, "Situated Actions and Vocabularies of Motive," *American Sociological Review* **5** (October 1940): 904–913.

26. For exploration, *see* Nelson N. Foote, "Identification as the Basis for a Theory of Motivation," *American Sociological Review* **16** (February 1951): 14–21.

27. Mills, *op. cit.,* p. 904.

28. *Ibid.,* p. 909.

29. William J. McGuire, "A Vaccine for Brainwash," *Psychology Today* **3** (February 1970): 36–64.

30. *See* Scott and Lyman, *op. cit.; also see* John P. Hewitt and Randall Stokes, "Disclaimers," *American Sociological Review* **40** (February 1975): 1–11; Gresham M. Sykes and David Matza, "Techniques of Neutralization," *American Sociological Review* **22** (December 1957): 664–670.

31. John Hocking, "Studies in Non-Verbal Behavior." Lecture delivered at University of Utah, April 1976.

32. *See* Daryl J. Bem, "Self-Perception: An Alternative Interpretation of Cognitive Dissonance Phenomena," *Psychological Review* **74** (1967): 183–200.

33. *See* Karl E. Weick, "Task Acceptance Dilemmas: A Site for Research on Cognition," in Feldman, *op. cit.,* p. 234.

34. *See* Susanne K. Langer, *Philosophy in a New Key* (New York: Mentor, 1951).

35. For an example, *see* Irving L. Janis and Bert T. King, "The Influence of Role Playing on Opinion Change," *Journal of Abnormal and Social Psychology* **49** (1954): 211–218.

36. Clyde Kluckhohn, "The Study of Values," in *Values in America,* ed. Donald N. Barrett (Notre Dame, Ind.: Notre Dame Press, 1961), pp. 17–18.

37. Florence Kluckhohn and Fred Stodtbeck, *Variations in Value Orientations* (1961; reprint ed., Westport, Conn.: Greenwood Press, 1973), p. 11.

38. Robin M. Williams, Jr., "Values and Modern Education in the United States," in Barrett, *op. cit.,* pp. 65–66. For additional explanation, *see* Robin M. Williams, Jr., *American Society,* 3rd ed. (New York: Knopf, 1970), pp. 452–502.

39. Joseph P. Fitzpatrick, "Individualism in American Industry," in Barrett, *op. cit.,* p. 94.

40. B. F. Skinner, *Beyond Freedom and Dignity* (New York: Bantam, 1971), p. 23.

41. Wally D. Jacobson, *Power and Interpersonal Relations* (Belmont, Calif.: Wadsworth, 1972), p. 3.

42. For examination of effective conditions of subliminal stimuli, *see* Mark Abrahamson, *Interpersonal Accommodation* (New York: Van Nostrand Reinhold, 1966), pp. 44–58.

43. Vance Packard, *The Hidden Persuaders* (New York: Pocket Books, 1958).

44. Everett L. Shostrom, *Man, The Manipulator* (New York: Bantam, 1968), pp. xi–xii.

45. For example of books concerned with manipulation, *see* George N. Gordon, *Persuasion: The Theory and Practice of Manipulative Communication* (New York: Hastings House, 1971).

46. For a view of the attitudes of exploitation, *see* Richard Christie and Florence Geis, *Studies in Machiavellianism* (New York: Academic Press, 1970).

47. For a summary of research findings on the specific variables inherent in the process of persuasion, *see* Philip Zimbardo and Ebbe B. Ebbesen, *Influencing Attitude and Changing Behavior* (Reading, Mass.: Addison-Wesley, 1969), pp. 20–23; H. Abelson and M. Karline, *Persuasion: How Opinions and Attitudes are Changed* (New York: Springer, 1959); and K. Anderson and T. Clevenger, "A Summary of Experimental Research in Ethos," *Speech Monographs* **30** (1963): 59–78.

Chapter 7

The Content Level of Communication

INTRODUCTION

The basic "stuff" of communication is content, or information—the ideas expressed in a communication setting. The way in which those ideas are communicated defines the relationship between the communicators. In other words, communication simultaneously offers both content and relationship.[1]

Communicators generally focus more on the content level than on the relationship level of interaction. The orientation is on trying to understand the message, on getting the meaning. Indeed, Watzlawick, Beavin, and Jackson go so far as to assert:

> Relationships are only rarely defined deliberately or with full awareness. In fact, it seems that the more spontaneous and "healthy" a relationship, the more the relationship aspect of communication recedes into the background. Conversely, "sick" relationships are characterized by a constant struggle about the nature of the relationship, with the content aspect of communication be coming less and less important.[2]

Nonetheless, the content and relationship levels do overlap. If you and a friend are in a restaurant, your friend's request to "please pass the salt" suggests a relationship quite different from that implied in the demand to "give me the salt, right now." The content level of the two statements is the same, but the relationship level is very different.

This distinction between content and relationship may be viewed as the difference between data and instructions. The numbers 3, 5, and 7, for example, are data; the words "sum the numbers 3, 5, and 7" constitute an instruction. Data are the report of things observed; instructions define the relationship of those observations.

Most writers in the field of communication focus on the relationship level of communication, because it is at this level that most problems in communication occur. The relationship aspect of a communication is generally not within the conscious awareness of the participants. However, although the content level in a communicative transaction generally does operate in the communicators' conscious awareness, problems may arise here too. The content of communication is information, a concept not always well understood or handled in the best possible way. The purpose of this chapter is to define the role of information in communication, describe the various ways in which information has been conceptualized, and offer a symbolic interactionist perspective on information as the content of communication.

THREE VIEWS OF INFORMATION

The word "information," like "communication," has been defined and used in many different ways. We will adopt the usage proposed by Colin Cherry, who classifies the uses of the term "information" according to the syntactic, semantic, and pragmatic views.[3] The essence of these three views can be described in three questions: (1) How much information is there? (syntactic view); (2) How accurate is the information? (semantic view); (3) How useful is the information? (pragmatic view). These three questions and the views they represent are extensions of our discussion in Chapter 2 about the syntactic, semantic, and pragmatic relationships among signs (sign to sign, sign to signified, and sign to sign user, respectively).

Syntactic Information

Derived from information theory, or the mathematical theory of communication, the syntactic view is that information reduces uncertainty.[4] But doubt or uncertainty can be reduced only if there are alternatives. If only one alternative exists, there can be no doubt or uncertainty and hence no information.

For example, suppose that a professor tells you that you did not fail a test. You have received information because your doubt about your test score has been reduced. Because you did not get an F, your grade must be A, B, C, or D; these are the alternatives. Seeking more information, you ask, "Did I get a C or lower?" "No." "Did I get a B?" "No." This response gives you all the possible information that exists in this set; there is now no doubt or uncertainty about your grade and hence no more information.

This question-and-answer sequence is syntactic because it deals with the relation of possible alternatives and nothing else. Cherry summarizes this point by saying that "signals have information content by virtue of their *potential for making selections*."[5]

Extending this notion of selection, Ashby asserts: "Communication thus necessarily demands a set of messages. Not only is this so, but the information carried by a particular message depends on the set it comes from. *The information conveyed is not an intrinsic property of the individual message*."[6] Consider Ashby's example of the message "I am well" sent by two prisoners of war to their wives.[7] One of the soldiers is held by a country that allows one of three messages to be sent: "I am well," "I am slightly ill," or "I am seriously ill." The other soldier is prisoner in a country that allows only the "I am well" message to be sent. The wife of the first soldier receives more information because he had a larger number of alternatives to choose from.

Redundancy Linked with the concept of information in the syntactic view is the notion of redundancy. A message is redundant when no alternative exists and therefore no information exchange can occur. Suppose you are jacking up your car and the spare tire is leaning against the side of the car. If someone comes up to you and asks, "Got a flat?" the question is redundant. In this case, however, the question was probably asked not for content purposes, but rather to express relationship.

Redundancy is used extensively in English. Many frequently used articles and conjunctions and other words contain little information. But redundancy nonetheless serves a purpose; it seems to reflect the fact that only a limited amount of information can be processed at a given time. It may also be used to confirm what is already known. For instance, in the example cited earlier about the test grade, we said that after the "no" response to your question "Did I get a B?" no more information was possible because all doubt and uncertainty had been removed. Even though your asking, "Did I get an A?" would be redundant in terms of information content, you might nonetheless ask, just to hear the response "yes."

Semantic Information

Most people are not interested in the amount of information available and its relationship to the set. Rather, they are more concerned about how useful, valuable, factual, reliable, precise, and/or true the information is. All of these questions focus on the semantic view of information—the relationship between the sign and the thing represented. In short, how accurate is the information?

The concept of *validity,* important in empirical measurement, is also useful in discussing semantic information. The debate over the concept of intelligence quotient (IQ) demonstrates the problem of empirical measurement. A student may be tested several times on several IQ tests and receive similar scores on all tests. However, although the IQ tests may therefore be called reliable, no one is sure of what exactly has been measured. Thus IQ has been defined by the measurement. In other words, because "something" can be measured, "something" must exist. The problem, however, is to discover what that "something" is.

Similar problems occur in semantic information. Labeling a reported observation presupposes the existence of information. The question is to determine whether that information is valid.

Testing the validity of information There are four typical ways to establish the validity of information in communication settings. First, several observers may *agree* among themselves. As a colleague of ours is fond of saying, "If it walks like a duck and quacks like a duck, it must be a duck." His statement suggests that if several people agree that the bird's walking and quacking behavior are those of a duck, they have found "truth"; the validity of the information has been established. Similarly, when the country shifts from daylight savings time to standard time, everyone agrees that the day before when it was 3:30 P.M., it is now 2:30 P.M. Accuracy of information has been established by agreement.

A second method of establishing the validity of information is through *inference*—the reasoning process of taking specific accumulated past experiences and drawing a conclusion before verification can be accomplished. For example, everyone has eaten a fairly large number of apples, and never was one of those apples without seeds in the core. If someone were to hold an apple in front of you and ask if it had seeds, your unhesitating response would be "yes." Your many past experiences with apples would lead you to infer that this apple too has seeds, even though the validity of this information has not been "tested" in this particular circumstance.

The accuracy of information may also be established by means of *concurrent measurement,* whereby several people find separate ways of measuring the same phenomenon. If each person's measurement is the same, the thing has been accurately labeled or accurate information found. For example, suppose that you are good at judging chocolate cakes by their color and texture, whereas your friend is an expert on the taste of chocolate cakes. A cake is presented to the two of you, and you look it over while your friend tastes it; if both of you conclude that it is a chocolate cake, you have found accurate information.

The fourth way to establish accuracy is through *definition*. How often have you started a paper by using a dictionary definition or tried to settle an argument by using the dictionary? Definitions are a neat, clean way to establish the validity of a thing, because the explanation is brief, offers clear-cut boundaries, and is based on "authority."

"But," you may say now, "how can one *really* establish truth?" When you conclude that none of these four methods can do so, you have learned a valuable lesson. The Ogden and Richards semantic triangle (see Fig. 2.2) demonstrates that there is never a direct, unmediated relation between the thing designated and its label, or information.

Precision of semantic information Accuracy of information is of interest not only for its own sake, but also because there are different levels of accuracy. If, for example, a duck hunter aims into a flock flying directly overhead and brings down a duck, the hunter was accurate, but only a minimal amount of precision was necessary. If, on the other hand, only one duck flies by, more precision is required for the hunter to be accurate. The analogy may be extended to information; to say that we reside in Utah is accurate but not very precise. Utah comprises 84,916 square miles, and our combined residences take up about one-half acre of the state's total land area.

Precision may be thought of as a continuum of accuracy. One can be quite ambiguous and still accurately represent the object; or, one can deal with the most minute detail of an object and still be accurate. Although communicators generally attempt to be accurate in their information, precision increases only when the communication interaction demands ever-increasing specificity of the objects of communication. Consider the following example of a person's address, each line of which is accurate yet represents a different level of precision.

Mary Wright	person within residence
888 Elm Drive	residence
Corvallis	city
South Dakota	state
U.S.A.	country

Pragmatic Information

The third view of information focuses on its usefulness and value. The pragmatic view is concerned with a person's ability to use the information; semantic information, by contrast, deals only with accuracy and precision.

A plane will leave from somewhere and go to somewhere else.

A plane flies between Fresno, California, and Reno, Nevada.

The only flight between Fresno, California, and Reno, Nevada leaves Fresno at 9:15 A.M. and arrives in Reno at 10:00 A.M.

Each statement is accurate and more precise than the preceding statement. But if you are not interested in these places, the semantic accuracy of the information is meaningless and has no pragmatic value for you.

Communication that is not regarded as useful is quickly discarded, no matter how much information is disseminated or how accurate it is. Communication is dependent on pragmatic information. Only when the participants see use for or value in information do they engage in communication.

Some may argue that sometimes people talk just because the topic is interesting. It is our conviction, however, that "interest" is tied to usefulness and/or value. Someone who is interested in the fact that Red Ryder's sidekick was Little Beaver or that the world's record for kissing is 96 hours probably enjoys stumping friends with trivia questions or perhaps wants to surpass the record. Even the factor of curiosity can be related to the pragmatic view. Someone who professes curiosity about something finds it of value because it is new; here again, pragmatic information forms the basis of communication.

A SYMBOLIC INTERACTIONIST PERSPECTIVE ON INFORMATION

A primary tenet of symbolic interactionism is that the human being is an active, interpreting, processing entity. Moreover, the human being does not act in isolation, but rather interacts with others to establish all facets of humanness. Specifically, as we noted in Chapter 1:

1. People's actions are based on the meaning they assign to the object;
2. The meaning of a thing is derived from social interaction;
3. Meanings have a degree of uniqueness because of people's individual interpretations.

Therefore, it is impossible to talk about an object as having information. A person imputes information by reason of a desire to act. In order to fully understand information, one must realize how one's perceptions and definitions of situations prepare one to use information. According to the perspective of symbolic interactionism, information about the world is a product of one's perceptual and definitional processes.

Perception of Objects

In writing about perception, Haney states, *"We never really come into direct contact with reality.* Everything we experience is a manufacture of our nervous systems."[8] The nervous system is not just physiological, according to Haney; rather, he implies, it is the entire mental process. Many instructors in perception are fond of the following classroom demonstration of the different ways people manufacture experience. They distribute slips of paper which have been treated with the chemical PTC. Without telling the students of the chemical treatment, they tell them to taste the paper. Some students find the taste sweet, others find it sour or bitter, and about half find it tasteless. In brief, even physical sensory inputs are not the same for all people.

The basic human monitoring equipment for sensing the external world varies from person to person. Even though everyone "knows" that people perceive things differently, nonetheless people tend to behave as if everyone perceived in a like manner. For instance, if an instructor held an orange up in class and asked everybody to identify it and a student in the back said "pear," that student would be ridiculed. However, perhaps the distance plus the student's tendency to see orange as pale yellow led to the logical answer "pear." The human eye is not a movie camera nor the ear a tape recorder, yet people often persist in behaving as if they were.

Information theorists assert that the eye is capable of processing 5 million bits of information per second; the brain, only 500 bits. The brain's ability to handle only 1 of every 10,000 bits of incoming information indicates that the human being is highly selective in attending to the stimuli in the visual field. In other words, individuals are relatively limited processors of sense data.

Social training What *do* people see or hear? Symbolic interactionists answer that an individual is trained by others—parents, friends, society, and culture —to assign meaning to things in certain ways. To most Americans, for example, Japanese, Arabic, or Hebrew writing looks like "chicken tracks," whereas the letters on this page are so recognizable that they do not require any conscious thought on the reader's part.

Another factor in perception is that this process is affected by one's expectations. Many police who expect to see crime and criminals *do* see more criminal types than do people not involved in law enforcement. Police officials, like everyone else, are cued to be aware of certain things. Similarly, all of us have had the experience of learning a new word, then becoming aware how frequently it seems to be used in conversation.

Transactional Perception

The transactional view of perception can be stated as follows: "Each percept, from the simplest to the most complex, is the product of a creative act."[9] This statement, in line with symbolic interactionism, suggests that a person is an active participant in rather than a passive observer of the environing world. In brief, there is no such thing as a stimulus without a response. The dependence of element on element "creates" perception. As a hypothetical baseball umpire cited by Cantril says, "Some's balls and some's strikes but they ain't nothin' till I calls 'em."[10] In this particular situation, the creative act of perception belongs to the umpire and the context of the game. As such, it reflects a primary tenet of transactional perception, namely, that people create what they see.

Wholeness of transactionalism Also implicit in the transactional perspective is that unlike the interactionists' concept of actor and acted upon, the perceptual process is a whole; the object of a perception cannot be separated from the perceiver.

A transaction has no specifiable beginning or end. Your seeing a tree depends on the tree's existence and being within your field of vision. Thus a small child who puts hands over eyes and states, "You can't see me" has a valid point. Once having constructed such a view, the child behaves in accordance with that view; the child has adequately defined the other person as being out of his or her perceptual view and consequently the environing world. Adults often do the same thing, as when they know of something but tell people not to mention it, so that they can ignore its existence.

Implications According to Toch and MacLean, the transactional view of perception has four distinct implications for our discussion of information.[11] First, shared experiences result in a commonality among people's perceptions. If several scholars have been trained in non-Newtonian physics, for example, their common base of experience will give them similar information as they observe a physical phenomenon. Communication is probably possible only because people have had similar experiences which lead to certain commonalities in the information they share. These commonalities are reinforced by social learning.

The second implication is that because all people have certain different experiences, a perceptual divergence occurs. By way of illustration, we and our colleagues in the field of communication have had different experiences: some have studied mechanistic models rather than systemic ones; some have backgrounds in literature, whereas others studied psychology, business, or forensics. Although we all principally study communication, we all view the communicative event differently, because of our varied experiences. Indeed, the subtitle of this book ("A Symbolic Interaction Perspective") is intended as a qualifier on the way two people perceive communication, yet ours is not the only symbolic interactionist interpretation.

A third implication is that differences in perceptual behavior can be produced, thereby changing the information available. Sherif's research demonstrates that social pressure may lead to changes in a person's perceptions.[12] Subjects were asked to make perceptual judgments in isolation and then with others (actually confederates of the experimenter). The subjects changed their perceptual judgments to match that of the confederates. When a follow-up was conducted by having the subjects make another judgment in isolation, they held to the perceptual evaluations made in the group situation.

Sherif's findings suggest that people seem to distrust their perceptions and are generally susceptible to group pressure. In applying this principle in a political context, Nimmo found that political campaigns should aim for perceptual shift rather than attitude change, because the latter is much more difficult and time consuming than the former.[13] For instance, a Democratic candidate who needs support in a heavily Republican area should show how his or her positions are in line with the constituency's values rather than try to change the voters' party affiliation.

The fourth implication of the transactional view is that different levels of perceptual complexity exist and that increased complexity will lead to more divergent perceptions. As Toch and MacLean state: "The more complex a perceptual situation becomes, the greater the tendency for variations in perception to occur . . . any standard *social* situation constitutes a veritable perceptual cafeteria."[14] If you and a classmate discuss the desk you sit at, for instance, whatever the "desk's information" is would be accurately and similarly perceived by both of you; the level of complexity in the desk is not great. If, on the other hand, the two of you talk about the "student riot" at a rock concert, the level of complexity is far higher; there exists far more information to be perceived. When moving from a "social reality" to an existential level, the complexity is so great that few people could agree on what is in the event unless they had had long periods of similar training. In other words, the level of perceptual complexity increases as the object of perception becomes more abstract.

Definition of the Situation

The symbolic interactionist defines the naming or labeling of the things being perceived as "definition of the situation." The implication of defining situations is broader and more communicative than merely labeling the perception; "perception" suggests recognition of a single element, whereas "definition of a situation" locates the process of observing an event and then finding symbols to communicate the event. Thus defining situations implies that events are symbolized so that they may be explained to others, and indeed this is the process of informing.

The events defined are not wholly a product of the individual. As Garretson has pointed out, "People are seen as responding not directly to a resistant outer reality but to meanings of objects which are defined within a cultural system and social organization."[15] A person's definition of an event is a product of his or her unique experience in a social unit located within a culture, and as such it reveals how the person was led to define a particular situation and suggests that information is communicated to others in a socially and culturally bound context.

Believability of the defined situation "If [people] define situations as real, they are real in their consequences."[16] Defining a situation makes it become real.

Earlier in this chapter we discussed how to know whether information is valid. Most people consider this question only rarely; more often than not, people believe that if something is defined, it exists. The only time this mode of operation is questioned occurs when a person becomes too deviant to be tolerated. The paranoid individual defines *too many* evil-force situations. However, even "normal" people define evil forces, occasionally feeling that they are being followed or will die of cancer or in an airplane crash. Rational discussion at such times is not always a deterrent; defining a situation as such makes it become real.

Benjamin Whorf offers a classic example of how a situation becomes real once it has been defined.[17] As an insurance investigator, he found a company that separated and labeled empty and full gasoline barrels. The workers lunched, smoked, and rough-housed around the empty barrels. Whorf noted that the workers defined the area of empty barrels as safe for smoking. They changed that definition, however, when he pointed out that empty gasoline barrels are highly explosive because of the large amounts of oxygen mixed with trapped gasoline vapors. In other words, "reality" can change with a change in the definition of a situation.

COLLECTING INFORMATION

Information may be defined as the report of personal perceptions and of social realities that are exchanged between people. Communication is the method most often used to exchange or collect information, because people rely on symbols to link themselves with other people. This content level of communication is the "stuff" of which enduring relationships are built. Information can be collected and disseminated in a variety of ways, and in our discussion of these methods, we focus on the information itself rather than on its use.

Participants in communicative interactions may seek information for a variety of reasons, e.g., in order to make decisions or to facilitate or regulate others or themselves. Moreover, one may collect information as either the communication initiator or respondent. Initiators seeking information activate or encourage communication with others. Respondents, by contrast, seek communicative events initiated by others. Both initiators and respondents enter a communication situation with a level of expectation, e.g., "This will be fruitful or meaningful to my needs for information."

The Interview

The interview is a dyadic form of communication in which two persons interact for a specific purpose and on a specific content area. The interview is a useful tool for collecting information because it focuses directly on information. Moreover, the interview's dyadic character eliminates much of the relational level of communication that is magnified in group or public communication, in which the additional influences of norms, social variables, and more participants make the exchange of information more complex. Thus the interview is not only a good tool for our analysis of collecting information, but also probably a primary method whereby people gain information from others. In other words, an interview is any dyadic communication used for the collection of information.

Even children use interviews to collect information. The child approaches mother, father, or other "big person" and begins the questioning in order to get information about things. The child's eager nature to learn starts with a specific question and then proceeds to an endless string of "whys." The child is the initiator—wanting information, directing the content, trying to control the interaction, and attempting to maintain it until satisfied with the explanation given.

The child's behavior is not essentially different from that of the employment counselor, the news reporter trying to get a story, the doctor attempting to find out where it hurts, or the consumer endeavoring to discover the disadvantages as well as the advantages of a product. Each asks questions, redirects questions, probes, then moves on to other areas with more questions.

Types of questions We have suggested that questions are the basic tool of the interviewer in trying to collect information. Different types of questions produce different configurations in the information obtained.

Although questions may be categorized in a variety of ways, there are five types that seem to "shape" the information obtained: open, direct, closed, bipolar, and leading questions. The open question, the broadest type, may allow the respondent to go in almost any direction. Some typical open questions are: "In general, what do you think . . . ?" or "Why or what does it all mean?" The respondent, hard-pressed to know what the initiator is after, will generally attempt to cover all bases or may become sidetracked in personal interests and not answer the initiator's intended question. For this reason open questions are probably more useful as follow-up questions. If the initiator's purpose is to get information, he or she would be well advised to first ask an information-eliciting question and then ask "why." This approach delineates the subject area and facilitates an exchange process—for the initiator an opportunity to gain information from the respondent, and for the latter an opportunity to give information in areas she or he deems crucial.

A direct question specifies a general topic but still gives the respondent broad latitude in framing an answer. The question specifies the content area of the information sought, but it also allows the respondent to answer in a number of ways and at length. Hence the initiator who has some prior knowledge of a topic may use a direct question to get a great deal of information relatively quickly.

We can use the following example to distinguish between open and direct questions. Suppose you want information about other students' views of college. An open question might be: "In general, what do you think about college?" A direct question, on the other hand, could be: "How do you think your college education has prepared you in your chosen career field?" The open question could lead to answers about fraternities or sororities, classes, athletics, career goals, administration, campus food services, etc. But the direct question forces the respondent into a well-defined topic area. Direct questions generally produce shorter answers, but they will also provide clues for follow-up questions about the topic.

The closed question, like a multiple-choice question, provides the respondent with a limited set of options from which to answer and places a demand characteristic of a very short answer. "What is your favorite color?" is a closed question. Your field of alternative responses is limited by the typical labels attached to the color spectrum, and the question also encourages a single-word response. Your answer "puce," however, would probably be deemed an inappropriate response, for although it is a single word, "puce" is not commonly used in everyday language. Similarly, your answer "blue with a light touch of green and somewhat like the side away from a sunset just before the sun sets in the water" would also be considered inappropriate. A follow-up question of "So your favorite color is blue?" most likely would elicit a "Well, yes" on your part. Although people do not often respond to direct questions with such inappropriate answers, the skillful collector of information knows that they can occur and therefore never expects a perfectly shaped answer.

The bipolar question is a more limited type of closed question in that only two options exist for the answer. Questions that can be answered with a simple yes or no are typical bipolar questions, but there are other types as well. In semantics, for example, there is the principle of polarization, whereby things are, erroneously, treated as dichotomies.[18] People often treat others as either beautiful or ugly, smart or dumb, good or bad, and so forth. For example, if two instructors are talking over coffee, one might ask, "Say, I noticed you had Leonard Carton in class last quarter, what about that kid?" The question is possibly a bipolar one in disguise; if so, the real question is "Is Leonard Carton dumb or smart?" A nonbipolar response to a bipolar question indicates that the respondent is trying to deal with pertinent middle-ground information.

The leading question, which can be any of the other four types, is basically an attempt to bias the respondent's answer. A supervisor's calling in a subordinate and asking, "Do you think our new management system is working as well as I do?" is seeking not information on the management system but rather personal verification. The bias introduced by leading questions elicits what is already known; in the words of the information theorist, the question seeks redundancy.

Structure Seldom can a single question provide all the information an interviewer needs. Instead, the interview becomes a structure of many questions. In addition to gaining information, it may also be used to determine how large the field of information is and how many alternative messages there are.

One typical method of interview structure is called the funnel technique, which starts with a broad, direct question, followed by a series of probing, specific questions. This procedure elicits an information set that is not only accurate but also precise.

Listening

When direct interaction is impossible, listening in public forms of communication may provide the needed information. Just as questioning is a primary skill for the initiator, so listening is a primary skill for the respondent. Although most people spend many of their waking hours listening, few make an effort to improve this skill.

Listening is more than a technique of facilitation. Listening, essential to the respondent's collecting of information, is both deliberative and empathic. Deliberative listening is the skill of getting the facts and understanding the speaker's information; empathic listening, gaining a "feeling" for the speaker and his or her position. These two types of listening are not mutually exclusive; in fact, the accuracy of the information collected is enhanced when the two are combined. The purpose of deliberative listening is to gather facts and test the facts mentally. Through empathic listening the listener seeks to learn why the speaker reached particular conclusions.

Although it is important to be a concerned listener when seeking information, one should also realize that listening is a perceptual process. A person does not simply hear and absorb each word spoken, but instead listens in a symbolic field, and this symbolic field influences the perception of what one hears and subsequently understands. People listen with culturally and socially trained ears. Therefore, listening is selective, based on the expectations the listener brings to an event. For example, the person who believes that the Equal Rights Amendment (ERA) is a way of upsetting societal balance will hear those types of messages. This person can believe that passage of the ERA will lead to sexually integrated restrooms. Or, this person can "know" that the salutation "Ms." is really a subversive way of greeting Marxist sisters. To the symbolic interactionist, listening is an active process. A person hears messages, interprets them, and defines the situation on the basis of a trained backlog of view of self and the self's current role.

Accuracy

Several techniques are available to both initiators and respondents for increasing the accuracy of information collected. Of course, one should be as systematic as possible in giving or collecting details. Accuracy increases as the specific details given become more orderly and well organized. Conversely, a listener should seek to find the speaker's organization.

Encouraging feedback in the communication event is another way of reducing the error of messages and hence increasing the accuracy of the content.

Using more than one medium of presentation can enhance accuracy. The use of drawings or gestures can facilitate others' understanding of the verbal content. Also, the initiator's use of attention catchers and summaries during the presentation of information helps listeners understand what has been said and what more may be coming.

Empathic listening can decrease the perceptual distortion inherent in information exchange. By "listening" to the speaker, one can learn the "why" behind a person's words or perceptions. Because of the variation in communicators' backgrounds and experiences, the mutual judging of each other's information is crucial to understanding. We may characterize this as a problem of social-psychological distance. People in the same role behave differently because of the different role models used for learning the role. Hence communicators must realize that communication is shaped by the participants' roles. Similarly, the way in which a person handles information depends on whether the person is acting from the Parent, Adult, or Child ego state. Accordingly, the distortion of information can be minimized by careful, empathic listening.

DISSEMINATING INFORMATION

How does society provide for the transmission of information? This question can be answered by two methodologies—(1) investigating the current mass media and developing an analysis of strengths and weaknesses and (2) exploring how interpersonal communication contacts guide the flow of information. These two processes are not mutually exclusive. Indeed, reliance on the mass media presupposes the existence of media to serve as initiators of messages.

Multistep Flow of Information

According to the two-step theory of communication flow, opinion leaders get information from the media and pass the information along to nonleaders.[19] This hypothesis also has implications for information dissemination. The hypothesis indicates that people do not always contact the original source of information. Sometimes information is passed along from media to person to another person. Today this basic notion is known as a multistep flow; that is, the information may go in a stepwise fashion farther than two people.

Immediately after the resignation of Vice-President Spiro T. Agnew, a class of University of Utah students surveyed Salt Lake City residents to find out how they had been informed of the resignation. The news was released at about noon M.S.T. and immediately broadcast over radio. People tuned in to their radios or watching TV were the first to acquire the information. They immediately told the first person they contacted about the news item. These people, who got the news second-hand, attempted to tell others. This pattern of verbal dissemination continued until about 3:30 P.M. By that time most people had heard the news, and information giving seemed to halt fairly abruptly.

The first step had been information dissemination. The next phenomenon was information seeking, which occurred a few hours later, during the national television news programs. People seemed to want to get the details and validate them. About two percent of the 450 people contacted in the survey said that they waited for the newspaper before actually believing the resignation story. Although the information was extraordinary and the survey a little "dirty" methodologically, the findings demonstrate the often-found concept of multi-step flow of communication through a large social unit.

Information Changes in Dissemination

As information flows through a social unit, the content of the information is susceptible to change. Higham, drawing on the work of many other research-ers, found in an experimental study that messages may be altered in one of three ways as they are passed from individual to individual.[20] Leveling, the first way in which the message may change, refers to the elimination of detail and nonessential elements, whereby the message becomes shorter, more concise, and easier to pass along. Leveling occurs relatively early in the process of mes-sage transmission.

In the next step the remaining details of the message are sharpened, thus highlighting what appear to be the essential elements. In fact, one piece of information may become so strong as to form the central core of the message.

Assimilation, the third way in which change may occur, refers to the way in which the receiver's prior attitudes, beliefs, and convictions influence the sharpening and leveling processes. As the message becomes shorter, for ex-ample, assimilation may expand the message in a new direction and change the content. In the Utah survey, this is exactly what happened. Along with the resignation news came the story that Agnew had pleaded no contest to charges of bribery. Some people reported that they had heard that Agnew had resigned because he was found guilty of bribery and income tax evasion. According to the altered message, the ex-Vice-President had been convicted of criminal charges.

Serial Transmission of Information

Serial transmission may be defined as the phenomenon of people passing on information without receiving much feedback. When messages are serially transmitted, they are distorted through leveling, sharpening, and assimilation. No matter how good people's intentions to be accurate and precise in passing along messages, the very act of transmission always distorts them. Selective perception, definition of situation, and wanting to be communicatively economical lead to these transmission errors. Distortion is so common that it is even the focus of a children's game, "gossip," in which everyone sits in a circle and a message is whispered from ear to ear. The last person to receive the message repeats it out loud, and everyone laughs at how little it resembles the original message.

The distortion inherent in serial transmission can be lessened if the receiver keeps in mind the three questions posed earlier in this chapter: (1) How much, and what set, of information? (2) How accurate and precise is the information? (3) How useable and reliable is the information? In addition, the distortion may be reduced if the participants are physically close together. Often distortion in serial transmission is magnified because of the distance separating those involved. A decrease in the physical distance permits the participants to more adequately deal with their respective personal attitudes, habits, and values that may lead to distortion. Also, once the participants know how serial transmission leads to distortion through leveling, sharpening, and assimilation, they may behave in more careful and responsible ways to obtain information with greater accuracy.

SUMMARY

No single definition of information is adequate; to look at information from the syntactic, semantic, and pragmatic points of view leads to different but equally important questions of information. To the symbolic interactionist, information is interwoven with perception and definition of a situation. Thus the following principles emerge:

1. People never perceive reality directly.
2. People manufacture sense data out of different physical and social differences.
3. Perception is a learned phenomenon and is acquired from the culture, social units, and significant others.
4. Perception is a creative act and depends on both the perceiver and the object of perception.
5. "Real" information is obtained from a person's definition of a situation.

These principles suggest that information is not a self-contained entity. Rather, it is given meaning and is treated as real on the basis of the person's assigning meaning to it through interpretation.

A person collects information through an active, communicative process of questioning and listening. These two skills are interdependent; the questioner, or interviewer, must listen to the respondent in order to gain information. Conversely, listening will often stimulate further questions. In other words, information collecting is a transactional process that becomes personal through the participants' definition of the situation.

The process of collecting information is not without pitfalls. It may lead to invading another's privacy or impinging on his or her human rights. In part to overcome this danger, for example, a December 1974 federal law stipulated that students' files were to be available to the students and their parents. Such a law is an attempt to ensure that the information collected about a person is both accurate and not damaging. In other words, the issue is not the collection of information per se, but rather the way in which that information is used to regulate the behavior of self and others.

Information is "public" in that it passes from person to person directly or more indirectly via the mass media to many people. But since the transmission of information entails distortion, communicators must strive to ensure the accuracy and precision of the information they collect and disseminate.

PROBLEMS AND ISSUES

1. In his studies on perception, Sherif found that people may change their perceptions on the basis of social pressure. Review such findings and attempt to explain why some people in his experiment did *not* alter their perceptions. (Abrahamson could offer you help.[21])

2. Healthy communication does not dwell on the relationship level. Identify and analyze a few situations in which people speak more about relationship than information and yet have "healthy" communication.

3. Conduct a survey on the multistep flow of information. How do your results differ and coincide with the findings in the Utah survey after Agnew's resignation? Can you explain the differences?

4. Write a position paper either supporting or attacking the idea that things are "real" because of the way a person defines the situation. Use communicative examples to help illustrate your thesis.

NOTES

1. Paul Watzlawick, Janet H. Beavin, and Don D. Jackson, *Pragmatics of Human Communication* (New York: Norton, 1967), pp. 51–54.

2. *Ibid.*, p. 52.

3. Colin Cherry, *On Human Communication*, 2d ed. (Cambridge, Mass.: M.I.T. Press, 1966), pp. 221–253.

4. C. E. Shannon and W. Weaver, *The Mathematical Theory of Communication* (Urbana: University of Illinois Press, 1949). This book was among the first to explicate the syntactic view of information.

5. Cherry, *op. cit.,* p. 171.

6. W. Ross Ashby, *An Introduction to Cybernetics* (New York: Wiley, 1956), p. 129.

7. *Ibid.,* pp. 129–130.

8. William V. Haney, *Communication and Organizational Behavior,* 3rd ed. (Homewood, Ill.: Richard D. Irwin, 1973), p. 55.

9. Hans Toch and Malcolm S. MacLean, Jr., "Perception and Communication: A Transactional View," *AV Communication Review* **10** (1967): 57.

10. Hadley Cantril, "Perception and Interpersonal Relations," *American Journal of Psychiatry* **114** (1957): 126.

11. Toch and MacLean, *op. cit.,* pp. 55–77.

12. M. Sherif, *The Psychology of Social Norms* (New York: Harper & Row, 1963).

13. Dan Nimmo, *The Political Persuaders* (Englewood Cliffs, N.J.: Prentice-Hall, Spectrum Books, 1970), pp. 179–183.

14. Toch and MacLean, *op. cit.,* p. 58.

15. Wyonna Smutz Garretson, "The Consensual Definition of Social Objects," *The Sociological Quarterly* **3** (April 1962): 107.

16. William I. Thomas and Dorothy Swaine Thomas, *The Child in America* (New York: Knopf, 1928), p. 571.

17. Benjamin Lee Whorf, *Language, Thought and Reality,* ed. J. B. Carroll (Cambridge, Mass.: M.I.T. Press, 1956), pp. 135–137.

18. For an excellent discussion of polarization, *see* Haney, *op. cit.,* pp. 305–318.

19. Elihu Katz and Paul F. Lazarsfeld, *Personal Influence* (New York: Free Press, 1955), pp. 309–320.

20. T. M. Higham, "The Experimental Study of the Transmission of Rumour," *British Journal of Psychology* **42** (1951): 42–55.

21. Mark Abrahamson, *Interpersonal Accommodation* (Princeton, N.J.: D. Van Nostrand, 1966), pp. 94–116.

Chapter 8

Processing
Decisions

INTRODUCTION

In each of the preceding chapters on facilitation, regulation, and information, we have stressed purposeful communication. But we have not dealt directly with a primary goal of many communication events—making a decision. This chapter explores various models of decision making and how they operate in communication.

There are two prevailing characteristics of decision-making models: (1) a claim of universality or generalizability; and (2) a specific notion of human nature. The claim of universality tends to be made not by the model builder, but rather by subsequent writers "buying" a particular theory of decision making. However, in fact, none of the models can be used in all situations; each is inappropriate in certain communication settings. Similarly, theorists who believe that the human being is a rational, analytical creature develop a rational, analytical model for processing decisions. By the same token, those who view the human as the product of a long history of shaping behaviors through reinforcement and other learning paradigms of a behavioral bent develop decision-making models predicated on reinforcement theory. Decision-making models can also be based on emotionality, the "evilness" of human nature, gestalt theory, and so on.

In brief, there is no universal model of decision making; there is no one "human nature." Instead, behavior is situational and calls for different methods of processing decisions. Hence it is our thesis that different communication situations require different forms of decision making. Furthermore, we will remain bound by our criterion that each decision model be compatible with symbolic interactionism. In this chapter we will look at five types of decision-making contexts: individual decision making, the interview, group decision making, the public forum, and organizational patterns of decision making.

INDIVIDUAL DECISION MAKING

A person's mental activity constitutes the interpretative process in the larger paradigm of symbolic interaction. Our purpose here is to explore how the individual processes decisions, so that we can place some general models of decision making in perspective and relate them to communication.

Dewey's Rational Model

During most of this century logical thought has been regarded as the basis for decision making. Dewey's statement of problem solving has become the primary tenet in this rational model. According to Dewey, there are five steps in the problem-solving process: "(i) a felt difficulty; (ii) its location and definition; (iii) suggestion of possible solution; (iv) development by reasoning of the bearings of the suggestion; (v) further observation and experiment leading to its acceptance or rejection . . ."[1] In other words, after perceiving a need, an individual defines the need, seeks solutions, develops arguments and evidence to support a solution, and further tests the preferred solution to determine whether it does in fact solve the problem.

To Dewey, these five steps described not the real-life decision-making process so much as an ideal formula to be learned and applied by reasonable people. To paraphrase his words, a trained, disciplined mind will better observe things, form ideas, reason, and experimentally test solutions.[2] He was calling for a unique and rational training of students' thinking patterns.

Despite Dewey's emphasis on training, many later writers have used his original concept to explain decision making as it actually occurs. (It does appear, however, that Dewey's five steps are useful in certain problem-solving situations, and we shall apply them to organizational behavior in a later section of this chapter.) For example, a recent book on decision making from a sociological perspective asserts: "The decision process consists of six phases customarily linked into a sequence: (1) identification of the problem; (2) obtaining necessary information; (3) production of possible solutions; (4) evaluation of such solutions (5) selection of a strategy for performance; and (6) actual performance of an action or actions, and subsequent learning and revision."[3] Thus what was first developed as a prescription of how a decision should be made has become a description of how the process actually works.

Lack of explanatory power There are several fallacies inherent in using a Dewey-like scheme to examine real-life decision making. First, the Dewey model cannot explain a seemingly irrational decision. As a real estate agent we know notes, people rarely buy a particular house for rational reasons. Lava rock fireplaces, pretty paint, and a brick exterior are major selling points.

A second fallacy of rational models is that they presuppose the existence of a problem to be solved; this structure equates problem solving with decision making. However, it may be possible to make decisions in the absence of a felt problem. On the other hand, many such problems never seem to get solved, despite the many decisions made about them.

When one gets up in the morning and makes a decision about what to wear, the decision is based not so much on the felt need to eliminate nudity as on what is available in the closet. Similarly, the whole notion of impulse buying is predicated not on need but on someone's presenting attractive alternatives consumers had not previously thought about.

A Descriptive Model

Our criticism of the rational models suggests that a model for individual decision making should meet the following criteria: (1) it need not be tied to problem solving; (2) it must consider seemingly nonrational behavior; (3) it must demonstrate process; (4) it should be explanatory rather than prescriptive; and (5) it must reflect the symbolic interactionist's idea of the mental interpretative process.

Leon Festinger has developed a concept of decision making that meets these criteria.[4] Festinger postulates three phases to individual decision making: conflict, decision, and dissonance. During the conflict phase, the individual notes alternative choices and objectively considers those choices. Next is the decision phase, during which one selects and becomes committed to one alternative. The last phase is dissonance, a postdecision period of instability during which the person seeks to justify the choice.

The primary assumption underlying this model of cognitive dissonance is that the human being is a balance-seeking system. In Chapter 6, on the regulation of behavior, we dealt with this idea under the broad category of consistency theory. To summarize this assumption, whenever a person is faced with two or more competing elements, he or she will seek ways to eliminate the competition. This assumption is based on the law of homeostasis, which states that organisms always move into equilibrium with their environment.

Conflict The conflict, or predecision, phase is a time for interpreting alternatives.[5] The conflict phase can begin only if the person perceives a set of alternatives from which to make a choice. Hence the first essential ingredient for decision making is the person's interpretation of at least two alternatives.

This step may be viewed as problem solving, but it can also be initiated by other forms of thinking. For example, suppose that your car completely failed you this morning and that you must have auto transportation to get around. You quickly see that your problem could be solved in one of at least three ways: (1) buy a new car; (2) buy a cheap used car; or (3) get your old car repaired. Once you see the alternatives, you have entered into the decision-making process.

You now begin an objective appraisal of the alternatives. By "objective," Festinger did not necessarily mean "rational," but rather treating all alternatives without bias. Your evidence and interpretation of the evidence may be emotional rather than intellectual. The objective appraisal could be likened to the behavior of a person in the Adult ego state; one tries to interpret the reality perceived in an objective manner—without bias or prejudgment, seeking to make evaluations based on the merits of each alternative.

But how does this model account for impulsive decisions? The concept of ego states is a possibility. For example, the Parent ego state contains ready-made answers to situations. When the alternatives to a decision are similar or in some way analogous to earlier situations, a response from the Parent is a quick way of making a decision. Buying a particular piece of clothing may seem very impulsive; however, past clothes-buying behavior helps give one the ready-made answer in this particular situation.

Decision The second phase of the cognitive dissonance process is the decision. Decision is not the same as selection of choice, because decision implies a commitment to the selection. Thus we may distinguish between preference and decision. Preference is selection without commitment. If you bring along a friend while you buy a car, your friend's behavior is different from yours. The friend can express preference, because there is no demand on your friend for payment or "living" with the car daily. Moreover, your preference may not be your choice. Your preference may be beyond your financial reality; therefore, you must choose something different. Preference is simply selection without commitment.

Dissonance Selecti n with commitment—decision—leads to dissonance. Once a person has made a decision, doubt or uncertainty about that selection sets in. This dissonance, or postdecision, phase is a part of the total process; moreover, the dissonance may alter the decision or affect later decisions.

Dissonance is also a part of the interpretative process. The person still sees certain alternatives, usually the same ones as before decision; now, however, they are treated subjectively, i.e., with a bias toward the alternative selected. This bias generally leads to the collection of two types of information —that supporting the decision, which ensures continued interpretation of the action as correct, and that about the other alternatives, so as to demean them. Thus much of a person's behavior in the dissonance phase reflects the Child ego state; one's interests are centered on self and the validity of one's choices. The bias position of the search indicates a certain petulance in wanting to be correct.

Dissonance may also explain why people change their minds after a decision seems final. If the biased information sought is unavailable or if the decision cannot be justified, the decision is likely to be changed. This too supports the idea that dissonance is handled in the Child ego state. The Child is variable and open to new directions, unlike the Parent and Adult ego states.

Commitment may be so strong that the person is unable to change the decision; however, the information found during the dissonance phase may eliminate alternatives in future decisions. For example, if you buy a new car that turns out to be a "lemon," you may vow never to buy that make of car again.

Much of the research by Festinger and his associates has been devoted to the topic of dissonance reduction. Dissonance reduction can be summarized in terms of an individual's interpretation process. Dissonance has been reduced and an acceptable state of balance exists when the individual can adequately define the situation. In Chapter 7, we said that defining the situation makes it become real. When the competing alternatives have been defined (interpreted) as satisfying justification in the choice, dissonance has been resolved.

Dissonance as process The three-phase cognitive dissonance process is an integrated movement progressing through time, with the alternatives in the conflict phase becoming the elements of dissonance. "The greater the conflict before the decision, the greater the dissonance afterward."[6] In other words, the amount of difficulty in making the decision indicates the amount of dissonance. This notion is not immediately validated by common sense, however. One would hope that by being careful and analytical in approaching all possible alternatives, the person's decision would be final and not subject to further doubt. The findings do not substantiate this view. The more information obtained in the objective, conflict phase, the more one must deal with that information subjectively in the dissonance phase. Thus people who seem to go through life rather blithely probably, according to Festinger, never approach decisions seriously, and therefore the consequences of those decisions do not become serious either.

DECISION MAKING IN THE INTERVIEW

The interview as a method of collecting information can be integrated with the concept of individual decision making to show how the individual makes decisions in a communicative interaction. In Chapter 7, we defined the interview as a two-person interaction designed for a specific purpose and focused on a specific content area. Whereas then our emphasis was on the content area of the communication event, we now look to the specific purposes of the interview.

The purpose of the interview is to make decisions or validate decisions (reduce dissonance). In any particular type of interview, the outcome hinges on a decision, be it employment, appraisal, or sales. The interviewer and interviewee agree to transact and exchange information so that a decision can be made. In making a hiring decision, for example, a personnel director usually has several applicants from which to choose. These applicants present a conflict phase in the director's decision making. Application forms do not give information about how the applicants may relate to the company, how verbal they are, and other interpersonal considerations. Festinger would argue that if many qualified people are interviewed, the personnel director will experience increased dissonance because of the difficulty in making a decision. If this is so, the personnel director can be expected to keep a close watch on the person chosen—not so much to find out if the person can do the job as to check whether the decision to hire that person was correct.

Salespersons often help a client make a decision on a seemingly rational basis, which should also result in lessened dissonance. A classic example is the so-called Ben Franklin close. When attempting to close a sale, the salesperson relates that when Ben Franklin was confronted with a tough decision, he divided a sheet of paper in half and then wrote all the pluses of the decision on one side and the minuses on the other. The salesperson then helps the client list all of the pluses, but leaves the client to think of the minuses. Of course, the plus list is longer than the minus column, and the client is therefore more inclined to buy the product.

The closing technique—whether or not this overt—is not objective but rather subjective. The salesperson helps list the pros but never the cons. The client generally assumes that a rational, objective field of information is present; in fact, however, the information is biased and looks more like dissonance reduction. The sales advantage to such techniques is that they encourage a rational-appearing decision plus give methods for dissonance reduction. But such a practice is neither healthy nor ethical; indeed, it is mostly likely to be used when the salesperson does not expect to deal with the client again.

In a healthy sales-client environment, there are several interviews: the first, an attempt to help the client see that a conflict exists and that a decision must be made; the second, a decision phase in which the salesperson attempts to help the client make a decision based on the *objective* data; and the third, a reinforcement of the client's decision and desire to continue using the product. This type of healthy sales-client situation is being encouraged by some companies; their sales interviews are conducted in line with a realistic model of the individual decision-making process.

Because the interview places the decision-making responsibility with only one of the two people present, decision making is therefore an individual process. The two roles—decision maker and information source—in the interview are interdependent; information is a prerequisite for decision making. Moreover, the individual decision-making process does not extend beyond the interview into other situations. When decision making moves from the individual to a group, social constraints and more interaction patterns change the process of decision making.

DECISION MAKING IN GROUPS

Not all groups are decision-making bodies; some are formed for social purposes, personal training, psychotherapy, etc. Our focus is on that communication transaction which seeks to make decisions in a small-group environment. Among the many writers in this field, one who integrates the work of others and views the group process of decision making as unique is Fisher.[7]

Types of Decisions

Decisions may be arrived at through either *consensus* or *technical expertise*. If a technical expert can make a decision, however, group decision making is not necessary, as demonstrated in the NASA game.[8] The object of the game is to correct a randomly ordered list of items necessary for human existence on the moon. There is only one right order, and knowledge of the correct solution requires technical expertise.

The type of decision most suited to group solution is one for which there is no technically correct answer, and members can therefore pool their resources and reach a consensus. This process is one of suggesting alternatives, discussing them, and eventually setting a course of action that can accommodate the group.

Decision Emergence

Although many scholars have stated that the agenda for group decision making should be Dewey's five steps in problem solving, the reality is a very different pattern; decisions emerge from the interaction within the group. A group may in fact make many small decisions which eventually lead to the prime, major decision. For example, suppose that the church deacons of a conservative Protestant denomination want to raise money for a new sanctuary. There are many possibilities, but the deacons' beliefs will eliminate many from further consideration in the discussion. Bingo is out because it is gambling, as is a raffle; a large dinner dance is out because dancing is sinful; an expensive donation dinner is out because the members of the congregation cannot afford $100 per ticket; and a charity fund raiser by a well-known personality would look like *charity*. After discussing and turning down these alternatives, the deacons' final decision emerges—to solicit long-term pledges from the church members and to conduct work activities.

Another element in decision emergence is that most groups cannot pinpoint the exact decision proposal. For example, according to Robert's Rules of Order, a motion is supposed to precede debate and a vote. Often, however, the person chairing a meeting says after some preliminary discussion, "I think we are decided, but we need a motion to vote on. Who will make the motion?"

This motion has emerged out of the discussion and is most representative of the way small groups behave.

Because of the way decisions emerge, unidirectional linear models, e.g., the Festinger—conflict-decision-dissonance—model fall short of explaning the process. Rather than moving from one problem to the next, Scheidel and Crowell found, groups generally behave in a spiral manner.[9] After forming and discussing an idea, the group goes to another idea, but the first idea may modify the second, and vice versa. Thus each idea leads to another but is modified in the process. In this model of mutual causality, effects go forward and backward and turn in on themselves for further modification. Groups, then, do not work at solving one large problem; rather, they make many small decisions which affect one another, and in turn these small decisions lead to the final group product. The final position of the group emerges from the many specific decisions it has made.

Phases of Group Decision Making

Many researchers have described the phases involved in group decision making. Fisher's investigations, for example, found four different phases.[10] Although our discussion of these phases suggests a linear movement in time, the spiral, or nonlinear, nature of the process is still applicable.

Orientation First, the group members must get to know one another. Most people feel socially inhibited with strangers, and members' statements during this first phase are likely to be tentative. The orientation phase establishes the group's social climate and the basic networks of communication.

In addition, many ambiguous decision proposals are introduced and generate a high degree of agreement. Here "ambiguous" refers to general proposals, e.g., "We need to carefully look at the whole system." The response to such a proposal might well be, "Sure, we must be thorough in our approach." Such ambiguous proposals and agreements do nonetheless begin to direct the course of the group. Thus the group may agree to collect a great deal of information, thereby committing the members to many lengthy meetings and some special information-collecting terms. In short, the orientation phase is a time for developing group rapport and setting tentative directions.

Conflict During the second phase the group begins to get down to the business at hand. Some members disagree with specific decision proposals, and proponents and opponents begin to "lock horns." Now the members are no longer tentative or socially inhibited.

As strongly held positions begin to emerge, disagreement increases. Members seek additional information to substantiate their positions. People develop counterarguments, exploring and analyzing many sides of an issue. As members begin to form coalitions, they attempt to discredit the decision proposals and arguments of the opposing coalitions. At this point the conflict phase becomes an ideational struggle.

Of course, conflict is not necessarily a screaming debate or all-out war. Rather, the conflict phase is simply that period when the members of the group are testing the direction and positions to be taken. This type of conflict is not dysfunctional, but instead serves as a time to weigh and carefully explore decision proposals. Conflict becomes dysfunctional if members rather than ideas are attacked or if the social norms of the group are violated. In short, the conflict phase is marked by "dissent, controversy, social conflict, and innovative deviance."[11]

Emergence In this phase the eventual outcome or final decision of the group becomes increasingly apparent. There is a return to ambiguous statements, but now their function is much different. Whereas ambiguity in the orientation phase was used to express tentative direction and a feeling-out process, it now serves to reduce conflict. Now an ambiguous statement is a method of saving face, and it also allows the predominant direction of the group to take over. Any remaining dissenter will find no support, and his or her positions and comments will be treated with ambiguity from former supporters. Ambiguity thus acts to dissipate coalitions and conflict, thereby facilitating the emergence of the group's final decisions.

Reinforcement Although final decisions emerged in the preceding phase, only during the reinforcement phase does group consensus occur. This last phase entails a return to more specific types of comment which, unlike those made during the conflict phase, reflect the final position adopted by the group. Dissent is all but nonexistent as the members continue to reinforce one another's statements with supportive statements of their own. These specific statements are used to take consensus one step further and establish the group's commitment to the final decisions. As commitment increases, the interaction becomes more jovial and the atmosphere one of happy accomplishment.

DECISION MAKING AND PUBLIC COMMUNICATION

Just as small-group decision making is generally consensus-oriented, so decision making in the public communication setting appears related to technical expertise. Although decisions of a technical type may indeed have a single correct answer, many such decisions are derived from problems whose solutions are improved through reliance on technical expertise. Even though there are no ultimate truths, there are optimal answers and solutions. For example, in a physical science class, students learn that the solar system hangs together and is governed by laws of gravity and centrifugal force. This explanation "works" because most people subscribe to Newtonian laws of physics. However, theoreticians have developed mathematical models of the solar system not based on gravity or centrifugal force. This newer explanation is not taught, however, because it requires a set of assumptions and postulates that most people cannot understand. In other words, technical experts make decisions about what explanation or element is best for the current cultural situation.

Public communication is generally not a decision-making mode; rather, previously made decisions are communicated in order to persuade people that those decisions are the best ones. This model of decision making comprises a flow. (1) Decision making by an expert or group leads to (2) communicating the decision to others with the intent of (3) having them arrive at the same decision. (Although the communication may be written, we will focus on the public-speaking event.) It would be a rare event to see a public speaker stand before an audience and have no idea about the conclusion of his or her speech or the point of view that will be advocated. We do know from studies of self-influence that a public statement on a decision will increase the speaker's commitment, but the decision must be made prior to a public statement.[12]

A public speaker's technical expertise is most often labeled "source credibility." Source credibility is not something possessed by the speaker; rather, it is an attribute conferred on the speaker by the individual members of the audience. For example, we could present our credentials as communication scholars by listing our degrees and the institutions we have attended, where and for how long we have taught, our previous publication records, and the consulting we have done; however, *you* must decide whether these credentials make us experts in the field, i.e., whether we have source credibility. This is *initial* source credibility; you decide beforehand whether the communicator can be of help to you. Later, after you have heard the speaker, you may or may not change your mind about the communicator's technical ability, and this is termed *terminal* source credibility. In other words, source credibility may change between the outset and conclusion of a public communication.[13]

In reality, source credibility is more than technical expertise. As a multidimensional concept, source credibility comprises several factors: competence, character, intention, personality, and dynamism.[14] The most important of these factors are competence, character, and dynamism.

Competence refers to the assessment of the speaker's expertise. How qualified is the speaker to address the topic?

The *character* dimension is expressed in the ancient Roman adage of rhetoric: "A good man speaking well." The character of the speaker must be seen as good in order for the credibility to have an effect. Here "good" means that the speaker can be trusted and respected and has the interest of the audience in mind.

Dynamism is the "speaking well" part of the adage. An expert may be seen as trustworthy and yet be dull. Consequently, a technical expert will have an effect on the audience's decision making to the extent that he or she is perceived to be not only competent, but also having a good character and a dynamic style.

Sometimes a single dimension may override the other components of credibility. One speaker may be regarded as so competent that dynamism is not important. For example, one of your instructors may be so brilliant that you attend class and learn despite his or her boring lecture style. Nonetheless, in most cases the speaker who wishes to make a decision known and advocate that decision will be hampered if the dimensions of competence, character, and dynamism are not positively perceived by the audience.

DECISION MAKING IN ORGANIZATIONS

Because of its task-goal orientation, an organization's decision-making process is a response to problems in the attainment of the goal. Hence only organizational decision making can be equated with problem solving.

Sources of Problems

An organization's problems may stem from either internal or external (environmental) sources. A myriad of internal problems, from participant or worker satisfaction to product quality, may cause the organizational framework to be put into decision-making motion. Similarly, everything from the economy to changing social mores may affect an organization. However, the nature of the problem situations is more limited:

> Three common situations that can give rise to decision-making activity are (1) a difference between performance and goals (aspirations), or between performance and expectations; (2) the prospect of some event that offers opportunities to, or threatens, the organization or some part of it; and (3) the occurrence of some recurring situation that must be resolved.[15]

An example of the first situation might occur if a cosmetic company sought to increase its sales by 20 percent by introducing a new cosmetic line for teenagers, but instead the company's sales went down 4 percent. An excellent example of the second situation occurred during the Arab oil embargo of 1973–74. Not only the oil companies, but also utility companies, Congress, and most energy-consuming corporations were suddenly faced with serious problems. Finally, examples of recurring organizational problems are contract bargaining and seasonal changes in the economy, e.g., the annual Christmas shopping rush.

Solving Problems

If an organization is large enough to have divisions of labor, as in most work organizations, various subunits will typically work to solve the problem, thus necessitating a "plan of attack." Most often this plan is a Dewey-type rational model of decision making. These models provide control and an apparently sensible way to proceed, as well as a familiar operating procedure.

Organizational decision making generally proceeds as follows. Seeing that a problem exists, management calls together other units of the organization to discuss the problem. By this act management is attempting to help the various units perceive the problem. Next, the organizational subgroups may be asked to consider the reasons for the problem and to propose solutions. Knowing that they will have to report back from their unique perspectives, the units may behave according to a small-group decision-making pattern. Thus, for example, the accounting, marketing, and production departments will provide the management decision-making unit with alternative solutions derived from a variety of perspectives. Now the management unit will weigh the information, consider each alternative in terms of the goal, and compare alternative to alternative for their respective advantages and disadvantages. After finding the best alternative solution, management calls on the appropriate unit to develop implementation procedures. Once the plan for implementation has been completed, the organization at large will enact the planned solution. If the planned solution demands a great deal of change, management may decide to test the change in only a few units, to check the feasibility of the solution before committing the entire organization to the new decision proposal.

Conflict over Decisions

Conflict may arise if one unit of the organization feels that it had a better decision proposal than the one adopted. When various units are exploring the problem and offering decision proposals to the management decision makers, an air of competition often arises. The perceived loser or losers in this competition may feel dissatisfaction.

In order to maintain satisfaction in the organization, units may be offered "side payments," e.g., offering commendation to all participating units or enhancing the position of dissatisfied units through organizational reform.[16] For example, if the marketing unit's proposal was adopted, the accounting unit may be given the "trusted responsibility" (i.e., side payment) of monitoring the change, and production may be promised a bonus for an exceptionally rapid changeover. The effectiveness of such side payments is tied to how well the management unit can communicate the need for organizationwide cooperation. If the side payment is perceived as a bribe or a gesture to placate the "losers," dissatisfaction will probably increase.

SUMMARY

No one model can explain decision making in all communication settings. The individual's decision making can most aptly be described in terms of a conflict-decision-dissonance model. The individual who must make a decision uses the interview to gain information in either the pre- or postdecision phase. Similarly, the interview is the tool for decision making when the individual is confronted with alternative elements.

In group decision making, the process is one of decision emergence reinforced by consensus and commitment of the group members. The many small decision proposals which modify one another in a nonlinear way shape the group's final decision. Each of the four decision-making phases is characterized by distinctive interaction patterns. The first phase—orientation—establishes the group's direction and permits basic proposals to be initiated. During the next, or conflict, phase, rigorous testing of all decision proposals occurs. The conflict dissipates during the emergence phase, and now the final decisions are set. Finally, reinforcement of the final decision occurs in the fourth phase, as members first consent and then become committed to the decisions.

In large, public communication settings, a technically expert answer often provides the basis for a decision. But the expertise must come from a highly credible source. Credibility depends on competence, which must be enhanced by the audience's perception of the speaker's good character and dynamic presentation.

Of the various types of decision-making models, the rational Dewey-type models are most appropriate for explaining organizational decision making. Because the organization is confronted with problems to solve, it sets its units to work in finding solutions. These solutions are tested against one another and the organizational goals, and then the "best" solution is selected. The solution is implemented, and at the same time side payments are made in order to maintain members' satisfaction.

PROBLEMS AND ISSUES

1. At the beginning of this chapter we stated our preference for description rather than prescription. Write an essay on whether students of communication should be taught through a descriptive or prescriptive ap-

proach. Alternatively, use one of the descriptions of a communication setting presented in this chapter and attempt to turn it into prescription (the two most challenging would be the interview and the group).

2. Several social psychologists have written criticisms of Festinger's dissonance theory. Read some of the criticisms, explain them, and decide whether they offer alternative ways of explaining individual decision making.

3. Several researchers of group processes have offered ways of labeling and explaining the phases of group decision making. Compare and contrast some of these views with the ones we presented. (Fisher's text is a good place to find some of these other classifications, as well as a list of other references.[17])

4. Listen to several public speakers and analyze their source credibility and the decision or decisions they want the listeners to accept.

5. If you work in an organization, attempt to observe a complete problem-solution cycle. How does it compare with and differ from our description of organizational decision making?

NOTES

1. John Dewey, *How We Think* (Boston: D. C. Heath, 1910), p. 72.

2. *Ibid.*, p. 78.

3. Orville G. Brim, Jr., David C. Glass, David E. Lavin, and Norman Goodman, *Personality and Decision Processes* (Stanford, Calif.: Stanford University Press, 1962), p. 9.

4. Leon Festinger, *Conflict, Decision, and Dissonance* (Stanford, Calif.: Stanford University Press, 1964), pp. 2–7.

5. *Ibid.*, pp. 152–158. Our discussion of each phase relies heavily on the basic ideas of Festinger's construct. However, Festinger has never related his model to symbolic interaction philosophy or to transactional analysis; in fact, he may disagree with parts of our discussion of the three phases. Also, for a critique and review of the cognitive dissonance model, *see* Chester A. Insko, *Theories of Attitude Change* (New York: Appleton-Century-Crofts, 1967), pp. 198–206, 281–284.

6. Festinger, *op. cit.*, p. 5.

7. B. Aubrey Fisher, *Small Group Decision Making* (New York: McGraw-Hill, 1974), pp. 125–153.

8. Larry L. Barker, *Communication Vibrations* (Englewood Cliffs, N.J.: Prentice-Hall, 1974), pp. 88–91.

9. Thomas M. Scheidel and Laura Crowell, "Idea Development in Small Discussion Groups," *Quarterly Journal of Speech* **50** (1964): 140–145.

10. Fisher, *op. cit.,* pp. 140–144; *see also* B. Audrey Fisher, "Decision Emergence: Phases in Group Decision Making," *Speech Monographs* **37** (1970): 53–66.

11. Fisher, *Small Group Decision Making, op. cit.,* p. 142.

12. Wallace Fotheringham, *Perspectives on Persuasion* (Boston: Allyn and Bacon, 1966), pp. 109–115.

13. James C. McCroskey, Carl E. Larson, and Mark L. Knapp, *An Introduction to Interpersonal Communication* (Englewood Cliffs, N.J.: Prentice-Hall, 1971), pp. 84–85.

14. *Ibid.,* p. 81.

15. Richard M. Cyert and Kenneth R. MacCrimmon, "Organizations," in *Handbook of Social Psychology,* Vol. I, 2d ed., ed. G. Lindzey and E. Aronson (Reading, Mass.: Addison-Wesley, 1968), p. 573.

16. *Ibid.*

17. Fisher, *Small Group Decision Making, op. cit.*

Part IV

How Organizations Use Communication

In Parts I and II we explored the concepts of communication and symbolic interaction; in Part III, the "relating" and "content" purposes of communication. Part IV enlarges our theoretical and philosophical perspective. Concepts such as self, role, and situation are of crucial importance to the organization. The multiple purposes of communication—facilitation, regulation, informing, and decision making—are instrumental in the survival of the organization. From our perspective, an organization is a system of interdependent interpersonal networks formulated, maintained, and altered through symbolic interaction.

Chapter 9 examines how organizations attempt to regulate behavior externally to ensure their continuity. This analysis is particularly important to understanding the process notion of communication. Focusing on the impact of self-image, situation, and communication cues, Chapter 10 describes a special purpose of organizational communication—evaluation of behavior. Chapter 11 applies communication principles to goal accommodation within the organization, with an emphasis on the processes of facilitation and regulation, and also explores the philosophy of negotiation and mutual gain. All three chapters are based on the assumption that you will be engaging in these organizational communication activities.

Chapter 9

Diffusion and Change

INTRODUCTION

This chapter will examine how organizations use communication to gain acceptance of their ideas. Important factors in organizational communication are the processes of diffusion and individual adoption, as well as the "connective tissue" provided by communication.

One of the goals of symbolic interaction is to explain how human groups operate and the pattern of activities that shape and form group life. Whereas in Chapter 1 we discussed the regulation of self and others, now we turn to how organizations attempt to regulate human behavior. People live not as isolated entities but in social units which attempt to shape behavior in ways to ensure the continuance of the social units or institutions. If churches, political parties, social clubs, and business organizations did not "sell" their ideas, recruit members, and market their products, they would not last, and people's livelihoods would fail along with the organizations. As social beings, humans are interdependent with institutions and their products, philosophies, and candidates. Our primary question in this chapter is: How do institutions disseminate their positions and garner support?

Before beginning to answer this question, we must state an assumption: Institutions, like individuals, are processing entities; therefore, they grow and are modified over time and thus always have something new to present or must seek populations which have not been exposed to their goals. For example, if you formed a company that produced a light bulb that would never burn out, your company would eventually have to either modify the light bulb so that it would have a limited lifespan or else find a new buying population. Institutions are perpetually involved with change or innovation and hence always have something new or different to present to their target populations. For example, the use of kerosene lamps is innovative in an electrical age; transcendental meditation and oriental religions seemed new and innovative to many people in the early 1970s.

THE DIFFUSION PROCESS

Institutions obtain change through *diffusion,* a process consisting of the innovation, communication, a social system, and time.[1] These four elements may be used to define the diffusion process as the communicating of an innovation to a social system over time.

Innovation The first requisite element for diffusion is quite obvious—innovation. An institution must have an innovation it can present. Without a recommended change, there is no need for the institution to enter the diffusion process.

Communication Communication is the principal means of linkage between an institution and the people it seeks to change. Communication during diffusion may take many different forms, ranging from use of mass media to personal forms of contact. (Specific forms of communication predominant in the several phases will be discussed later in this chapter.)

Social system The social system as an element of the diffusion process must be considered from two perspectives—the culture and the individual. Any innovation presented by an institution must be in keeping with the cultural norms of the social system. If the recommended change cannot be brought within the norms of the group, most likely, it will be rejected. For example, some years ago an effort was made to induce a Southwest Indian tribe to replace its strain of corn with a new, high-yield hybrid corn.[2] The first year, a small test plot of the hybrid variety planted next to the village produced three times the yield of the old corn. The following year almost everyone planted the new corn, but only after the harvest did the villagers discover that the corn was unsuitable for making tortillas, the tribe's food staple. Needless to say, the next year the villagers returned to growing corn that could be made into their dietary staple. In this instance, what at first appeared to be a beneficial innovation in fact violated the norms of the society by disrupting the people's diet, and therefore the change was rejected.

Just as cultural norms are important in the social system, so too are the individuals who comprise that social system. In articulating the assumptions of mass persuasion, Nimmo states that "certain tendencies are common to all members of this mass, but for the most part people respond in different ways at different times to different stimuli."[3] Although certain response tendencies are shaped by the culture and are therefore generalized, individual differences ensure unique definitions of any given situation.

For example, most Americans respond favorably to an appeal for "fair play," because fairness is a value in American culture. However, it is the individual, not the culture, who defines fair play. Consequently, some may say that all politics is dirty and that "playing fair" is being the equal of other political candidates. Since they make promises they cannot keep or discuss irrelevant issues, such actions are fair because all candidates do it. Indeed, this argument was used by many of President Nixon's defenders during the "Watergate affair." In fact, however, fair play and ethics were not the main issues that finally emerged; rather, the downfall of the Nixon administration was caused by discovery of the "smoking pistol"—proof of obstruction of justice in the cover-up.

Time Innovations are diffused over long periods of time. As many authors in the field of persuasion have noted, few changes are made by people on the basis of a "one-shot appeal."[4] If this were the case, people would switch brands of soap or coffee with the broadcast of each commercial. Instead, in diffusion the innovation is presented many times and in various contexts over time so that the target population can receive many messages demonstrating the use of the innovation in various circumstances. Also, diffusion is a lengthy process because most people need time to make decisions. Since people do not make decisions from a variety of data bases, the innovation must be diffused in several ways with different information. Finally, seldom can a single presentation be offered to everyone in the target population at the same time. Hence, we may define diffusion as the process of communicating change over time to a social system.

THE ADOPTION PROCESS

The goal of the diffusion of innovation is adoption, a particular type of personal decision making. The adoption process does not replace our explanation in Chapter 8 of the individual decision-making process; rather, it is a five-phase process pertaining to a decision made on a wholly new idea.[5]

Awareness An individual's first introduction to the innovation constitutes *awareness* that such an innovation exists and is being used by some people. Awareness occurs in a somewhat accidental fashion, because the person does not know that the idea or product exists and therefore cannot go looking for it. In the awareness phase, the person learns the name of the idea or product and has only a rudimentary knowledge of what it will do. Awareness serves as a catalyst for a person's initiation of the adoption process. The purpose of this function is to arouse the person's curiosity by introducing the label or name of the innovation in hopes that the individual will want to delve deeper into the process.

Mass media seem to be the most important types of awareness-generating communications. Through exposure to radio or television commercials, news items, and colorful magazine ads, people hear and may see the name of the innovation. The next most effective type of communication that fosters awareness is for the person to talk with friends who may serve as opinion leaders. The least influential type of communication occurs when the person communicates with salespersons or other advocates (change agents) who personally contact people about the innovation.[6] These sources of awareness-inducing information come primarily from outside the target population. That is, personal contact is not an important element of communication at the awareness stage.

Interest   After becoming aware that an innovation exists and is available, the person enters the *interest* phase of the adoption process, which is characterized by the seeking of semantic information (see Chapter 7). Now the person takes a more active interest in the innovation, asking questions about the nature of the idea or product, how it works, and what its potentials are. The person is interested in getting to know the name of the innovation as a real thing or entity.

Whereas the behavior of the person in the awareness stage is generally nonpurposive, in the interest stage it becomes purposive. In other words, people become aware of most innovations by accident, but thereafter act in specific ways to gain information about the new idea or product. For example, during our first winter in Utah we both heard of "waffle-stompers." We quickly understood that when our students talked about waffle-stompers, they were referring to a type of footgear. From this awareness, we began to find out just exactly what waffle-stompers are and what function they serve. (They are hiking boots with a variegated sole for traction in snow.)

Although we gained the information on a personal level, information in the interest phase generally comes from mass media dissemination, followed in importance by personal contact and change agents. Even though the sources have the same order of importance as occurs in the awareness phase, there are differences. First, the mass media used in the second phase are closer to the target population. For example, an individual who first hears of an innovation on a national television broadcast may gain information from local newspapers. This is what happened in the emergence of the environmental issue. Many people first heard of the environmentalist movement from national media, but generally people became interested when local ecological problems were reported in local media.

Another difference is that in the second stage, the person begins to seek out those people who can give information, and the personal communication begins to take the form of information-seeking interviews. Some conversations will be initiated for the specific purpose of discussing the innovation;

in the earlier phase, by contrast, the topic of the innovation might be "mentioned in passing."

Evaluation If the individual retains an attentiveness toward the innovation through the awareness and interest phases, he or she will enter the *evaluation* phase of adoption. During this period the person tries out the innovation in a sort of mental trial-and-error process. Now the person seeks pragmatic rather than semantic information, e.g., How useful is it? Can it benefit me?

The need for pragmatic information is probably attributable to the fact that the evaluation phase culminates in a decision to either try or forget about the innovation. To make such decisions, people want information that will help them determine how good the innovation will be for them. In the waffle-stomper example cited earlier, one of the authors decided that boots did not look good with suits and sport coats; the other decided that they fit his more casual style of dress and anything that might help on snowy sidewalks would be beneficial. Decisions made at the end of the evaluation phase are judgments of personal usefulness based on information about the innovation's value.

Personal forms of communication become more important than the mass media in the evaluation phase, apparently because a person seeking pragmatic information needs others who know him or her well enough to help in the judgmental process. People do not rely on mass media sources to tell them what is best for them as unique individuals. Such information comes from friends or possibly change agents communicating with clients.

Trial After deciding in favor of the innovation, the individual will try it for a period of time. Whereas the evaluation phase concludes with a mental judgment, the trial phase is a period of physical judgment. Usually a person will attempt to test the innovation on the smallest possible scale, but even if it must be used in total, the early use of the idea or product is a probationary period. If, for example, your first new car is a Chevrolet, you cannot be called a Chevy or GM person, because later you might find that GM does not make the product you want or that after driving your new car, you never want to buy another GM automobile.

During this phase personal sources of information are still the most important. Information of a reinforcement nature is sought, e.g., Am I doing it correctly? Does it work this way for you? Is this the right way? Reinforcement may also come from mass media. For example, most auto makers send colorful magazines to people who have purchased their cars. The magazines show the wonderful vacations people are taking in their new cars and extol the virtue of the customers' discriminating taste. Nonetheless, although mass media may be used at this stage of adoption, personal contact is the overwhelming reinforcer.

Adoption By the adoption, or final, phase, the person has entered into a wholehearted acceptance of the innovation. No longer is use of the idea or product tentative or on a small scale. The individual takes the innovation and puts it to the broadest possible use.

No longer does the person seek information and reinforcement. Instead, the person may become a source of information for others and thereby become an opinion leader for friends who have not yet adopted the innovation.

Adoption and Decision-Making Models

Adoption is a special type of individual decision making. One of the unique characteristics of adoption is that the innovation to be adopted is a totally new idea or concept that calls for a decision. Hence the adoption process is activated not by a conflict phase, but rather by awareness of a single innovation. This aspect of adoption may be considered as a phase prior to the individual decision process of conflict-decision-dissonance. In a general model of decision making, one usually starts the analysis with conflict, i.e., the point where the individual feels a need to make a decision. However, in adoption the novelty of one element to the individual demands a new starting point of analysis—awareness.

The interest and evaluation phases of adoption are related to the general model in that they represent the conflict phase, with decision coming at the end of evaluation. Moreover, one must understand these phases as components in the diffusion of information in order to understand differences in the sources of information; the general model, by contrast, seeks only to demonstrate that conflict requires information seeking, with no regard to the sources of the information. In both adoption and the general model, the actual decision occupies little space along the time dimension. The decision act is of short duration; the pre- and postdecision phases are lengthy.

The trial phase is equivalent to the dissonance phase of the general model; however, whereas "trial" suggests the tentativeness of adoption (decision) and the sources of information, "dissonance" implies the use of information in a subjective manner. Adoption occurs *after* dissonance, the last stage in the general model. Adoption demonstrates how a person who has made a full commitment to a decision may now become a disseminator of information to others going through earlier phases of the adoption process.

During the awareness, interest, or evaluation phases the innovation may be rejected; during the trial phase it may be discontinued. In short, the adoption process can be stopped at any point. Simply because a person is made aware of an innovation does not mean that she or he must go through all five phases. The challenge to the organization seeking to diffuse an innovation is to find ways to help individuals move through the five-phase process to adoption.

Diffusion and Adoption

In relating diffusion to the adoption process, one can begin to realize that a single message would seldom lead to a person's adopting an innovation. Rather, a well-coordinated campaign employing a mixture of interpersonal and mass media forms of communication is called for. Information in an adoption campaign must be diffused by means of sources appropriate to the various phases.

Awareness and mass media An ideal organizational campaign to adopt an innovation would begin with short name-identification messages presented in a far-reaching mass media channel, e.g., brief television commercials showing the innovation and attracting attention to the product's name. At this point the messages are geared toward making people take notice (become aware) of the innovation.

Interest and mass media As people begin to realize that the innovation exists and is available, a variety of mass media should be used to offer detailed information about the innovation. Newspapers could carry advertisements highlighting the innovation's features. Public affairs radio and television programs could be used to feature institutional representatives talking about the innovation.

This phase of the campaign should be aimed at the interest phase of adoption—giving people information about what the innovation can do and how it works. This type of approach was used in 1975, when most car makers came out with a small-sized sedan. Shortly before sales of its new Granada began, for example, Ford followed up by full-page magazine and newspaper ads describing the features of the Granada.

Evaluation and personal contact The next phase of diffusion would be to have the communication campaign offer personal contact, which helps diffuse pragmatic information. This could be accomplished in two ways. First, the multistep flow of communication would aid the campaign. Second, perhaps the company could send trained representatives to personally contact people in order to extol the virtues of the innovation.

The multistep flow occurs as people take the information from mass media sources and begin to tell others. In effect, people in the target population become an "extra sales" force for the organization; they take the messages presented in the second stage of the campaign and begin to talk to others, reshaping the semantic information to pragmatic information. Similarly, trained representatives of the organization serve the same function; they help people take semantic information and turn it into information showing how the innovation will be beneficial to the adopter.

To continue with our Ford Granada example, the sales staff is given information on how to relate the auto's features to a client's needs. Moreover, the salespeople do not simply wait for people to walk into the showroom, but instead telephone former customers and invite them in to see the Granada. Not only the salespeople, but also other people begin to take the information about the car and discuss it among themselves.

Trial and communication During the trial stage the content of communication turns from a presentation of information for a decision to reinforcement of a decision already made. Personal contact is very important now. It immediately brings to light any problems that specific individuals are having while trying the innovation. When the problems are noticed, the organizational representatives can correct them or offer the person a new focus on the innovation. In our Ford Granada example, the salespeople might be encouraged to watch for past customers in the service area and to talk with them and help solve their problems. Moreover, the service department people are trained to be pleasant and helpful while indicating that any problems are relatively minor and easily solved.

Mass media may be used to supplement the personal contact. Special magazines printed for the adopters of an innovation may be distributed. Many of the short television commercials used earlier may be used as reinforcers. Similarly, about four months after the Ford Granada promotion started, the theme of many of the commercials changed from an emphasis on an affordable American type of Mercedes-Benz to one of the Granada's outselling all other competitive models combined. This shift in emphasis became a bandwagon reinforcement message, which said to many Granada owners: "Your decision was right because many people agree with you."

Limitations of an idealized campaign Earlier we stated that a complete campaign based on the adoption process to diffuse information is idealized, because most organizations experience limitations in the use of media.

Resources. A primary limitation in campaigns of diffusion is the amount of organizational resources available. Huge expenditures of time and money are required to conduct a national media campaign. However, even unlimited resources are interdependent with the innovation. If the innovation is relatively small and must be adopted by many people, resources may have to be used creatively. For example, it would be unrealistic to develop a personal salesforce to sell coffee by the pound on a door-to-door basis. Therefore, a coffee maker, realizing the value of personal contact in the evaluation stage, might create for its ads a surrogate neighbor who discusses the pragmatic information about the product—it tastes better than other brands, will save marriages, turn the users into hits at PTA, and please mothers-in-law. None of these ideas explains what coffee is (which would relate to the interest stage); rather, they offer statements of use and value which belong in the personal-contact aspect of the evaluation stage.

If one begins to analyze commercials that use testimonials by famous people, you will note that the information is of a pragmatic nature. Such messages attempt to have a "substitute friend" talk to you the consumer in an evaluation phase of the adoption process. However, such surrogate personal contact is best suited to television, the only medium that combines visual and language elements to make a "living" situation.

Legal restrictions. Many organizations are restricted in the types of campaigns they can conduct. For example, it is illegal to transmit certain messages over certain media. In many states it is illegal to give information about birth control or to advertise contraceptive devices on radio or television. Thus Planned Parenthood may have difficulty in many communities in diffusing its information.

Since people rely so heavily on mass media in the awareness and interest phases, any type of restriction on their use raises the problem of how to start the flow of information without using mass media. The answers all involve greater amounts of time spent and fewer people contacted. Planned Parenthood in such a community, for example, could develop a speakers' bureau and contact civic organizations, teachers' groups, and women's service clubs.

Message interpretation. Another limitation is the sender's inability to hold interpretation of the message constant in the multistep flow during the evaluation phase. As discussed in Chapter 7, information becomes leveled, sharpened, and assimilated in the multistep flow of information diffusion.

We recently observed the distortion of messages in two recent adoption campaigns in Utah. The first involved an effort by the legislature to pass a uniform statewide land-use act. A group of citizens was successful in getting the act placed on the general election ballot. Some people campaigned against the act on the grounds that passage would lead to state determination of the colors people could use on their houses. Similarly, opponents of the Equal Rights Amendment argued that its ratification would result in the elimination of separate public bathrooms for men and women and the drafting of women into the army. Such claims were substantiated only in that they were passed along among people. Both examples are based on resistance to change, the topic of the last section of this chapter.

ADOPTERS

So far we have discussed the institutional diffusion in the general way that a person processes the information leading to the adoption. However, people adopt at different times during the diffusion process. Although all people proceed through the adoption process, they do so at different times because of the types of information they use and their sociological position in the target population.

Categories

Through the research of Rogers and others, five distinct categories of adopter types have been recognized and documented: innovators, early adopters, early majority, late majority, and laggards.[7]

Researchers generally find a normal distribution of adopters' categories in a population. Innovators comprise about 2.5 percent of the population; early adopters approximately 13.5 percent; early majority and late majority 34 percent each; and 16 percent laggards. Note that the first two categories combined are the percentage equivalent of the laggards category at the other end of the distribution. Since most studies in the diffusion of innovation focus more on adoptions than on explaining the people who adopt late, if at all, in a campaign, more is known about the earlier adoption categories and how people can be differentiated here.

Innovators People who adopt first may be characterized as highly venturesome or high risk takers. Their risk-taking orientation comes from having adequate resources with which to gamble on an innovation. These people tend to be younger and better educated than the general population. By virtue of their resources, education, and venturesome attitude, the innovators have high social status, but since most community members regard that status as unapproachable, the innovators are somewhat isolated from the rest of the population.

Innovators maintain many contacts outside the community and spend as much time communicating with members of other communities as with members of their own community. Their influence as opinion leaders is usually on other innovators and some early adopters. Their use of mass media is of a highly technical and specialized nature; their greatest reliance for information is on impersonal sources.

Early adopters The respected leaders of the community, early adopters hold the elective and appointive positions of leadership in the organizations of the community. Although not as wealthy in resources, as young, and as educated as the innovators, people in this second category are nonetheless much above the average. They are viewed as more temperate than the innovators by the members of the community. Their respected positions of leadership and moderation in approaching change make them the most important opinion leaders in the community. They have a great deal of interpersonal contact and are often sought-after communicators. Their use of mass media is fairly technical and specialized, but less so than that of the innovators.

Early majority This large segment of the population comprises the belongers to the organizations led by the early adopters. Although generally favorable to change, members of the early majority are deliberate because they do not have the resources. These people are a shade above average in wealth, education, and age. They use the mass media in a general way and recognize its information value, but their sources are informative rather than technical. They put as much weight on what people tell them personally as on what they obtain from their media sources. Their principal arena of influence is as opinion leaders for some members of the late majority.

Late majority Although very much members of the community, people in this category are not leaders or belongers, but rather followers. They tend to be skeptical of change and adopt only after it can be shown that the innovation works for a majority of the people. Only when a new idea or product is seen as necessary will members of the late majority adopt. Their low status and limited resources and education make them wary of all change and suspicious that many innovations are for innovation's sake.

Their main sources of information leading to change are peer pressure and personal contact. Since these people regard the mass media primarily as sources of entertainment, they find relatively little information value in the media. The sphere of influence of the late majority is generally to other members of that category.

Laggards This group of people is highly tradition-bound and oriented to the past. Like the innovators, laggards are somewhat isolated from the community, mainly because they believe that the community adopts and changes too quickly and that tried and true practices have been discarded. Ultraconservative in their approach to change, laggards adopt an innovation only after it is no longer regarded as such by most other members of the community. Laggards' principal sources of information are close friends and relatives who share their values.

Although there are no direct data, we suspect that a small percentage of the laggards should be classified as nonadopters. Certain people may live their entire lives without accepting an innovation. Some religious sects are even dedicated to preserving a centuries-old way of life and resisting all change.

The laggard and late majority categories are often viewed in deprecatory fashion by those interested in change; however, the members of these categories may serve a vital function in society by braking the rapid acceleration of change. The role of slowing down the rate of adoption probably ensures the continuance of the social order.

Category shifting A note of caution: We are describing adopter *categories,* not people. A particular person may be in different categories for different innovations. This shift in categories can be explained in terms of the community or target population. Although we have used these interchangeably in this chapter, we prefer "target population." A target population is a collection of people with shared cultural and social norms who are the object of given diffusion strategies. Consequently, all people belong to a variety of target populations; a person may be an innovator in one and a member of the early majority in another. However, since people do have general response tendencies, an innovator in one situation would be unlikely to be a laggard in another. In fact, we may posit that people will usually not vary over more than three categories.[8]

Time and Adoption

Just as people adopt innovations at various times in a target population, so too the rate of adoption is uneven. As Fig. 9.1 shows, the cumulative adoption over time is shaped like an "s" curve. Adoption among innovators is slow to occur because few of them become aware of the proposed change simultaneously. For early adopters the rate of adoption increases as more people become aware and start to react. The rate of adoption is quickest during the time of acceptance by the early and late majorities. Many people are communicating with one another, and the mass media "blitz" the information during this time. In the laggard category the rate of adoption slows down as the thrust of the diffusion of change concludes. It may be assumed that few if any innovations ever reach 100 percent adoption.

Diffusion and the Adopter Categories

Earlier we presented a campaign model for diffusion that was based on the adoption process of the individual. Having described adopter categories, we may now extend that idealized campaign for the diffusion of change. First,

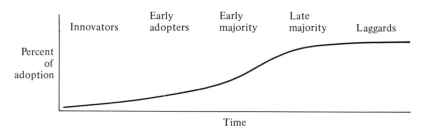

Fig. 9.1 The rate of adoption.

however, we point out that the campaign model discussed earlier is most reflective of the early majority category, because this category comprises the largest segment of possible, reachable adopters and displays the general norms of the target population.

Innovators and the campaign Innovators rely so heavily on technical, impersonal sources of information that they omit the awareness phase via mass media. Rather, since they become aware before the general population does, an organization may seek to identify the innovators before beginning the general campaign, giving them the advanced research or reports of the innovation. This material, which serves to arouse the innovators' awareness, also provides enough information for the interest phase of adoption. In the evaluation phase the innovators can use the technical information and interpret the pragmatic application with minimal assistance from an organization's representatives. Instead, they most need personal assistance as the trial phase begins, when they put the idea or product into practice for a "trial run."

An innovator's actual adoption is based on personal reflection about the utility of the change. The sources of information for the innovator, who generally adopts before the diffusion campaign even begins for the target population, are technical data and personal contact with the organization. For example, the first Ford Granadas were sold on the initial day of showing, but orders for these cars had been placed earlier. The innovators received their information from special magazines that previewed the Granada, and these early buyers were probably treated to an "early look" at the car on the dealers' back lots.

As innovators enter the trial and adoption phases, an organization begins its more general campaign, giving special attention to the early adopters, whose awareness was gained through both mass media dissemination and personal contact with the innovators. The mass media employed at the start of the campaign are specialized sources rather than technical or popular media. For example, suppose that a new method of financial investment has been proposed in the stock market. The innovators, using technical sources, would read market analyses of the proposal. The early adopters, using specialized sources, would read articles about the proposal in the *Wall Street Journal* and *Forbes* financial magazine. Members of the early majority would see advertisements and read articles in the business and economy sections of *Time* and *Newsweek*. Members of the late majority might rely on a more popular source, such as *Reader's Digest*. Of course, each of these sources would carry the information at different times—a story might appear months or even years earlier in *Forbes* than in *Reader's Digest*.

Early adopters and the campaign As the early adopters become aware of the proposed change and enter the interest phase, they seek more information in the specialized media sources in order to gain a better understanding of the innovation. In the evaluation phase they still rely on media and impersonal contacts, but their main communication focus shifts to personal contact with the innovators and institutional representatives. Early adopters seek help in explaining how the innovation will be useful and need to see that it has worked for a few other people. During the interest and evaluation phases, the early adopters need substantially more information than innovators do. The early adopters, though often predisposed to change, must assure themselves that the innovation is practical and will not fail, which would harm their respected leadership positions.

Early majority and the campaign With the onset of the trial and adoption phases in the early adopters, the organization begins the full popular media campaign for the early majority. Such coordination is necessary in diffusion because as the early majority becomes aware of the innovation, the early adopters have to be prepared for their opinion-leadership role.

Those in the early majority seek a balance between impersonal and personal communication during the awareness, interest, and evaluation phases. The impersonal sources are the popular forms of mass media—television, radio, local newspapers, and general-interest magazines; the personal communication, contact with the early adopters, who now become the important opinion leaders for this large percentage of the population. Contact with organizational representatives is sought only to the degree that people in the early majority need them to actually make the decision and obtain the innovation.

During trial and adoption, members of the early majority rely most heavily on peers and early adopters for reinforcement about the correctness of their decision. Even in campaigns based initially on surrogate personal contact, the trial and adoption phases require personal reinforcement communication.

Late majority and the campaign Only the most popular mass media are useful in stimulating awareness and interest among the late majority. Even though the media may stimulate these phases, members of the late majority will be skeptical about a possible media "hustle" and consequently will turn quickly to see how the innovation is working for others. People in this category develop a "show me" attitude and must find that the change works well for many people—mainly those in the early majority and others in the late majority who are going through the adoption phase. People in the late majority want as little contact as possible with the representatives of the organization advocating change; consequently, they seek out the representative only when necessary and resist most contact initiated by the representatives of an institution.

Laggards' place in diffusion The people in this category are generally so late in adopting an innovation that the force of the campaign has ended before they even begin the adoption process. Therefore, diffusion among laggards goes on without organizational support. (It should be noted, however, that an organization may offer messages for the purpose of continuing support for a product.) The diffusion occurs principally by "word of mouth." Most organizations do not attempt to invest time or money in this last 16 percent of the population. Organizations operate under the law of diminishing returns and realize that the cost of innovation overrides the gains to be made in the laggards' adoption.

Laggards adopt an innovation when most other people in the general population no longer consider the idea or product innovative. Many laggards may be forced to adopt simply because the old way is no longer feasible or practical. The last people in our society to switch from iceboxes to refrigerators, for example, probably did so because ice was no longer delivered door to door or new iceboxes were no longer being produced. Thus adoption by the laggard may be viewed as an attempt to catch up to the status quo. For these reasons the primary communication contacts of laggards are other people; the media have already moved on to other campaigns of diffusion.

Diffusion and the Change Agent

The change agent, or organizational representative, is the professional who seeks to influence members of the target population to adopt the organization's innovation. Thus the change agent is the personal communication link between the organization and the general population and as such is in an unusual position. Change agents typically are members of the target population, yet earn their living by attempting to regulate the behavior of other members of that population. The change agent's position, then, is located midway between the target population and the organization. For although the agents may subscribe to some values of the community, they also hold some values of an organization trying to change the community.

Link to the institution Change agents must recognize their interdependence with other elements of the organization.[9] Organizational diffusion of innovation requires the coordination of all parts of the organization; production, research, and marketing are related in that each succeeds only because the others also succeed. Several years ago the Alpo pet food company created an attractive, well-designed national media campaign. The advertisement was so successful that the demand for Alpo outstripped the company's production supply, and the company had to offer a public apology on television about its inability to deliver the product.

Such an incident can be viewed as an unawareness of the interdependence of all elements of the company. A change agent who has influenced the decision of a client and then cannot deliver the innovation is in danger of creating poor public relations and a lack of confidence in the organization. The change agent must therefore see his or her role in relation to the organization's coordinated efforts of diffusion.

Link to the population The change agent is especially important as a communicator to the early-adopter category, and the skillful agent will develop ways of identifying the members of this category.[10] Given what is known about early adopters, the change agent will look for the leaders in the target population. Another method is to check mailing lists of specialized publications in the general field of the proposed information. The change agent may also talk to people in the target population and ask them to identify the opinion leaders. All of these devices help the change agent pinpoint who should receive the major amount of the agent's communicative effort.

The change agent serves the client best in the evaluation and trial stages of adoption, presenting information and demonstrating its utility.[11] Moreover, the change agent is not simply a salesperson, but also helps to service and maintain the innovation for the adopter. It should be noted here that the responsible change agent does not try to gain adoption for adoption's sake, but rather helps the client evaluate the innovation for personal utility. In this vein the change agent should understand the consequence of change and help the adopter adjust, because any change an adopter accepts will have consequences on other behaviors of the adopter.

The role of the change agent is both difficult and multifaceted. Agents must serve both organization and adopter with integrity. They must realize who relies on their information most and at what phases of the adoption process they have influence. Also, change agents need to see their role as an interdependent element in organization's coordinated diffusion process.

Resistance to Change

It would be easy to say that resistance to change is located in the categories of late adopters and laggards. It is true that change is often resisted simply out of skepticism and a preference for tradition; however, such explanations are not complete. Some innovations may die out before a major portion of the population has had a chance to adopt. Other innovations are law, and yet still are resisted.

Risk One reason for resisting change may be the perceived risk the innovation entails. If an innovation is seen as producing a great deal of risk, people may resist the change. Much of the resistance to ratification of the Equal Rights Amendment has been generated by the unknown (risky) consequences of the amendment. Some people, for example, are afraid that women would be drafted into the army in case of a military emergency. These people consider this too great a risk to support such measures of equality.

Change may be resisted because other avenues of behavior are available. Many people argued against the ERA amendment on the grounds that specific pieces of legislation could accomplish the same ends and yet be clearer and more manageable. Specifically, these people called for legislation on given issues of sex discrimination, such as credit, alimony laws, land sales, and equal pay for equal work.

Motivation Lack of motivation may lead to a resistance of innovation. People may not see that a need exists or that anything is being threatened so as to demand a change. In the ERA debates many women argued that they had never been discriminated against and saw no reason for the controversy. Some even asserted that they felt privileged to be on the pedestals men had placed them on.

Competing needs In these days of energy shortage, many people would like to reduce their fuel consumption. However, they also argue that they have to drive their own cars to work because of their erratic work schedules. Or, parents may want to keep their home warmer than recommended because a young baby or ill older person also lives in the house.

Other factors Opposing campaigns may occur concurrently, necessarily leading to people's resisting one or the other. For example, a person cannot accept in equal measure the appeals of the American Cancer Society and other health organizations to stop smoking while believing the cigarette companies' advertisements to find springtime freshness in smoking.

Resistance to change may also result from a lack of confidence in the change agent's credibility. If one believes that all used car salespersons are crooks, for example, one will not buy a used car.

Some innovations fail because they are intrinsically bad. Both the Edsel and the Corvair were thought to be poor products by many automotive engineers. The hypothesis that fluorocarbons destroy the earth's ozone layer led many people to stop using aerosol sprays in 1975.

Any adopter may find ways to resist or delay an innovation. Moreover, these avenues of resistance are not independent of one another. For example, the perception of risk may be tied to one's holding of a traditional value. Or, several of the means may be used by one individual. In other words, simply because an organization conducts a well-coordinated campaign to diffuse change is no guarantee that the innovation will be adopted.

SUMMARY

Organizations introduce change in a planned, coordinated effort that leads to adoption of an innovation. The adoption process is a five-phase special form of decision making consisting of awareness, interest, evaluation, trial, and adoption. Understanding the adoption process leads to managing the diffusion of information about the innovation. Different sources of information become important during the various phases of adoption.

Although the adoption process represents the individual's method of deciding on change, people may also be grouped according to how they use information, sociological factors, and when they accept change. The categories of adopters are: innovators, early adopters, early majority, late majority, and laggards. Because these categories vary in the types of media they use and the persons they look to as opinion leaders, the general diffusion campaign must employ various media and people at different stages.

The rate of adoption in the campaign starts slowly, gains momentum, and slows again in the laggards category. The change agent is the organizational representative who serves as the communication link between the target population and the organization. Although some resistance to change is generated in the late majority and laggards categories, anyone may resist change in a variety of ways for motivational, personal, or behavioral reasons. Finally, there is no certainty that each innovation campaign will be successful in having change adopted.

PROBLEMS AND ISSUES

1. Examine statements in a current community campaign aimed at encouraging people not to adopt the change. Into what categories for resisting change do the statements fall? What other categories do you need for grouping all of the statements?

2. Identify some change agents in your community. Interview them to discover what values they hold, how they see their role, and what responsibilities for change they have.

3. In a single innovation or product, find media sources of technical, specialized, and popular natures. How does the information differ in each source? How would you relate particular messages to both the categories of adopters and the adoption process?

4. Construct a position paper with examples that demonstrate the effectiveness of a single persuasive message.

NOTES

1. Everett M. Rogers, *Diffusion of Innovations* (New York: Free Press, 1962), pp. 13–20. Much of this chapter is based on Rogers's work, and where possible, we have directly noted his influence.

2. Anacleto Apodaca, "Corn and Custom: Introduction of Hybrid Corn to Spanish American Farmers in New Mexico," in *Human Problems in Technological Change,* ed. Edward H. Spicer (New York: Russell Sage Foundation, 1952), pp. 35–39.

3. Dan Nimmo, *The Political Persuaders* (Englewood Cliffs, N.J.: Prentice-Hall/Spectrum, 1970), p. 31.

4. Charles U. Larson, *Persuasion: Reception and Responsibility* (Belmont, Calif.: Wadsworth, 1973), p. 162.

5. For further description and documentation of adoption, *see* Rogers, *op. cit.,* pp. 81–86.

6. The types of communication at each stage are drawn from the works of George M. Beal and Joe M. Bohlen, *The Diffusion Process,* Special Report No. 18 (Ames, Iowa: Cooperative Extension Service, 1962) and Rogers, *op. cit.,* pp. 98–105.

7. Rogers, *op. cit.,* pp. 148–192.

8. *Ibid.,* pp. 189–191.

9. Wallace C. Fotheringham, *Perspectives on Persuasion* (Boston: Allyn and Bacon, 1966), pp. 233–235.

10. Rogers, *op. cit.,* p. 257.

11. *Ibid.,* p. 263.

Chapter 10

Evaluation of Behavior

INTRODUCTION

A person acquires and sustains his or her self-image through the symbol process, and the negative and positive values attached to those symbols are critical to one's world view and view of self. All of us must make discriminations and judgments about others, and all of us are judged by others in one way or another. Evaluation is an emotionally charged process, and the way in which it is done has considerable import to those involved. The nature of the communication in the evaluative process can ensure better performance and can also sustain values that are humane and equitable.

Communication for evaluation is an internal organizational process Everyone—whether teacher, supervisor, or businessperson—is involved in this process. In this chapter we are concerned not with the judgmental decision-making aspect of evaluation, but rather with the role of communication in reducing the problems inherent in evaluation, e.g., feeling uncomfortable about being judged until after one has been judged favorably, and the implication of superiority engendered in the evaluator's role.

It is appealing on face value to think about eliminating evaluation altogether. One way to do this, of course, is to judge everyone favorably. For example, a teacher may give high grades to everyone and create a great deal of temporary happiness. However, this approach also creates anxiety in the students, because it fails to discriminate among them and discriminates against the high performers. Moreover, since an employer seeks quality, potential, and wants to know who might best fulfill these expectations, it seems shortsighted to send students from a nondiscriminating situation into a society that does discriminate and foster competition and the production of quality. Individuals need to have an honest grasp of their strengths and weaknesses on various competencies.

Much of today's literature about interpersonal communication has been influenced by various approaches to mental therapy. Such literature provides insights into the kinds of communication that facilitate human understanding and principles that can be applied to various settings. However, one cannot generalize from the therapeutic setting to all others. A therapist is likely to withhold evaluation and watch for self-growth in the client. In the organizational setting both organizational and individual needs must be met, and the organization cannot afford to focus exclusively on the individual.

Earlier we talked about "nonevaluative listening" and its part in facilitating interpersonal relationships. Those principles are still operative in the organizational setting. Although evaluation may be inevitable, the way in which it is done, the time at which it occurs, and what is evaluated are critical to both individual and organization.

PURPOSES OF EVALUATION

Organizations sustain themselves by providing their membership with knowledge of role expectations and subsequent evaluation of role execution. It is important to remember that this evaluation takes place between individuals within the larger organizational framework. Thus the individual tends to view the organization in terms of the behavior of the person doing the evaluating. In other words, an evaluator may be the most personalized contact an individual has with the organizational hierarchy. It is therefore crucial for evaluators to possess both knowledge and attitudes that allow them to recognize the purposes and functions of evaluation.

Underlying Assumptions

One's concept of humans determines what purposes are perceived in the evaluation process and thereby the kind of communication directed toward individuals. If one conceives of humans as being motivated primarily by external factors, the communication will emphasize one-way messages, material rewards, and stringent role behaviors that focus on the organization's operational needs. For example, managers who think this way are unlikely to make an effort to find out what really makes their people "tick." Communication from these managers would be limited to telling subordinates what they must do for a particular reward or what to do to avoid punishment. Consequently, knowledge of personal aspirations, which could be constructive, is lacking.

If one believes that the qualities inherent in human nature are detrimental to the goals of an organization, the communication to motivate will emphasize manipulation and correction. Evaluation may even be used as a threat, on the assumption that individuals do not really see any intrinsic value in their work, but instead seek only economic rewards and the avoidance of punishment. For example, a teacher may use the threat of a low grade to get students to achieve and meet a particular standard. This may work in the short term, but it can also detract substantially from long-range goals. In other words, it is important for students to not only learn, but also have a positive feeling about the learning experience. Most situations demand continual learning and self-learning. The threat situation is not conducive to self-development.

If one views humans as being motivated by internalized symbols, one uses "interactional" communication and evaluation focused on self-development. Here evaluation involves the determination of what has meaning for the individual and how she or he can best achieve. Evaluation is not a "cut and dried" matter of observing and then rating some behavior. Instead, the evaluator is as much coach as judge. If a person is viewed as having potential qualities that will meet both individualistic and organizational needs, the evaluator's communication will be directed toward inner motivation to make those two types of needs consonant.

Any single explanation of human behavior is likely to be insufficient, and single views tend to obscure the multiple purposes of evaluation. Evaluators must be aware of their beliefs about human nature and how they might affect their role in the evaluation process. After some studies on teacher evaluation, for example, Wrightsman concluded that evaluations are affected by the evaluator's beliefs about human nature and the extent of differences in human nature.[1]

Most students of human behavior would agree that humans are complex individualities rather than predictable, controllable machines. This complexity is revealed in the symbol process and what the symbols mean to each individual. An evaluator who believes in developing human resources must understand the symboling process revealed through communication.

Meeting Operational Needs

Evaluative behavior serves the operational needs of the organization by providing feedback to each unit so as to link quality of performance with desired outcomes. For example, if the goal of a university is to produce a highly educated and competent individual, one should evaluate those responsible for that outcome—faculty, departments, colleges, administration, and students. The same process holds true for business enterprises. It is necessary to know how well both individuals and groups are carrying out the operations of the organization. This type of evaluation ensures the continuance of the organization and also provides information for future decision making.

Motivation

Evaluative behavior is utilized to motivate individuals to greater effort. The very term "evaluation" implies that some sort of standard exists. Part of meeting a standard, or established level of excellence, is to know what it is and what the organization's expectations are in relation to that standard. Of course, individuals differ in their reactions to evaluation, and simply knowing about the expectations will not necessarily motivate a person toward a particular goal. However, for those who are achievement-oriented, evaluation can clearly serve as a motivator.

Self-Development

Evaluative behavior is also designed for personal self-development. We start from the assumption that each individual has growth potential—the capability and desire to improve one's competencies. Therefore, an evaluation program should be geared toward the development of human resources. Evaluation should allow individuals to engage in self-examination and appraisal. It is a wasteful practice to look on evaluation as a means of discarding those persons who do not meet needs immediately. Evaluation can enable individuals to develop so that organizational needs can be met.

Validation of Self and Role

Appraisal is necessary for the validation of self and role. In Chapter 4 we noted the close association between certain qualities and roles and said that individuals differ in their self-perceptions of how well they match these qualities. A person may use evaluation to relieve the uncertainty and anxiety stemming from the effort to match self and role. Self is a process molded by communication, and evaluation is a significant factor in the communication that occurs in the social setting. Evaluation, then, is social confirmation of the individual and his or her role.

FACTORS AFFECTING EVALUATION

If the purposes of evaluation are to be achieved, the evaluator must be knowledgeable about what might affect its outcome. Although evaluation can produce anxiety, there is a substantial body of commonsense and empirical data to indicate that knowledge of performance is desirable. According to Leavitt and Mueller, for example, feedback increases accuracy of performance, confidence between participants, and a feeling of amity.[2] In addition, Stolz and Tannenbaum have found that individuals prefer situations of negative feedback to no feedback at all.[3] Even negative feedback acknowledges one's existence and is a form of social confirmation. But it is *how* the evaluation is interpreted that is critical to the outcomes. In addition to the personality structures of the individuals involved, the context, content, and nature of communication have considerable influence on reactions to evaluation.

Impact of Self-Image

The evaluator who desires change must take into account both his or her own self-image and that of the other. A person who does not think well of self is unlikely to think well of others; by contrast, one who sees self as in process and in continual change is more likely to see others as capable of change and growth.

An evaluator with a strong self-image is less likely to project personal shortcomings onto others. Bruner and Tagiuri maintain that many of the cues used in judging another person are cues that the perceiver is instrumental in producing.[4] Why do people tend to see their own shortcomings in others? Perhaps concern about adjusting to a particular role limits the range of qualities a person focuses on. The self-image of a respondent is important in a similar way. The messages one initiates are influenced by self-image, as is one's interpretation of those messages.

This raises a very real problem in giving any kind of advice about the best kind of communication to use in the evaluative setting. Some behaviorists use a variation of hedonistic philosophy, maintaining that people work for pleasure and to avoid pain. According to this theory, praise operates as a positive reinforcer of desired behavior; criticism, as an inhibitor of undesired behavior. However, human complexity confounds this kind of simplicity; "pleasurable" and "painful" do not have the same meanings for all individuals.

McDavid and Schroeder compared the interpretation of approval and disapproval by delinquent and nondelinquent adolescents and found a tendency for delinquents to interpret praise as criticism and criticism as praise.[5] Perhaps the self-image of the delinquents did not allow them to accept praise; praise might have left them with guilt feelings. In addition, an individual with a poor self-image might be suspicious of anyone who judged him or her favorably. If these findings are applied to the work setting, it is important to gain as much knowledge as possible about the individuals being evaluated.

Communication Behavior

The amount and type of information obtained from those being evaluated depend in part on the behavior of the evaluator. Facilitative communication must be a continual process; it cannot start at the time of evaluation. The evaluator must be capable of communicating trust and positive regard toward others from the outset. A climate which allows for open communication must be established. An evaluator who does not engage in self-disclosure cannot expect a subordinate to do so. Again, evaluation is not just a matter of looking at someone's ability and then making a judgment. Rather, an individual's abilities must be released and developed, and this is one of the major functions of evaluation.

In the evaluation process the ability to delay judgment is as important as the final evaluation itself. More reliable information can be gathered, and the attitude it communicates to subordinates produces an atmosphere of trust in which individuals are given ample opportunity to adjust to expectations.

Perceived Performance and Credibility of the Evaluator

Reactions toward both the source and content of criticism depend on several interrelated factors. For example, Deutsch and Solomon found that individuals receiving negative evaluations of their work regarded the source of the criticism favorably if they thought poorly of their own performance and unfavorably if they thought well of it.[6] Since it is necessary for the evaluator to have credibility and gain the confidence of his or her workers, much of the evaluative communication should be directed at listening and determining how others view the quality of their own work. Because much of any appraisal involves subjective judgment, agreement about work standards needs to be reached in advance of evaluation.

The reaction to evaluation will have more impact if the evaluator is perceived as competent to hold the role of evaluator. Expertise and experience would certainly be among the competencies associated with the role of evaluator. However, one does not always take these qualities of a role into the evaluation setting. Suppose, for example, that a supervisor with expertise has the task of evaluating others who have far more experience. The supervisor in this case must be willing to communicate an attitude that says, "I am willing to learn from the experience of others, but I will also carry out my responsibilities on the basis of the knowledge I have and can obtain."

Perceived Roles and Social Context

Social context and role have a decided effect on how praise and criticism are interpreted. According to Deutsch:

> Evaluations made by a superordinate to a subordinate are interpreted most favorably, evaluations by a peer next most favorable, evaluations by a subordinate least favorably. The immediate emotional impact of evaluations by superordinates is expected to be greater than those made by subordinates. The "holding of tongue" in response to intense criticism is expected to be greatest by subordinates and least by superordinates.[7]

The role expectations, then, should guide communication behavior in several ways. A subordinate expects to be evaluated and is sensitive to what a superior has to say. A supervisor is perceived to have the right to make evaluations. Because of the roles involved, participants need to be aware of the impact one may have on the other's behavior. Even a facetious comment about another's work or person can have a damaging effect if it is not in the context of a unique relationship.

Direct communication must be established so that individuals do not think of a supervisor or manager as only an evaluator. The meanings attached to a supervisor's remarks are quite different from those attached to the same remarks made by a peer. Similarly, a teacher's casual remark about the general quality of a class may have much more impact than intended. The role expectations involved in the evaluative setting may inhibit free and open communication because the "holding of tongue" is part of normative behavior. This barrier must be broken if all relevant information is to be discovered in the evaluative process.

In his study of the interpretation of praise and criticism, Deutsch noted:

> Evaluative acts are interpreted most favorable within the family, somewhat less favorably in school and work, and least favorably within the military context. The effects of status differences upon the interpretation of an evaluative act are seen to be most marked within the military and least marked within the family.[8]

These differences in reaction to evaluation may be due to what is perceived in a particular context. For example, each family member perceives that all of the other members have their best interests in mind. Reactions to criticism in the family may have strong emotional impact because the individual members are significant to one another. Also, members of the family may be perceived to have the right to evaluate because each act has an effect on the well-being of the family unit.

In short, the climate of any particular context has a great deal to do with how evaluative acts are interpreted. Therefore, communication should try to establish a supportive climate in which evaluation is viewed as a joint process toward common goals. Evaluation will have its greatest impact when a cohesive climate exists. It seems trite to refer to an organization as a family, but the principles of behavior in a family are very much at play if an ideal organizational climate exists.

METHODS OF EVALUATIVE COMMUNICATION

What method of communication is most effective in getting others to improve their performance? Although individuals do not respond to the "same" messages in the same way, several general methods of communicating do reflect different philosophies and also have the capacity to produce different outcomes. The American Management Association has illustrated some of these methods and the projected outcomes (see Table 10.1).[9] However, the terms "cause and effect relations" in the title may be overstated; individual differences make it difficult to predict reactions to evaluations. Although the material in the table refers to performance appraisal in the managerial setting, it may be applicable to the educational situation as well. The three methods of appraisal interviews provide an opportunity to reexamine and apply principles of communication discussed at the outset of this text.

Tell and Sell

S-R orientation The "tell and sell" approach is representative of the stimulus-response model of communication, in which an individual conceptualizes the recipient of a message as a passive object. S-R is a model of one-way influence; the evaluator does something to the recipient. The communication is linear, and the power is vested in the evaluator. The communicator who uses this particular approach will also probably be very message-oriented and will concentrate on finding the magic words that motivate all individuals.

Ignores mutuality This type of model ignores the development of a relationship and the mutual exchange of symbols. One of the major assumptions of "tell and sell" is that an evaluator who wants someone to do something just tells the person to do so. In other words, the message is "delivered," much as anything else would be delivered. The "tell it like it is" approach suffers the disadvantage of ignoring the "like it is" to the recipient of the appraisal. In addition, persuasion becomes viewed as an external process in which the evaluator is assumed to have more control than is probably true in fact. This model ignores the fact that the ultimate decision to do anything about one's performance lies with the individual being evaluated.

Error-oriented This approach tends to emphasize correction and the detection of error instead of the positive aspects of performance. The critical aspect of an individual's view of his or her own performance is lost if the communication is sufficiently one-sided. The nature of the communication stimulated by the tell-and-sell method can be damaging to the evaluator, who may forget that much of the evaluation material is opinion and not fact. So much effort may be placed in convincing another that the message takes on the ring of absolute truth, and additional facts may not be sought or perceived. The role of judge is reinforced and that of coach is lost.

Assumes shared reality Throughout this text we have emphasized the importance of learning the symbolic world of others. The tell-and-sell approach does not lend itself to this advice. An evaluator who utilizes the one-way communication approach is likely to make an assumption about the symbolic makeup of others and to generalize his or her approach to all individuals.

Table 10.1 Cause and Effect Relations in Three Types of Appraisal Interviews

Method:	Tell and Sell	Tell and Listen	Problem Solving
Role of interviewer:	Judge	Judge	Helper
Objective:	To communicate evaluation To persuade employee to improve	To communicate evaluation To release defensive feelings	To stimulate growth and development in employee
Assumptions:	Employee desires to correct weaknesses if he knows them Any person can improve if he so chooses A superior is qualified to evaluate a subordinate	People will change if defensive feelings are removed	Growth can occur without correcting faults Discussing job problems leads to improved performance
Reactions:	Defensive behavior suppressed Attempts to cover hostility	Defensive behavior expressed Employee feels accepted	Problem-solving behavior
Skills:	Salesmanship Patience	Listening and reflecting feelings Summarizing	Listening and reflecting feelings Reflecting ideas Using exploratory questions Summarizing
Attitude:	People profit from criticism and appreciate help	One can respect the feelings of others if one understands them	Discussion develops new ideas and mutual interests
Motivation:	Use of positive or negative incentives or both (Extrinsic in that motivation is added to the job itself)	Resistance to change reduced Positive incentive (Extrinsic and some intrinsic motivation)	Increased freedom Increased responsibility (Intrinsic motivation in that interest is inherent in the task)

Gains:	Success most probable when employee respects interviewer	Develops favorable attitude to superior which increases probability of success	Almost assured of improvement in some respect
Risks:	Loss of loyalty Inhibition of independent judgment Face-saving problems created	Need for change may not be developed	Employee may lack ideas Change may be other than what superior had in mind
Values:	Perpetuates existing practices and values	Permits interviewer to change his views in the light of employee's responses Some upward communication	Both learn since experience and views are pooled Change is facilitated

Reprinted by permission of the publisher from *Personnel*, March/April 1958 © 1958 by American Management Association, Inc. This table originally appeared in N. Maier, *The Appraisal Interview*, copyright © 1958 by John Wiley & Sons, Inc.

In so doing, the evaluator will bypass certain individuals and at the same time be unaware of changes in values that may be occurring in society at large.

Suppresses open exchange When defensive behaviors are suppressed, they often build into irreconcilable differences. One of the purposes of evaluation is to develop human resources; therefore, an organization that suffers unusually high turnover not only loses potential resources, but also must pay the price of recruitment and training.

Facilitative communication allows the expression of hostility, as well as any other emotion, but the tell-and-sell method is normally counter to the principles of open, honest communication. Sometimes tell and sell results in the evaluator's "talking down" to individuals. When individuals come to feel that they are being "sold" or "talked to," they are likely to be suspicious and resentful. Of course, it might be contended that if the salesmanship is good enough, those feelings are not likely to emerge. Unfortunately, one-way communication does not permit one to find out if such feelings exist.

Table 10.1 points out that patience is one of the skills needed in the tell-and-sell method. Although the teller must wait to see what happens to the performance, patience is not limited to that approach. In fact, the other approaches may demand more patience.

Criticism may inhibit performance According to Table 10.1, the attitude of the individual practicing the tell-and-sell method is that people profit from criticism. In addition to the notion of individual differences in reaction to criticism, there is evidence that criticism may be an inhibiting factor in performance. In a study of performance appraisal, Meyer, Kay, and French found that the more criticism received, the more defensively the recipient reacted: "Frequent criticism constitutes so strong a threat to self-esteem that it disrupts rather than improves subsequent performance."[10] We do not mean to imply that an evaluation should not contain criticism or that criticism is the same as frequent criticism. However, the tell-and-sell approach may well lend itself to confusion between criticism and help, because of its focus on detecting errors and dispensing judgments.

Narrows motives The tell-and-sell approach also tends to limit one's view of motives to external considerations. In other words, the "carrot" and "stick" version of motivation is applied, and particular rewards or punishments are dangled in front of the person being evaluated. The notion of psychological compensation and the individual's desire to do good work are given secondary consideration. The symbolic field of humans may be limited to the significance attached to material gains.

Risks If the evaluator has high credibility, the tell-and-sell method can achieve some success. However, this method of communication entails certain risks. First, since it does not allow for the release of defensive behaviors, there is a loss of information about the feelings and growth potential of the individual being evaluated. Second, individuals who are not permitted to negotiate or save face become resentful and overcautious. Their independent judgment is inhibited, and they may not learn to deal in self-appraisal. Third, if too much reliance is placed on the evaluator, one of the major functions of evaluation may be suppressed. Fourth, tell and sell does little to implement upward communication in the organization. The assumption is that the existing practices are sound and should be sold. This attitude discourages change, and the organization in which this occurs does little to help itself engage in self-examination and improvement.

Tell and Listen

Some reciprocity The "tell and listen" approach has the elements of the circular, or interaction, model of communication. There is some reciprocity between the evaluator and the individual being evaluated, and this feedback loop ensures some reciprocal influence. Nonetheless, the evaluator is still judge focusing on the evaluation.

The material in Table 10.1 notes the importance of releasing defensive feelings. However, the tell-and-listen approach encourages the evaluator to elicit factual information relevant to the work setting, and therefore not all responses should be labeled as defensive. The evaluator should listen for ways to improve the work setting and not just hear an individual out.

The tell-and-listen method has the virtue of fostering discovery of the symbolic world of the person being evaluated and allowing the evaluator to learn about what is important to the other person. Listening behavior in an evaluator tends to promote listening behavior in the individuals being evaluated. People who have an opportunity to say what is on their minds tend to be more receptive to new ideas. Once defensive feelings have been released, there is room for other thoughts to emerge. It is important that the evaluator communicate acceptance of a subordinate and willingness to listen to any ideas she or he might have.

Employs listening skills and attitudes The primary technique in this approach is listening and reflecting another's feelings. This involves not only skill but also an attitude whereby the evaluator can engage in exchange without becoming defensive. For example, an angry student confronted one of the authors in his office: "I don't see how you can expect us to do all this work! We haven't received any direction, and the term project is due this week.

You seem to favor some of the students, and they get all the breaks." "Now just a minute, Bill, that isn't fair!" About to launch into a speech, the author realized that his response had been defensive and that the probable outcome would have been an argument and more defensive behaviors. The two started over again, and this time the author reflected the feelings he was hearing from the student: "You feel that you have too much work to do. You think, then, that you need some assistance." In response to these comments, the student revealed that he had just had a test. He felt that he had performed poorly on it because his outside job prevented him from studying as much as he should, and therefore he felt a distinct disadvantage to other students. After discussing these problems, the student could concentrate on ways of completing the term project.

To reflect another person's ideas and feelings may seem trite, but this method "primes the pump," facilitating exchange that might not take place otherwise. A good listener is also able to summarize the conversation to the satisfaction of all participants. In other words, areas of agreement and disagreement can be summed up, as well as the feelings of the participants involved.

Listening to someone does not mean making a commitment to agree. However, it is necessary for the evaluator to possess an attitude of respect for others' feelings. Individuals view the world through a symbolic screen, and symbolic behavior affects other behavior—especially perceptual behavior. Therefore, it is important to keep in mind that from the other person's point of view, he or she is right.

Reduces resistance to change Listening can reduce resistance to change because it gives individuals a hearing, thus relieving them of the burden of suppressed feelings. Then they are more receptive to new ideas. Listening operates as a positive incentive by conveying a powerful nonverbal message, namely, that an individual is worth listening to and has important feelings. Realizing that an evaluator has the other's best interests in mind, the person being evaluated finds it easier to look at different ways of doing things. An evaluator can use not only the customary extrinsic rewards, but also the listening process to discover the intrinsic motive structure of the person being evaluated. It is important to know what the task means to the individual being evaluated, the qualities of role associated with the task, and the perceived qualities of the individual.

Generates useful information The tell-and-listen approach has the advantage of developing more favorable attitudes toward the evaluator, which in turn may make the evaluation process more effective. Gaining more insight into the problems of the subordinate, the evaluator can adjust the evaluation accordingly. The tell-and-listen method ensures some upward communication, which may be valuable in adjusting organizational policies.

Risk The major risk involved in the tell-and-listen approach is that there may be a lack of mutuality. In other words, a dual monologue may result from a lack of focus on the problems to be solved. The tell-and-sell method could be described as a monologue, in which the evaluator makes a speech to the subordinate. The tell-and-listen approach can result in a dual monologue, or a speech by the evaluator and a speech by the subordinate. If the process stops here, the need for improvement and how to achieve that improvement may be lost.

Problem Solving

Relationship-centered The problem-solving approach to evaluation most nearly represents an idealized view of communication. Its major departure from the other methods of communication discussed is its focus on the relationship between participants. Evaluation must still be conveyed, but it is done so within the context of coach and learner. The multiple functions of evaluation are undertaken, in an effort to ensure the subordinate's growth and development. The problems of the subordinate are those of the evaluator, and both concentrate on attaining specific goals. There is less emphasis on detecting error and passing judgment and more on specific problem areas and how to solve them. Discussion centers on job problems and how they are perceived by both participants involved in the evaluation process.

Problem-oriented Problem-solving behavior requires a different method of communication. With a performance problem, there is no need to determine who is at fault, but rather to discover how to solve the problem. A spirit of inquiry is maintained, and judgments are delayed until various alternatives have been explored. Problem-solving behavior stimulates more suggestions from a subordinate and also makes that person more open to suggestions. When the focus is on the problem or objective, a subordinate is less likely to be defensive, because his or her abilities are not being criticized directly. Besides, defensive behaviors do not help solve problems, and this fact is most clear to the subordinate when the problem-solving approach is utilized.

Employs listening skills and attitudes The listening skills discussed in the tell-and-listen approach to evaluation are also applicable in the problem-solving method. It is necessary to obtain as much relevant data as possible, and therefore both participants must be willing to talk. This willingness is stimulated when an evaluator listens and reflects the other person's ideas and feelings. The process is less effective if it is mechanical in nature. The importance of feelings must be recognized, and the evaluator will have the most success when engaged in empathic listening. Communication is facilitated by the use of exploratory questions and summarizing points of view. Again, these methods are as much attitude as technique. An evaluator must feel enough self-confidence to be able to view a problem from a subordinate's point of view. One should not obtain another's point of view just because it makes the other feel good, but because that point of view may make a substantial contribution to the solving of a problem. The role of facilitator entails the techniques of reflection, exploring, summarizing, and the withholding of immediate judgment.

Mutuality The problem-solving approach has the potential of facilitating the development of new ideas and mutual concerns. It creates an atmosphere of not only freedom but also responsibility. Both participants have the responsibility of solving problems associated with improving performance. Thus it is the subordinate who must eventually decide how to use his or her abilities.

Much of the emphasis on motivation focuses on the task, on the assumption that it is satisfying to solve a particular problem and improve one's performance. If one believes in the potential for human growth and self-actualization, it should follow that a growth-stimulating approach should be satisfying and motivating. Increased responsibility, then, is regarded not as a burden but as an opportunity, and communication can operate as a motivating force when the evaluator recognizes that a subordinate has the capacity to solve problems. The problem-solving procedure itself suggests that the subordinate is worthy of partnership and deemphasizes the role of superior and judge.

Although the outcomes of this approach may be the most productive, the approach itself is difficult to undertake. It demands patience and the ability to teach. There is a considerable difference between telling someone something and teaching someone something. For example, one of the authors observed a Little League baseball practice in which the coach told his players to throw the ball to first base and then "cover the bag." When a ground ball was hit to the third baseman, he scooped it up and relayed to first. After the throw he remained motionless, not moving to the third-base bag for a return throw. The coach stopped play and engaged in several minutes of public ridicule. "When I tell you guys to do something, I want you to do it! Third base, I want you to quit dogging it! We are out here to play ball!"

This sequence of events aroused the author's curiosity, and at the conclusion of the practice he approached the player and asked, "What did your coach mean when he said 'cover the bag'?" The player expressed confusion and said that he wasn't sure. Some patience and an exploratory question would have been much more effective in this case. The coach had assumed that the meaning was in the message. In addition, he imputed the motive of laziness to the player. He also made it more difficult for the players to ask questions and learn. The implication was that these young boys should already know the fundamentals of baseball.

It is important to realize that in mutual exchange the participants both teach and learn. Lacking ideas at first, the subordinate may move in a number of unproductive directions. However, this searching process can ultimately be most productive, for when the person learns and examines the reasons for change, change is facilitated.

Risk According to Table 10.1, one of the risks of the problem-solving approach is that change may be other than what a superior had in mind. However, this is not a risk—if the particular change solves the problem. A superior is not always right and does not necessarily know the best ways of accomplishing tasks. This is epecially true if both participants in the evaluative process are willing to learn.

Although we have discussed these three communication approaches to appraisal interviews separately, we do not mean to imply that each is exclusive of the others. It is a matter of emphasis, and elements of each method may be found in the others. Each method has its merits and will produce results if done skillfully. Also, a particular method may be best suited to particular types of individuals—both evaluators and subordinates.

However, in our opinion the problem-solving approach best fits our view of communication and holds the most promise for fulfilling the multiple purposes of evaluation. The problem-solving method is most consistent with the philosophy of a "mutual influence" approach to communication acts. Power does not reside solely in the evaluator, and attention is paid to exchange that is mutually beneficial. It is useful for an evaluator to be aware of the communication methods she or he is using and the kinds of behavior that might be stimulated by that particular method. In addition, the evaluator should be sensitive to communication cues inherent in the evaluative setting.

COMMUNICATION CUES

Role

Certain communication cues extraneous to the message have considerable impact on respondents. The roles themselves can inhibit free and open communication in the evaluation process. It is difficult to break down the role barrier even when the evaluator role is redefined as one of helper and coach. Subordinates still realize that an evaluation is going to be made, and they may be reluctant to give information detrimental to their position. As Read states, "High mobility aspirations strongly militate against accurate communication of potentially threatening information *even when high trust prevails.*"[11]

Although mutual role taking is important to communication occurring in the evaluation process, it must not be allowed to dominate all of the interaction. Thus an evaluator must achieve role distance by communicating roles other than that of evaluator. The achievement of a unique role set will allow an evaluator to convey a more realistic picture of evaluation. In other words, a subordinate is expected to make errors, and a certain amount of compensation for error is both necessary and expected. Evaluators who live under an illusion of perfection may well convey that illusion to others, who in turn may rationalize or cover up errors. When this occurs, the information needed for problem solving and self-examination may not be forthcoming.

Relationship Function of Communication

An evaluator must not only be willing to "interact" with individuals, but also communicate that willingness. The interpretation of the content of a message depends largely on the relationship between evaluator and subordinate. The nature and amount of content are also dependent on the relationship. The evaluator who is tight-lipped about his or her own feelings and who wishes to convey an aura of infallibility will generate the same type of behavior in the individuals being evaluated.

How does one convey willingness to relate to others beyond a traditional role set? A study by Chaikin and Derlega of dialogue between strangers gives some insight into this question. Subjects were given written accounts of what one had said, and they then watched a videotape of the response of the other. Although intimate disclosures to strangers were questioned, "subjects liked best the character who answered straight facts with straight facts and intimacies with intimacies."[12] In other words, reciprocity is an operative norm in most communicative exchanges. An evaluator who is willing to share part of self with others thereby gives a cue calling for reciprocal action. When an evaluator makes known his or her humanness, a subordinate is more likely to do the same.

The content of a message sets forth not only what that message is about, but also the relationship that exists between sender and receiver. In one university, for example, a group of teaching fellows disgruntled with their supervisor had less and less communication with that person. The problem stemmed from an incident which created unintended consequences. The teaching fellows had given a departmental examination to their classes. The supervisor told them that the answer sheet to the test could be obtained in his office and should be used in his outer office. What the supervisor interpreted as a move toward efficiency, the teaching fellows interpreted as a general lack of trust. In their view, the supervisor thought that they might lose the answers to the test or pass some of the answers along to students.

In this particular situation the content of the message was limited, and the supervisor had not given reasons for his instruction. Had he explained his reasoning and asked for suggestions, the problem probably would not have occurred.

The relationship communicated in the evaluative setting is even more sensitive to these kinds of interpretations. There is no way to ensure that messages will not be interpreted negatively when no negative meanings are intended. However, the problem-solving method of appraisal lends itself to more complete exchanges and also implies the existence of an Adult-Adult rather than a Parent-Child relationship.

Use of Criticism

The amount of criticism and the frequency of discussions about performance communicate distinct messages to those being evaluated. An individual performing a task for the first time is likely to need considerable instruction. If all of the instruction and criticism are given at one time, a subordinate is likely to interpret the message as saying, "You are hopeless." A supervisor, manager, or teacher can get carried away with the role of evaluator. A corrected paper that looks as though it had been dipped in red ink may show the ignorance of the teacher rather than that of the student.

Learning is an accumulative process, and that message should be part of evaluation. In addition, as Meyer, Kay, and French conclude, "Employees become clearly more prone to reject criticisms as the number of criticisms mount."[13] When individuals have feelings of hopelessness, they are likely to behave defensively. Having frequent discussions about performance not only allows for well-planned criticism, but also conveys the evaluator's interest in preparing a subordinate before any final determination is made about his or her work.

Opening Channels

It is necessary to keep the lines of communication open and to obtain as much data as possible about the other person. In order to empathize with and discover another's world view, symbolic interaction must take place. The amount of exchange is governed in large part by subtle communication cues. Experiments in verbal conditioning have demonstrated that the number of opinions an individual gives can be traced to the type of communication received.[14] When one's opinions are met with agreement or paraphrasing, the person feels reinforced, and this generates more opinions. On the other hand, when someone of status simply disagrees or ignores one's opinion, one is less likely to give more opinions or to show more of one's self.

We are not recommending that an evaluator engage in false agreement with a subordinate. But it is important to realize that the opinions of others are important; then there should be an awareness of the communication cues conducive to generating those opinions. Opinions can be elicited by asking questions, paraphrasing, indicating acceptance of the opinions, and by being attentive to others. There is a difference between agreeing with the opinions of others and indicating acceptance of those opinions. It is rewarding to talk to those who will listen to what one has to say and respect one's opinion, even though disagreeing with them. In the evaluative setting, communication cues convey the attention paid to a subordinate's opinion and the value attached to such opinions.

Nonverbal Cues

Nonverbal behaviors can have considerable impact on the outcomes of evaluation. These behaviors can be best examined in the problem-solving context, framed against the assumptions of that approach. Underlying the problem-solving mode is the assumption that both participants are engaged in a joint enterprise and have something to offer toward the solution of the problem. The accuracy of this assumption is reflected in the consistency between what is said verbally and nonverbally. Certain nonverbal cues can be associated with joint problem solving. Individuals involved in problem solving are attentive to one another, listen to one another, and attempt to remove outside distractions. They tend to remove physical barriers so as to achieve a closer physical proximity. In other words, an evaluator who sits behind a desk seems more like a judge than a coach or helper. Two people who are involved in mutual effort are careful with criticism of each other around each other's peers or in front of other groups. The two have a stake in each other and allow for face-saving in the privacy of an evaluation.

Perhaps the most significant nonverbal cue in evaluation and subsequent interchange is *time*. The phrase "spending time" has considerable import, because time is a precious commodity in American culture, and willingness to spend it communicates one's interests and intentions toward others. An evaluator whose interests are indeed mutual will make the time to engage in problem solving. If the evaluation seems mechanical and cursory, the entire notion of mutual problem solving may be regarded as hypocritical. Of course, evaluators do not have unlimited time to give to all individuals. Some individuals will need more time than others, and therefore it is helpful to think of evaluation as an ongoing process rather than as a one-shot affair. It is necessary to communicate this notion of continuous problem solving and adjustment to subordinates.

Often there is a reliance on nonverbal behavior to terminate interviews. For example, an interviewer, finding that the allowable time has been spent, may stand up, extend a hand, and explain that the available time has elapsed, whereupon another meeting might be arranged. Other forms of nonverbal behavior are less desirable. The teacher, supervisor, or manager who continually looks at a watch, for example, unwittingly communicates lack of desire to spend time with others. Subordinates in this situation may come to feel that they are being processed on an assembly line.

In the office setting it is not uncommon for secretaries to help regulate the time schedule. A secretary may interrupt a conference to remind an evaluator of another appointment. Many times this interruption is prearranged to make sure that the interviewer does not spend so much time with one individual that other appointments become impossible. This procedure may communicate deceit and gamesmanship if it is not handled in a straightforward manner. Thus is is better to explain to a subordinate that the secretary has been asked to interrupt at a designated time than to pretend that forces beyond one's control have suddenly made a decision. Individuals who are involved in a mutual enterprise do not need to engage in gamesmanship.

One of our colleagues terminated interviews by using a contrived signal —moving a pencil from the right side of a desk to the left after a certain amount of time. A secretary in an outer office would watch for this signal and then interrupt to remind our colleague of another appointment or commitment. These nonverbal behaviors communicated deceit, disinterest, and became an irritant to others. One of the authors reacted as follows.

> At first, a number of schemes ran through my mind. What would happen if I pointed up at the ceiling during a conversation and snatched the pencil away so that no signal could be given? Why not be bold and break the pencil in half and then inform the secretary that my time was not up? What would happen if I saw the secretary looking for the signal and gave her an obscene gesture? Some schemes will remain unreported.
>
> I found myself talking to this individual as little as possible and when I did, the pencil was seldom moved, because my message was the length of an inexpensive telegram. The pencil maneuver had made me feel as though I was not to be trusted with the precious commodity of time and that I was under pressure to say something significant, or the pencil would move against me. Today I can see the humor involved in the situation and can refer to it as the "old pencil trick." However, there is little question in my mind that because of reliance on a gimmick, both of us lost something and never came to know each other.

Nonverbal behaviors are especially potent because they are conceived to be less controlled and therefore reflections of the communicators' real feelings.

Therefore, as much or more attention should be paid to communication cues that are extraneous to verbal messages.

THE EVALUATION PROCESS

The purposes and functions of evaluation are best met by approaching the act of evaluation as an evolutionary process. Coaching should be done on a day-to-day basis rather than in a one-time, formal evaluation session. According to Wilhelms, the test of an evaluation system is: "Does it deliver the feedback that is needed, when it is needed, to the persons or groups who need it?"[15] Different kinds of communication are needed at various stages of the process.

Phases

An *orientation* phase allows the respondent to understand expectations and the evaluator to understand what is significant to the respondent. It is a time to clarify work assignments, expected results, standards, and possible difficulties. The evaluator must allow for several thorough exchanges of information during this period. A subordinate ought to have the opportunity for ample feedback and discussion during this stage. A judgment needs to be made about how much information an individual can handle, but the information that is given should be explicit and direct. A person who is performing a task for the first time may rely heavily on the evaluator. However, the problem-solving climate ought to be established at the outset.

A *review* phase allows for transaction, mutual goal setting, and commitment to specific objectives. An individual who has had an opportunity to perform is in a better position to enter into mutual problem solving.

A judgment, or *decision,* phase permits evaluator and respondent to view the amount of disparity between objectives and performance. Most of the discussion should focus on ways of reducing this disparity. At this stage an evaluator should help individuals recognize and capitalize on their strengths. A *follow-up* phase ensures continued problem solving and gives the evaluator an opportunity to reinforce desired behavior.

Providing a Communication Framework

Earlier in this chapter we examined conditions leading to various reactions to evaluation. However, we did not deal directly with the question of which has the greater impact on performance—praise or blame. The experimental findings relevant to this question are inconsistent.[16] Some studies have found that the performance of certain individuals remains the same whether they are given praise or blame. In other studies praise has been found to enhance performance; blame, cause a decline. It would seem that individual characteristics, the social context, and the nature of the communication decide in large part the reaction to praise and criticism. The main point is that no single element serves as a reliable predictor of response to criticism and praise. Praise may very well be expected normative behavior in most situations, and as such it is probably preferable to criticism in terms of improving performance. However, praise must be linked to success if it is to have an impact on performance. The evaluator needs to keep in mind that "nothing succeeds like success." It is useful, then, to provide a framework for positive reinforcement. In their studies of performance appraisal, Meyer, Kay, and French concluded that criticism has a negative effect on achievement of goals, praise little effect one way or the other, and that performance improves most when specific goals are established.[17] Again, this stresses the importance of providing a situation geared to achievement and positive reinforcement.

One management procedure with the potential to provide a useful communication framework is "management by objectives."[18] Although these programs vary, most of them include the following steps. (1) At the beginning of a specified time period, a set of job objectives is mutually agreed on by evaluator and subordinate. (2) The objectives are directly related to specific job responsibilities and may also include personal-improvement objectives. (3) Once the objectives have been agreed on, they become goals. (4) Both individuals sit down at the end of the specified time period and discuss which objectives were met and how well.

The success of this procedure is highly dependent on the human exchange that takes place. The mechanics are less important than the bond built between individuals. Mutual agreement allows for exploration and the sharing of values. The "identity" function of communication is met by listening to the personal aspirations and aims of each individual. When there is a focus on mutual problem solving, the roles of superior and subordinate become deemphasized, and teamwork can result. The evaluator who believes that all humans have growth potential becomes a coach rather than a judge. It is critical that the communication behavior convey the mutual search for the melding of individual and organizational goals. Of course, judgments must eventually be made about individuals' value to an organization, and not all individuals possess the same abilities. What is important, however, is how one proceeds toward those decisions. With a belief in the basic value of humans, an evaluator's behavior will be aimed at giving each person ample opportunity to develop and demonstrate his or her worth.

Ethics

Because so much responsibility is entailed in the evaluation process, ethics are very much a part of this process. The following is a list of considerations for managers involved in employee appraisal.

1. Know the reason for appraisal.
2. Appraise on the basis of representative information.
3. Appraise on the basis of sufficient information.
4. Appraise on the basis of relevant information.
5. Make an honest appraisal.
6. Keep written and oral appraisals consistent.
7. Present appraisal as opinion.
8. Give appraisal information only to those who have a good reason to know it.
9. Don't imply the existence of an appraisal that hasn't been made.
10. Don't accept another's appraisal without knowing the basis for it.*

Appraisals that describe the behavior of individuals rather than impute motives or attribute personality characteristics have the best chance of meeting ethical standards. An evaluator would need to get inside the defining process of an individual in order to understand his or her actions. Although this is appropriate when working with someone, the data consist of inferences, and the distribution of such inferences must be done with great care. Generalizations about individuals should be preceded by descriptive data from which the conclusions were drawn. An evaluator should keep in mind that the description of the individual's behavior is limited to a particular setting at a particular moment. Description of level of achievement is more fitting than hanging symbolic tags around someone's neck that must be lived down. This point becomes even more crucial when one realizes that the person being evaluated may internalize the symbols and come to believe that they represent the self.

RECEPTION OF EVALUATION

Although the focus of this chapter has been on the evaluator, the principles can also be applied to the recipients of evaluation.

Attitude

The value of the evaluation depends largely on one's attitudes. It is important for one being evaluated to seek knowledge about how to improve oneself and how to engage in self-examination for greater effectiveness. A person who believes in this approach will be able to receive evaluation more easily.

---

* Reprinted by permission of the publisher from *What to Do About Performance Appraisal* by Marion S. Kellogg, p. 29. © 1965 by the American Management Association, Inc.

Much of what is communicated to any individual in the evaluation process is *opinion*. Sometimes the task being performed can be reported in an objective manner. For example, if you can run 100 yards in 9.2 seconds, we might conclude that you are fast. Even in such cases, however, a question remains as to how much speed may be necessary for a particular task. This is not to say that others' opinions should be ignored, only that they should form a part of self-examination that looks for strengths *and* weaknesses.

Because of the human potential for growth, an opinion is not an eternal indictment. This growth potential is stifled when individuals impute motives to evaluators, e.g., "The teacher doesn't like me"; "The coach has certain 'pets' "; "We have a personality conflict, and the boss is afraid that I might get his job." These phrases can be defensive maneuvers that inhibit self-improvement.

It is equally damaging when individuals internalize negative symbols and fail to see their own growth potential. Individuals who regard negative evaluation as truth rather than as opinion may actually perform those negative behaviors, which further reinforces the original evaluation. When this is done it is difficult to accept the self, and more importantly an individual is less likely to see the self in process. What can a person who receives evaluation do about avoiding some of the foregoing pitfalls?

Employ Communication Principles

In addition to attitudes, the procedures by which one operates can have a decided effect on the reception of evaluation. Rather than imputing motives to an evaluator, it is more beneficial to get "meaning-centered." What does the evaluator mean? How is the evaluator viewing a particular task? What specific items support which statements? In other words, the individual being evaluated should seek as much specific information as possible.

The person being evaluated should also get "problem-centered." The spirit of inquiry will focus on what must be done to improve and what assistance will be needed to solve particular problems. This will be more likely to promote self-improvement than trying to assign fault for a weakness.

An attitude of information seeking and mutual problem solving serves both the rights and obligations of the counterrole in the evaluation process. The behavior of a respondent can do much to ensure maximum information. The respondent should not be reluctant to communicate his or her feelings about specific criticisms. Rather, openness is a stimulus for the evaluator, who then is more likely to expand on the evaluation and seek additional information.

Earlier in this chapter we advised the evaluator to delay judgment until an individual has had time to perform. The same principle should apply in reverse. It is unethical to make judgments about evaluators until all the facts are in. Even then, such opinions may be valid only for that particular situation. It is helpful to perceive evaluators as people who exist for the success of both the organization and its members. The needs of each must be negotiated, and evaluation is part of that process.

SUMMARY

Evaluation serves multiple purposes in the organization. It meets operational needs, motivates, stimulates self-development, and validates self and role. An important aspect of evaluation is one's concept of humans, and this view directs the communication used in evaluation. Reactions to evaluations are dependent on the participants' self-images, communication behavior, perceived performance, credibility of the evaluator, perceived roles, and social context.

We have looked at three methods of communication in the evaluative process—tell and sell, tell and listen, and problem solving. In our view it is problem solving that is most appropriate for a mutual-influence model of communication.

Whatever the method of communication used in evaluation, cues irrelevant to the message may have as much impact on the respondents as the content of the message. One such factor is *role,* which may remain an insurmountable barrier to free, open communication. Similarly, communication between evaluator and respondent may be inhibited by the evaluator's inability or reluctance to convey *willingness* to interact interpersonally. A third potential impediment is too much *criticism* by the evaluator, which may result in defensive behavior on the part of the respondent.

Evaluators who are aware of the pitfalls entailed in these extraneous cues can work to maintain open channels of communication. This can be done by soliciting subordinates' opinions and communicating acceptance of—though not necessarily agreement with—those opinions. In addition, evaluators can make sure to take the time necessary to engage in mutual problem solving.

The general framework within which evaluation occurs can become more realistic (and therefore more effective) if evaluators keep the following points in mind. (1) Evaluation is an evolutionary process, moving through phases of orientation, review, judgment, follow-up, and reinforcement. (2) Praise must be linked to performance. (3) Management by objectives is one useful communication framework for conducting evaluation. (4) Evaluation entails ethical responsibilities on the part of the evaluator.

Finally, evaluation depends on not only the evaluator, but also the person being evaluated. If evaluation is to be characterized by open, free communication and mutual problem solving, the respondent, or person being evaluated, too shares in the evaluation process. The recipient who is able and willing to engage in self-examination will derive more benefit from being evaluated. In other words, recipients should strive to view evaluation and the evaluator in a judicious manner. In addition, evaluation is most meaningful when the person being evaluated becomes meaning- and problem-centered, willing to engage with the evaluator in open communication directed toward mutual problem solving through symbolic interaction.

PROBLEMS AND ISSUES

1. Is there too much emphasis on evaluation in our society and educational system? Why or why not?

2. What kind of evaluation system in education is most appropriate to adapt one to society, or should there be a change in society?

3. Must someone always lose in a competitive society?

4. What personal experiences have you had with evaluation that either detracted from or enhanced your personal development? What kinds of communication were associated with each?

5. Examine the evaluation procedures in a local organization and determine the reactions to those procedures by both evaluators and respondents. What kinds of communication behaviors are the participants aware of?

6. What functions are attributed to evaluation in the educational setting, and how are they met? What kinds of evaluation receive the most favorable reaction?

7. Adopt a management-by-objectives program for your class. What are the strengths and weaknesses of your program?

NOTES

1. Lawrence S. Wrightsman, *Social Psychology in the Seventies* (Monterey, Calif.: Brooks/Cole, 1972), p. 86.

2. Harold J. Leavitt and Ronald A. H. Mueller, "Some Effects of Feedback on Communication," *Human Relations* **4** (1951): 401–410.

3. William Stolz and Percy Tannenbaum, "Effects of Feedback on Oral Encoding Behavior," *Language and Speech* **6** (1963): 218–228.

4. Jerome Bruner and Renato Tagiuri, "The Perception of People," *Handbook of Social Psychology*, Vol. II, ed. Gardner Lindzey (Reading, Mass.: Addison-Wesley, 1954), pp. 634–650.

5. John R. McDavid and Harold M. Schroder, "The Interpretation of Approval and Disapproval by Delinquent and Non-Delinquent Adolescents," *Journal of Personality* **25** (1957): 239–249.

6. Morton Deutsch and L. Solomon, "Reactions to Evaluations by Others as Influenced by Self-Evaluations," *Sociometry* **22** (1959): 93–112.

7. Morton Deutsch, "The Interpretation of Praise and Criticism as a Function of Their Social Context," *Journal of Abnormal and Social Psychology* **62** (1961): 400.

8. *Ibid.*

9. American Management Association, *Personnel* **34** (1958): 39. *See also* N. Maier, *The Appraisal Interview* (New York: Wiley, 1958).

10. Herbert Meyer, Emanuel Kay, and John French, Jr., "Split Roles in Performance Appraisal," *Harvard Business Review* **43** (1965): 126.

11. William H. Read, "Upward Communication in Industrial Hierarchies," *Human Relations* **15** (1962): 13.

12. The research of Alan Chaikin and Valerian Derlega was cited in "Human Behavior Reports," *Human Behavior* (August 1974): 36.

13. Meyer, Kay, and French, *op. cit.,* p. 127.

14. *See* W. S. Verplanck, "The Control of the Content of Conversation: Reinforcement of Statements of Opinion," *Journal of Abnormal Social Psychology* **51** (1955): 676.

15. Fred T. Wilhelms, ed., *Evaluation as Feedback and Guide* (Washington, D.C.: NEA, 1967), p. 4.

16. For examples, *see* Robert Bostrom, "Classroom Criticism and Speech Attitudes," *The Central States Speech Journal* **14** (1963): 27–32: W. A. Kennedy, A. J. Turner, and R. Lindner, "Effectiveness of Praise and Blame as a Function of Intelligence," *Perceptual and Motor Skills* **15** (1962): 143–149; W. A. Kennedy and H. Willcutt, "Motivation of School Children," Cooperative Research Project No. 1929, Tallahassee, Florida: United States Department of Health, Education and Welfare, October 1963.

17. Meyer, Kay, and French, *op. cit.,* p. 127.

18. *See* George Odiorne, *Management by Objectives* (New York: Pitman, 1965).

Chapter 11

Goal
Accommodation

INTRODUCTION

Social welfare has come to depend largely on collective effort, and the inter-dependence between individuals and organizations is more apparent now than ever before. When organizations shut down, entire cities may stagnate; when certain groups decide to strike, cities may be left at the mercy of ac-cumulated garbage, criminals, fire, and inadequate transportation. Humans have come to rely on organizations for a certain quality of life, and in turn organizations can exist only with the support of individuals. Organizations exist to provide services and make a profit, and their continued existence is impor-tant in any societal scheme.

An organization's ability to survive is directly related to its ability to accommodate its goals with those of the individuals who accomplish those goals. This accommodation process takes place via communication and human interaction. Organizational functioning depends not on some strange inner dynamics, but on people acting on the basis of how they define a situation.

Goal accommodation also occurs between organization and environment because organizations use environmental resources—land, air, energy, and human resources. Organizations design communication programs to convince those outside the organization that the benefits derived from organizational activity are beneficial to the larger community. In addition, external com-munication may be used to sell a product or help recruit well-qualified em-ployees. In turn, organizations need information from the external environ-ment in order to adjust and survive in that environment.

This last chapter deals with individual-organizational goal accommoda-tion, the framework within which the multiple purposes of communication become clear. Goal accommodation requires the processes of facilitation, in-formation, regulation, and decision making within a societal setting bounded by a value system. In the first section of this chapter, we stress the significance of integrating individual and organizational goals and discuss the role of com-munication in this integration. Next we show how communication is used to obtain commitment to organizational goals. Then we explore the role of communication in integrating group goals with organizational goals and in managing conflict. Finally, we set forth principles of bargaining which meet our communication philosophy of mutual influence and mutual gain.

INTEGRATION OF GOALS

Individual and Organizational Goals

One major organizational task is to obtain commitment to goals. No legal force or law obligates an individual to comply, however. In fact, when organizational goals are perceived to be at variance with individual goals, an individual is unlikely to put forth his or her best effort.

Lack of involvement can also result from felt inequities in goal achievement. For example, as Form writes: "In our society, the question is ubiquitously posed: 'who has the profit, the power, and the glory?' Short of an imminent national catastrophe which threatened everybody, the bulk of employees in large organizations feel a sense of detachment from work."[1] This statement is not limited to large industrial organizations. A bargaining process takes place within all organizations, and individuals' cooperation can best be acquired by enabling them to achieve their personal needs and satisfactions and to pursue their personal values as much as possible within the framework of the organization. The development of individuals should enhance the organization and its goals.

Although educational organizations differ in many respects from profit-based ones, they provide an interesting perspective on the linkage between individual and organizational goals. McMurrin states:

> The broad purposes of education can be distinguished under three orders: (a) the satisfaction of the intellectual interests of the individual, (b) the criticism and perpetuation of the social institutions, and (c) the renewal and strengthening of the culture. It is a primary assumption of a democratic society that there is a happy coincidence of these three, so that when we effectively pursue the interests of the individual, bringing him to the full appreciation and use of his rational and creative powers, not only do we contribute to his economic, intellectual, moral, artistic, and spiritual life, but we also bring increased vitality and strength to the culture and to those institutions of society which merit preservation.[2]

In other words, one's pursuit of personal interests may not be irrelevant to what the organization seeks; the goals of individuals and organizations are not necessarily mutually exclusive.

It seems realistic to assume that most participants in the work setting make a distinction between personal and organizational aspirations.

The hope in an organization is to create a climate in which one of two things occurs. The individuals in the organization (both managers and workers) either perceive their goals as being the same as the goals of the organization, or, although different, they see their own goals being satisfied as a direct result of working for the goals of the organization. Consequently, the closer we can get the individual's goals and objectives to the organization's goals, the greater will be the organizational performance.[3]

In the integration process, the latter part of the statement above seems most workable, in that individuals are more likely to compare personal goals and organizational goals. If individual-organization goal integration is to take place, organizations must not only clearly inform participants of organizational objectives and goals, but also have an understanding of their personal goals. This understanding forms the basis for striking a bargain.

Assessing Individuals' Goals

The most common approach to determining the goals of individuals has been to speculate about the nature of human beings. In Chapter 5 we explored some conceptualizations of humans and their impact on communication behavior. We also warned about the danger of applying simple and sovereign theories about motives and values to all humans. However, that is precisely what happens in many large organizations.

Motives McGregor observed two theories of motives prevalent in industry. Table 11.1 summarizes these two theories, which are (1) contradictory, (2) extreme views of human nature, and (3) unitary explanations. These two theories, which have provoked considerable discussions about managerial behavior, appear to fail to either provide a middle ground or recognize individual differences.[4] It is misleading to place either employees or managers solely in one category or the other. However, these underlying beliefs about human behavior can shape one's perception of others' goals.

A manager who believes that people are inherently lazy and must be controlled will readily assume that the goals of those people are related to material needs—economic compensation, job security, etc. Communication is therefore aimed at the lower-level needs advanced by Maslow and the maintenance factors outlined by Herzberg.[5] Communication functions become severely limited, and a "telling" atmosphere antithetical to integration of individual and organizational goals ensues.

Because most models of management are aimed at "workability" and none can account for all situations or individual differences, a common conclusion has been that managerial style should "fit the task and the people."[6] This makes sense—*if* one is saying that since goals and people are different,

Table 11.1 Assumptions of McGregor's Theory X and Theory Y*

Theory X	Theory Y
The average human being has an inherent dislike of work and will try to avoid it.	The expenditure of physical and mental effort in work is as natural as play or rest.
Therefore, management must coerce, control, direct, and threaten workers with punishment in order to get them to put forth adequate effort toward the achievement of organizational objectives.	External control and the threat of punishment are not the only means for bringing about effort toward organizational objectives. People will exercise self-direction and self-control in the service of objectives to which they are committed.
The average human prefers to be directed, wishes to avoid responsibility, has relatively little ambition, and wants security above all else.	Commitment to objectives is a function of rewards associated with their achievement.
	The average human being learns, under proper conditions, not only to accept but also to seek responsibility.
	The capacity to exercise a relatively high degree of imagination, ingenuity, and creativity in the solution of organizational problems is widely, not narrowly, distributed in the population.
	Under the conditions of modern industrial life, the intellectual potentialities of the average human being are only partially utilized.

* Summarized with permission from Douglas McGregor, *The Human Side of Enterprise* (New York: McGraw-Hill, 1960), pp. 33–48.

accommodations will be different. However, such statements contain pitfalls. It should not be assumed that one should use theory X when it will "work." When one uses threats and they "work," one is reinforced to use threats again. The person who is threatened and controlled may be of little use to self or the organization unless under threat and control. This not only stunts individual growth, but also limits the quality of organizational goals.

Attributed motives The words "people differences" should not be used to refer to "class differences" or to "differences in rank." People tend to believe that their own motives are unique and that therefore a "shape up or ship out" attitude is the only one that others will understand. In other words, the notion of "differences" can be used as an excuse to apply theory X at will and to ignore the goals of others.

Likert's data illustrate how superiors may perceive their subordinates (see Table 11.2).[7] Workers were asked to rate the importance of various job factors. Their superiors were then asked to make the same ratings in the way they thought the workers would, as well as for themselves. Another level of management was asked to repeat the process for the next lower rank. The data show that the superiors in this study had a rather pessimistic view for everyone but themselves.

In order to assess goals and work toward goal integration, one must have some knowledge of what others value and what motives are at work. Various motivation schemes may reveal possible motivators and may suggest assumptions underlying a person's behavior toward others, but they should not be superimposed on every individual.

Motives as social justification A symbolic interaction approach stresses the importance of the social justifications that people give for their behaviors.

Table 11.2 Attitudes Toward Others' Satisfactions

What Subordinates Want in a Job Compared to Their Superior's Estimates

	As Men: Rated Selves	As Foremen: Men Would Rate	As General Foremen: Foremen Rated Selves	Foremen Would Rate	Rated Selves
Economic variables:					
Steady work–steady wages	61%	79%	62%	86%	52%
High wages	28	61	17	58	11
Pensions and security	13	17	12	29	15
Not to work too hard	13	30	4	25	2
Human satisfaction variables:					
Get along with people	36	17	39	22	43
Get along with superior	28	14	28	15	24
To do good quality work	16	11	18	13	27
To do interesting work	22	12	38	14	43
Chance for promotion	25	23	42	24	47
Good working conditions	21	19	18	4	11
Total	*	*	*	*	*
number of cases	2499	196	196	45	45

* Percentages total over 100 because they include three rankings for each person.

From Robert L. Kahn, "Human Relations on the Shop Floor," in E. M. Hugh-Jones, ed., *Human Relations and Modern Management* (Amsterdam: North-Holland Publishing Co., 1958). Reprinted by permission.

Such justifications arise out of a value system that is part of an individual at a particular moment. This approach implies that the *only* basic nature of humans is that of action. In our discussion of using motives to regulate behavior (see Chapter 6), we stressed that social justifications may be either discovered in people or created. The communication of accommodation does both. The communication process should reveal an individual's lines of conduct and self-conception, thereby providing insight into how goals can be made more attractive to that person. Two essential questions are: *What does the organizational context mean to the individual?* and *What is the "work" vocabulary of the individual?*

Impact of Values on Integration

Values in transition With maturity, a person acquires different social justifications and hence different motives and values. Goal integration must take these changing values into account.

Values are centered at the core of one's belief system and tend to resist change. Therefore, they change slowly. Because not everyone embraces new values at the same rate, discrepant interpersonal communication occurs. It is difficult to find extensive empirical evidence of change in basic values. However, both personal experience and the literature on organizational behavior show that values are in transition, with new ones gaining in importance.

Trist contends that most advanced countries have a postindustrial society, yet still tend to cling to the values of an industrial culture. According to Trist, the following changes in cultural values are taking place:

From	*Toward*
Achievement	Self-actualization
Self-control	Self-expression
Independence	Interdependence
Endurance of distress	Capacity for joy[8]

In examining these two sets of values, it is clear that they would have differing effects on how one communicates to another and on what communication can be expected in return.

The notion of *achievement* takes on new meanings; in addition to communicating that an individual is completing a work task, the concept of achievement suggests relating tasks to personal growth needs. Cooperation is gained by enrolling individuals to pursue personal needs and satisfactions within the framework of an organization. This requires listening to others in order to determine their aspirations. In this view, the individual's growth is an asset to the organization, not a threat.

The value of *self-control* puts forth a stoic philosophy whereby individuals do what they are told and refrain from questioning or challenging. In the past, individuals may have questioned the system but refrained from speaking out because they had little protection or opportunity for other positions and were conditioned to value deference. Thus organizations showed little inclination to develop a new level of decision makers or seek consensus at lower levels of the organization.

Today's educational system, by contrast, is based on a philosophy of "being yourself" and "expressing yourself." Individuals are encouraged to speak out; "do your own thing" is a widely acclaimed philosophy. Television and films have suggested an entirely new perspective on what one may say and to whom. In addition to the security offered by unions and civil service, workers with technical training are mobile and can seek positions elsewhere that offer more than economic security. Today's managers or supervisors cannot afford to be so attached to a role that they forget to communicate at a personal level with their subordinates.

The concept of *interdependence* does not mean that people are giving up their own freedom, but rather that they are seeking greater insight into how and where they stand in relation to others. Communicating the individual-organization-environment interdependence is a way of increasing personal identity by relating the tasks of individuals to the total enterprise. It also conveys a more realistic world view, namely, that individuals and organizations cannot be separated from their larger environment.

Today the issues of common welfare are intensified. What is the responsibility of an organization in the utilization of human and material resources? Do organizations have the right to utilize natural resources as they see fit? Are people used and discarded? When is business everybody's business? Because one act on the part of one aspect of the system has such far-reaching effects on the total system, independence has become not only difficult but indeed detrimental.

The issue of social responsibility is more important now than ever before. External communication programs are typically aimed at convincing the general public that the organization embraces the value of common welfare. For example, oil companies attempt to justify price increases by maintaining that higher profits are needed to pay for further exploration for oil and ensure a continuing supply of energy. Whether or not such external communications are manipulatory and selfish, organizations *are* feeling some accountability to the public.

In the past, workers were supposed to be pleased that they had a job and were expected to "grin and bear" the work conditions. There was virtue in working hard and *enduring distress;* work was good in itself. Today that philosophy is being questioned. Although an older work ethic is still operative and some people work in order to earn leisure time, many others seek meaning in their work, self-development, and enjoyment in what they do. Therefore, managers must recognize the achievements of individuals within group efforts and communicate that feeling of achievement.

Why values change The change of values arises from a changing environment —more wealth, more choice, more mobility, more education, and more leisure time. In addition, values are reflected, created, and altered through the mass media. Thus people are exposed to a variety of values and can reflect on them.

The term "generation gap" would be more appropriately labeled "value gap." It is difficult for those who have lived in the symbolic environment of an economic depression to understand or communicate with those who have the luxury of expecting a job that pays more than simply economic rewards. People accustomed to showing deference for authority and following instructions have difficulty understanding a younger generation that questions authority and expects more from communication than instructions.

The environmental impact on human values and conceptualizations is affected by a variety of models. Observing that machines condition one's thinking about humans, Alvin Toffler points out that the clock came along before the Newtonian image of the world as a great clocklike mechanism.[9] Today, in fact, ideas about humans are generated by the computer. The view of human as machine has provided some insight into the possible ways that information is processed, but it has also had the detrimental effect of oversimplifying the process of communication. In addition, to regard the human as a machine clashes with a value system that demands more personalized treatment. The symbolic needs of persons require more than an approach that limits communication to the transfer and processing of information.

Communicating across value systems Communicating from one value system to another is like communicating from one culture to another. Both attempts can be disastrous, especially if one is not aware of the premises underlying the communication. A real-life incident illustrates the impact of values on communication. One of our students worked in a local organization and brought a memo to our attention that had angered him and his coworkers. The unsigned memo had been distributed to employees and a copy posted on the company bulletin board:

"I Am Your Job"

You had better take care of me. Perhaps you don't think much of me at times, but if you were to wake up some morning and realize you did not have one, you would start the day with an uneasy feeling.

From me you get food, clothing, shelter, and such luxuries as you can enjoy.

If you want me to—badly enough—I'll get you the best automobile and a home on Park Avenue.

But I am exacting! I am a jealous mistress. Sometimes you appear hardly to appreciate me at all. In fact, you make slighting remarks about me at times and neglect me. Considering the fact you need me not only for the material things in life, but spiritually as well, I wonder sometimes that you neglect me as you do. What if I should get away from you? Your happiness would flee for a time at least, and your friends would worry, and your bank account would dwindle.

So, after all, I am pretty important to you. Cherish me. Take good care of me, and I'll take care of you. I am your job.

The student and his coworkers perceived this memo as a threat. They felt that they were being told that they did not appreciate their jobs and were more interested in getting a paycheck than in doing good work.

Although meanings may change in the transfer from message to recipient, it seems safe to say that this memo does stress material rewards and therefore underplays other values held by the employees. Our student was much happier with a second, again unsigned, memo posted within a week of the first. He assumed that it had been written by an employee in response to the first memo.

"I Am Your Employee"

Myself, and others like me, are the life blood of your business. We supply the creativity and the means for the making and display of your products. What we do and say greatly determines the reputation of your business to the outside world.

If I am treated unfairly, made to work under poor working conditions, or paid on a scale below that of other people in the same position and stature as myself, I cannot put forth my best efforts for you. In some cases I may even leave and seek employment elsewhere! Often I go to your competitor.

If I am treated with respect, paid an honest and fair wage, and in general shown that I am a valued and trusted employee, then I will do everything that I can to improve on and increase your business. If, on the other hand, I am belittled, treated as though I have no mind of my own, and given the impression that I am of little value to you and can be easily replaced, I will not and can not put forth my best efforts for you.

Think of me as an investment. I work at a skilled trade, and in most cases your business paid to train me to work within your organization. How much time and expense would be involved to find and train someone new to take my place? What are the effects on your business while you are training someone new?

After all, I am pretty important to you. If you will only take good care of me, then I will take good care of you.

This response to the first memo makes it clear that economic security is only one aspect of a job. The employee who wrote the second memo not only speaks out, but also calls for accommodation and the organization's recognition of the employees' worth as human beings. The writer also recognizes the interdependence between workers and organization; the employees do not have to "endure," but may seek employment in an organization where their value will be recognized and validated.

Again, the goals of both individuals and the organization must be considered for maximum organizational effectiveness. There must be mutual respect; thus workers who want fair wages, trust, etc., without putting forth their best efforts are engaging in unethical behavior. Taken together, both memos suggest the interdependence that we have been stressing. However, it should be remembered that the first memo produced hostility because it did not give proper emphasis to values held by the employees. This type of communication can result in a "we" versus "they" situation, with a subsequent loss of the concept of interdependence.

But how realistic are such values during an economic recession, for example? Many workers may not have the mobility available during an economic boom. Nonetheless, workers may engage in slowdowns, sabotage, mediocre effort, and lack of interest in their work. Similarly, a parental attitude on the part of employers produces dependent employees who do not utilize their creative abilities to further the organization's goals. Human values should not be dependent on the vitality of the economy. First, exchanges that develop individuals present an economic advantage to an organization. Second, the bargain struck between employers and employees should involve fair exchange based on positive human values.

Changing values and communication The change in values requires a corresponding change in communication behavior. The following list shows what Tannenbaum and Davis consider to be values in transition.[10] Their items are in italics; our description of the effect such a value might have on communication follows, in parentheses.

1. *"Away from a view of man as essentially bad toward a view of him as basically good."* (Communication aimed at the positive growth tendencies of humans and conveys acceptance of the individual for his or her human worth.)

2. *"Away from avoidance or negative evaluation of individuals toward confirming them as human beings."* (Personalized communication that compensates for error rather than retaliates or focuses on individuals' shortcomings.)

3. *"Away from a view of individuals as fixed toward seeing them as being in process."* (Recognizing that individuals change and are capable of growth and communicating accordingly.)

4. *"Away from resisting and fearing individual differences toward accepting and utilizing them."* (Communicating respect and acceptance for other points of view and values, thereby opening communication channels.)

5. *"Away from utilizing an individual primarily with reference to his job description toward viewing him as a whole person."* (Communicating the large picture and allowing the individual to cross boundaries in interpersonal and intergroup communication.)

6. *"Away from walling off the expression of feelings toward making possible both appropriate expression and effective use."* (Creating an atmosphere in which feelings can be communicated and explored in an honest, open manner.)

7. *"Away from maskmanship and game-playing toward authentic behavior."* (Communication between people rather than roles. Communication that is honest, direct, and personal.)

8. *"Away from use of status for maintaining power and personal prestige toward use of status for organizationally relevant purposes."* (Utilizing problem-centered communication with a focus on reasonableness rather than superiority.)

9. *"Away from distrusting people toward trusting them."* (Communicating the belief that individuals are capable of negotiating their own set of responsibilities and permitting that exchange to take place.)

10. *"Away from avoiding others with relevant data toward making appropriate confrontation."* (Communication that "levels" with people, even when conflict is present.)

11. *"Away from avoidance of risk-taking toward willingness to risk."* (Communicating the organization's willingness to allow decision making and possible error at all levels of the organization.)

12. *"Away from a view of process work as being unproductive effort toward seeing it as essential to effective task accomplishment."* (Placing more importance on communication activities and the way in which a task gets done and how individuals feel about the outcome.)

13. *"Away from a primary emphasis on competition toward a much greater emphasis on collaboration."* (Utilizing an open communication system in which teamwork is developed by stressing the interdependence between individuals and work units.)

Much more could be said about each item on the list above, and one might speculate as to how much each change in value has actually taken place.

The important point is that underlying most of the Tannenbaum and Davis statements is an emphasis on communication that is open, personalized, and negotiated. According to the traditional set of values, the purpose of communication is to pass information along designated channels so that others can carry out instructions; the newer set of values broadens that perspective to include a personal, negotiated exchange of information.

COMMITMENT TO GOALS

Individuals bring their goals with them when they enter organizations. Most individuals have a concept of who they are and select behaviors accordingly. In addition, people may seek to identify with the organization, which may even operate as a change agent. The individual may internalize organizational goals, accepting them as one's own. An organization may use communication to accomplish both personal integration with and commitment to its goals.

Master Symbols

A master symbol is one of supreme importance. An organization wishing to utilize such symbols should have several criteria for doing so. First, master symbols should generate images with which participants can identify. Second, they should be tied directly to goals and objectives. Third, they must be easily understood and capable of penetrating all levels of an organization.

The internal communication program at Geneva Works–U.S. Steel is one example of how master symbols can be used.[11] George Jedenoff, Vice President of Western Steel Operations, summarized the basis of the program: "The role of internal communication should be to create the awareness of common economic interest among fellow employees of each plant . . . and then, on this base of understanding, to build cooperative action to compete profitably."[12] The central theme (master symbol) of the communication program is "shared competitive responsibility." In order for the steel plant to survive and provide jobs, it must be able to compete with a margin of profit. Derivative master symbols, therefore, include "competition," "teamwork," and "survival." A program label (master symbol) provides the means by which each person can compete, engage in teamwork, and ensure mutual survival. That label is "errors zero," or "reduce errors–produce quality."[13]

This program appears to meet the criteria advanced for usage of master symbols. (1) Competition is not used in an abstract sense, but becomes what everyone must do if the plant is to remain open. (2) Unless the organization engages in quality production and teamwork, it will cease to exist. (3) The symbol "errors zero" is clear enough to reach everyone in the organization.

Master symbols may initiate activity, but they cannot stand by themselves.

Before people can become committed to goals, they must understand and become involved in them.

Understanding Goals

Katz and Kahn have observed:

> Though organizational leaders are quick to recognize the importance of involving their followers in system goals, they are slow to utilize the most natural devices available to them in the form of job rationale . . . the understanding of one's role and how it relates to other roles is a good bridge to involvement in organizational goals.[14]

The linkage between individual roles and organizational goals should be built into a communication program. The team concept may help implement such involvement by making communication between individuals necessary. An individual who receives job information and understands how his or her role is related to organizational objectives can more easily identify with the organizational mission.

Geneva Works–U.S. Steel shows how this procedure works in practice. Messages about specific developments in the industry are sent to all employees to inform them of external competitive threats. Both media communications and meetings focus on foreign imports, new processes, and ways to become more competitive in the world market. Organizational goals and objectives are executed as follows. First, the general superintendents review market conditions with all supervisors and set team goals. Next, foremen and crews cooperate in setting up their own goals; thus departmental goals are linked with overall plant objectives. Third, "huddle" meetings are held weekly between a foreman and his men. Fourth, all employees contribute through an errors-zero suggestion form. The program is augmented by various media presentations and a recognition phase for employee contributions. For both initiating and responding to messages, the communication loop involves all levels of the organization.

After a study of 9796 people in a large industrial corporation, Maher and Piersol concluded that job satisfaction is related to the clear perception of both individual job objectives and the overall objectives or mission of a person's location.[15] For example, workers who perceived the overall objectives or mission of their locations also tended to perceive a high degree of cohesiveness within their working units and between their units and other units at the location. The direct involvement of employees in establishing objectives led to greater clarity and increased mutual commitment to achieving agreed on results.

Some schemes of motivation seem to assume that once a certain individual need is satisfied, organizational objectives will be satisfied. Other models focus on assessing the importance of certain goals to employees and then measuring their perceptions of how important they view organizational objectives in relation to achieving their own personal goals.[16] This second model might be best implemented by the "management by objectives" approach discussed in Chapter 10. Within that framework, organizational and personal goals can be identified and commitment generated. This commitment is more than a mechanical matter of goal disclosure; the process is most likely to be fruitful in a healthy organizational climate.

Generating a Healthy Climate

Empirical evidence suggests that managerial climate is related to commitment to organizational goals. Although study findings differ on the relationship of managerial climate to production, our intent is to briefly review factors of climate that have the potential to influence goal commitment. In one study, Indik, Georgopoulos, and Seashore examined 975 nonsupervisory employees in 27 work stations of a package delivery firm to determine the relationship between supervision and performance.[17] Using both objective records and managerial ratings as criteria of performance or effectiveness, they found that a high level of performance tended to be related to: (1) openness of communication channels between superiors and subordinates, (2) subordinates' satisfaction with supervisors' supportive behavior, (3) a mutual understanding of others' viewpoints and problems, and (4) a high degree of local influence and autonomy on work-related matters.

The climate necessary for the achievement of individual and organizational goals may vary and the components may be different in various settings, but certain factors are generally applicable. Redding proposes five components of an "ideal managerial climate": (1) supportiveness, (2) participative decision making, (3) trust, confidence, and credibility, (4) openness and candor, and (5) emphasis on high performance goals.[18]

Supportiveness This factor can be best explained by examining defensive and supportive behaviors (see Chapter 5). The important question here is: To what extent is there a prevalence of defensive communication attitudes and behaviors? In a supportive climate the personal worth of everyone is recognized and communicated.

PDM Participative decision making, or PDM, refers to the participants' opportunity to shape their own tasks and destinies within the organization.[19] In this situation there is a flow and exchange of information both up and down in the organization. Throughout, emphasis is placed on mutual goal setting and appraisal.

Trust, confidence, and credibility The amount of commitment generated in the organization is related to the amount of trust and confidence shown by the organization. When one is confronted by a distrusting and suspicious superior, it is difficult to maintain a high level of performance, because failure might bring further recriminations. Credibility is having belief in others and conveying that belief. When one places another in an impossible situation and says, "I believe in you" or "Everything will work out," one loses credibility. Credibility is not built by using the themes of trust and confidence for purposes of being "nice"; rather, one builds credibility and commitment by being honest.

Openness and candor Openness and candor are part of initiating messages and responding to them. In Chapter 5 we stressed the importance of achieving "role distance" and avoiding those role behaviors that shut people out. Openness refers to one's willingness to listen to the bad as well as to the good. This dimension of organizational climate is not just a part of interpersonal relationships within the organization. A key question is to what extent employees are informed about policies and external factors that might affect their lives. The antithesis of this component is "tell the employees only what they need to know," an attitude based on the assumption that workers are not capable of taking on responsibility. However, responsibility and commitment to goals are bound together. One can hardly accuse others of being ignorant yet withhold information from them.

Performance goals Performance goals must be balanced with concern for people, and the methods employed to achieve those goals should be a part of a healthy climate. Thus organizational members should understand both general expectations and specific task goals.

Sustained communication A healthy communication climate develops over time. Crisis-oriented organizations that decide to act when the climate has deteriorated find that openness and concern then will be met with suspicion and hostility. Communication and commitment are ongoing processes and require sustained contact among organizational members. Part of this contact can be accomplished by coaching workers.

The following suggestions are in keeping with the maintenance of a healthy climate:

1. Tell participants why a job is done in a certain way and why it is done. Help them see the importance of the job.
2. Avoid overinstructing. Individuals can process only so much information at one time; in addition, they should be able to fashion their own tasks.

3. Obtain feedback about participants' ideas and feelings about tasks and organization. Solicit ideas.

4. Utilize criticism by criticizing privately, being constructive by showing a better way, and directing comments toward the work rather than the participant.

5. Recognize the participant's progress. Do not be error-oriented only.

6. Make use of group problem solving.

7. Ensure stability by (a) making expectations clear, (b) making penalties for poor performance firm, fair, and clearly understood, and (c) giving credit for good work freely and promptly.

GROUP GOALS

Most organizations depend on groups to perform specialized tasks, and these groups have their own task goals, or organizational subgoals. The groups—whether formal or informal—carrying out these tasks, as well as their individual members, must be integrated into the overall organizational structure.

Integration

Workers called on to meet organizational subgoals may come to restrict their vision to those goals. Lawrence and Lorsch observe:

> Since groups, once formed, will evolve their own distinctive task-related characteristics, they will have different points of view that necessarily complicate the coordination process. This often generates serious intergroup problems whose symptoms are destructive competition, secretiveness, and hostility. The integration process must cope with these issues to achieve unity of effort.[20]

Two classes of problems often result from organizational divisions. First, groups may concentrate so much on subgoals that they are uninformed about what others are doing and how they actually relate to one another. For example, each group may think (erroneously) that the other is carrying out tasks that need to be done. Second, groups can concentrate so much on subgoals that they forget their role in the organization. This typically results in their playing a "win-lose" game with one another, and the resulting conflict detracts from the accomplishment of organizational objectives.

Just as individual roles should be related to group and organizational objectives, so too linkage should be made between group efforts and organizational objectives. This effort requires both vertical and horizontal communication within the organization. The role of communication in the linkage of groups can be served by media and meetings of representatives from various groups.

Conflict

The handling of conflict has always presented a complex problem for both theorists and practitioners. The very term "conflict" suggests that something is wrong and requires resolution. However, conflict may not only be a normal state, but also serve a useful function.[21] Karl Weick, for example, maintains that a certain level of conflict provides information and alternatives that may be necessary for adapting to a changing environment.[22] In our view, conflict is a continuous phenomenon that requires management. Some conflict is inevitable if people are searching for better ways of doing things or if there is a continual effort to allocate resources in the most useful way. Our major concern is with the conflict level that detracts from organizational goals.

What should be done when groups reach a level of conflict that places each in the role of protecting subgoals to the "bitter end"? Communication functions become extremely difficult to carry out when groups view one another as "the enemy."[23] Groups tend to isolate and fortify themselves with distorted perceptions that make others look bad and themselves good. Through this process it becomes easier for the groups to dehumanize the objects of questionable action or sanitize that action. Isolation means that little communication takes place; therefore, representatives of a group may be looked on as "unrepresentative" or as the carriers of falsehoods.

Why not just bring the groups together, forcing them to communicate? Does increased communication result in increased agreement in conflict situations? The research evidence is contradictory. Some theorists have argued that increased communication means increased conflict and fewer settlements.[24] Others have found the opposite, namely, that communication increases available strategies of bargaining.[25] We can conclude that different experimental conditions will yield different results on the effect of communication. Observation also suggests that this variability is probably representative of real-life conflict situations. Whether or not communication helps is dependent on the conditions in and complexity of the situation. Furthermore, communication alone is not a sufficient condition for "resolving" conflict.

Eventually groups must learn to communicate and work together if organizational goals are to be served. Functionally interdependent groups cannot remain isolated from one another. It has been observed that functional interdependence and the perception of trust in a nonthreatening situation are the conditions under which communication can function to reduce conflict.[26] It is important, then, to establish these conditions and create an atmosphere in which groups can view one another realistically. The first task might be to establish a nonthreatening communication situation. This is part of the model advanced by Blake and Mouton; groups are asked to describe their images of one another and how they came to feel that way.[27] Eventually the groups work together to determine how they can relate to one another differently.

Rather than throwing groups together and going immediately to issues, an effort to alter the atmosphere may be much more effective as a first step. Communication can then be utilized to stress the interdependence of the groups, and superordinate goals can begin to receive some attention. There is no substitute for prevention; unless groups come to understand their dependence on one another, conflict may reach such a high level that it cripples intergroup relationships.

Monitoring Significant Symbols

We are not suggesting that every move of a group should be monitored; indeed, groups are more effective when given some autonomy. However, it is helpful to know if organizational master symbols are having impact and what behaviors are receiving group reinforcement. Geneva Works–U.S. Steel provides a real-life example of how this procedure has worked.

The interview is an integral part of the internal communication program at Geneva Works. During a four-year period approximately 500 interviews were conducted as part of an employee "recognition" program. The interviews (made primarily with hourly employees) focused on the description of job tasks and their relationship to company goals, as well as on the overall principles of the "errors zero program." As in the Geneva Works program, such interviews serve several purposes.

1. Devised as a means of recognition, the interview seems to do just that. The "relationship function" of the interview says: "You are important enough to the overall operation for us to solicit your ideas and suggestions."

2. The central themes of the "errors zero program" are reinforced through employee verbalization. In other words, a positive attitude on the part of an employee is reinforced when he or she receives the interviewer's approval for stating the importance of his or her job.

3. The interview provides an opportunity for the employee to relate his or her job and its importance to the overall operation. Subgoals are connected to the larger goals of the organization.

4. The interview provides data for adjustments and reveals areas needing further investigation.

5. Because the interviews touch all segments of the organization, they provide feedback from all levels of the organization and serve as a check on the effectiveness of the communication program.

In sum, the interview method helps determine what symbols have been internalized and also aids in assessing group climate. There are other ways to monitor symbols, but this one has the virtue of reaching into the ranks.

CONDITIONS OF BARGAINING

Regulation

Throughout the text we have maintained that: (1) "regulation" refers in part to a bargain struck between individuals, individuals and organization, and individuals and the state; (2) facilitation and regulation are not antithetical, but instead are part of the negotiation process; and (3) mutual persuasion or regulation should not be equated with exploitation. In our discussion of ethics, we opted for a set of conditions that allow for alternatives and for both willing and informed consent on the part of those being regulated. Here we will present some of the conditions of bargaining that help implement those principles. Although our focus is on the organization in this chapter, the conditions are equally applicable in the interpersonal context.

Relationship Maintenance

David Smith points out that relationships can be regarded as fixed sum or variable sum:

> In fixed-sum situations strategic considerations dictate that our gains will come necessarily at the expense of the other(s). In variable-sum situations we believe that if we behave appropriately, the total rewards available may be increased; hence both parties may benefit by acting to increase the total benefits from the transaction.[28]

We are most interested in the variable-sum situation, the approach most consistent with the theme of mutual gain. Smith discusses several principles applicable in both the organizational and interpersonal setting in terms of achieving accommodation.

1. *Bargaining in good faith.* Bargaining in good faith means in negotiation that once you have agreed to an arrangement, you will not later withdraw your agreement or fail to fulfill the terms agreed upon. In ordinary interaction it means that you keep your promises. Failure to bargain in good faith quickly destroys variable-sum relationships.

2. *The convention of reciprocal concessions.* Within our society bargaining usually operates on a convention of reciprocal concessions. We talk about the give and take of bargaining. Concessions don't have to be equal to be reciprocal, but in order for a variable-sum relationship to be maintained, each party must perceive the other to be making appropriate responses to the attempts he makes at accommodation. . . . In those relationships wherein we feel that we are making all the concessions to the other, the force of that perception pushes the relationship in the fixed-sum direction.

3. *Maintenance of multiple issues.* When a number of issues or reward dimensions are bargained for simultaneously, the possibilities for reciprocal

concessions mentioned above are increased. Narrowing the number of issues reduces the possibility of reciprocal concessions.

4. *Revealing information about utilities.* When parties' information about one another's preferences is limited, they lack the essential basis for finding ways for increasing the available rewards. They must know what each values highly in order to develop the elegant solution which takes advantage of the variable-sum relationship. But the revelation of a party's preferences gives to the other the information he needs to use a hard strategy successfully in treating the situation as fixed sum. In order for a relationship to be variable sum, the parties must reveal information about their utilities, but to protect against the exploitation of that information it may be necessary to treat it incrementally by applying the reciprocity convention mentioned above.

5. *Commitment.* A commitment strategy is employed in bargaining when a party makes a credible "this or nothing" move. "If you won't do things my way, I'll leave you", or "I'll take my marbles and go home." ... Early commitment by one party, however, engenders the possibility that the other will withdraw from the relationship and virtually guarantees that a variable-sum relationship is impossible.

6. *Manipulation of communication opportunity.* We can all recall the frustration we feel when someone seems to do all the talking without ever listening to us. ... My own research has demonstrated that increased agreement accompanies increased communication opportunity.

7. *Repetitive bargains.* If the entire nature of our relationship must be decided once and for all time at a single time, an important group of creative solutions may be excluded. If I must regard a concession made now as a permanent one, I will be more reluctant to make it than if I expect to be able to renegotiate the matter later on. ... By making moves which indicate a willingness to renegotiate at a future date, a party may increase the possibility of a variable-sum relationship.[29]

These seven strategies suggest ways of maintaining relationships so that communication channels can remain open and trust developed. The variable-sum relationship presents a flexible situation in which individuals are most likely to give their best and honestly consider the goals of others. The bargaining may include a wide range of activities within the organization and is not limited to economic considerations. The essential question is whether individuals have the opportunity to participate in shaping their own destinies.

SUMMARY

Organizations use communication in a variety of ways to achieve goal accommodation. The integration of individual and organizational goals can be accomplished by an assessment process based on open and personalized communication which forms the basis for an individual-organization bargain.

Although such communication may be initiated from the point of human values, members of the organization hierarchy must also be alert to value differences and changes in values.

Whereas values vary with individuals and thereby create differences in the nature of the communication and resultant bargaining, organizations generate commitment to their goals through the use of master symbols, ensuring understanding of organizational goals, and creating a healthy organizational climate. Commitment to organizational goals must be accomplished at two levels—individual and group.

Group-level integration requires a flow of information so that the various groups know what the others are doing and recognize their interdependence. A certain level of intergroup conflict may be inevitable and even desirable, but when it threatens organizational goals, communication should be aimed at establishing the conditions conducive to problem solving. In other words, communication can be used to *manage* conflict. Conflict management can be accomplished through the monitoring of significant symbols to determine whether there is a balance between group autonomy and interdependence.

Throughout the accommodation process—whether between individuals and the organization or between groups and the organization—relationships can be maintained and trust developed through bargaining. The conditions of bargaining facilitate accommodation by ensuring the maintenance of relationships and developing trust among the participants. These conditions are best accomplished through strategies and communication that maintain a variable-sum relationship.

PROBLEMS AND ISSUES

1. If you were asked by an organization to conduct a motivation program for its employees, how would you proceed?
2. What individual goals will you seek inside a work organization?
3. What individual goals do you seek in your university or college? Can those goals be met within the framework of the educational institution?
4. Examine a local organization and determine its master symbols. Are they conducive to integration of goals?
5. Survey organizational members to determine their understanding of and commitment to goals. Is a distinction made between personal and organizational goals?
6. Study a department within your university or college. Do members make a distinction between subgoals and departmental goals? What devices are used to maintain focus on departmental and larger goals?

7. Set up an experimental bargaining setting. Vary the techniques that were suggested for a variable-sum relationship. What differences in communication occur? How do the results change?

NOTES

1. William H. Form, "Toward Re-evaluation of Individualism in Industry," *Values in America,* ed. Donald Barrett (Notre Dame: University of Notre Dame Press, 1967), p. 115.

2. Sterling M. McMurrin, "Purposes and Problems in Higher Education," *AAUP Bulletin* (Spring 1974): 5. Reprinted by permission.

3. Paul Hersey and K. Blanchard, *Management of Organizational Behavior* (Englewood Cliffs, N.J.: Prentice-Hall, 1969), pp. 116–117.

4. For further explanation, *see* Douglas McGregor, *Professional Manager* (New York: McGraw-Hill, 1967).

5. Abraham Maslow, *Motivation and Personality,* 2d ed. (New York: Harper & Row, 1970); Frederick Herzberg, B. Mausner, and B. Snyderman, *The Motivation to Work* (New York: Wiley, 1959).

6. *See* J. J. Morse and J. W. Lorsch, "Beyond Theory Y," *Harvard Business Review* **48** (May-June 1970): 146–155.

7. Rensis Likert, *New Patterns of Management* (New York: McGraw-Hill, 1961), p. 50.

8. Eric L. Trist, "Urban North America: The Challenge of the Next Thirty Years," in *Organizational Frontiers and Human Values,* ed. Warren H. Schmidt (Belmont, Calif.: Wadsworth, 1970), p. 82. This work has been further developed in F. E. Emery and E. L. Trist, *Towards a Social Ecology* (New York and London: Plenum Press, 1973).

9. Alvin Toffler, *Future Shock* (New York: Bantam, 1970), p. 29.

10. Robert Tannenbaum and Sheldon A. Davis, "Values, Man, and Organizations," in *Organizational Frontiers and Human Values,* ed. Warren H. Schmidt (Belmont, Calif.: Wadsworth, 1970), pp. 131–146. This article also appeared in the Winter 1969 issue of the *Sloan Management Review,* formerly the *Industrial Management Review.*

11. This program is described in Don F. Faules and David Bigler, "A Model Internal Communication Program: Analysis and Measurement of Effectiveness" (unpublished manuscript, 1971).

12. George A. Jedenoff, "To Share the Duty," a presentation at the American Newspaper Publishers Association Convention, New York City, April 22, 1970.

13. We use this term to illustrate the use of master symbols. For a more complete discussion of the pro's and con's of "zero defects" programs, *see* Edgar F. Huse, "Do Zero Defects Programs Really Motivate Workers?" *Personnel* **43** (1966): 14–21.

14. Daniel Katz and Robert Kahn, "Communication: The Flow of Information," in *Dimensions in Communication*, ed. James H. Campbell and Hal W. Hepler (Belmont, Calif.: Wadsworth, 1970), p. 98.

15. John R. Maher and Darrell T. Piersol, "Perceived Clarity of Individual Job Objectives and of Group Mission as Correlates of Organizational Morale," *Journal of Communication* **20** (1970): 125–133.

16. *See* V. Vroom, *Work and Motivation* (New York: Wiley, 1964).

17. Bernard P. Indik, Basils Georgopoulos, and Stanley E. Seashore, "Superior-Subordinate Relationships and Performance," *Personnel Psychology* **14** (1961): 357–374.

18. For an interpretive review of theory and research of these components, *see* Charles Redding, *Communication within the Organization* (New York: Industrial Communication Council, 1973).

19. For in-depth exploration, *see* Rensis Likert, *op. cit.*, and *The Human Organization* (New York: McGraw-Hill, 1967).

20. Paul Lawrence and Jay Lorsch, *Developing Organizations: Diagnosis and Action* (Reading, Mass.: Addison-Wesley, 1969), p. 6.

21. *See* Georg Simmel, *Conflict, and the Web of Group-Affiliations*, trans. Kurt H. Wolff and Reinhard Bendix (New York: Free Press, 1964). *Also see* Lewis Coser, *The Functions of Social Conflict* (New York: Free Press, 1956).

22. Karl Weick, *The Social Psychology of Organizing* (Reading, Mass.: Addison-Wesley, 1969), pp. 103–105.

23. For elaboration, *see* Edgar Schein, *Process Consultation: Its Role in Organization Development* (Reading, Mass.: Addison-Wesley, 1969), pp. 70–75.

24. *See* Sidney Siegel and Lawrence Fouraker, *Bargaining and Group Decision Making* (New York: McGraw-Hill, 1960), p. 100.

25. *See* David H. Smith, "An Experimental Study of Communication Restriction and Knowledge of the Opponents' Minimum Disposition as Variables Influencing Negotiation Outcome" (Ph.D. diss., Ohio State University, 1966).

26. *See* Morton Deutsch and Robert Krauss, "Studies of Interpersonal Bargaining," *Journal of Conflict Resolution* **6** (1962): 52–76.

27. Robert Blake and Jane Mouton, "Reactions to Intergroup Competition Under Win-Lose Conditions," *Management Science* **7** (1961): 420–435.

28. David H. Smith, "Applications from Research on Bargaining and Negotiation." Paper presented at the Central States Speech Convention, April 7, 1972, p. 6.

29. *Ibid.*, pp. 7–9.

Author Index

Subject Index